Suffrage Outside Suffragism

Suffrage Outside Suffragism

Women's Vote in Britain, 1880–1914

Edited by

Myriam Boussahba-Bravard

palgrave
macmillan

Softcover reprint of the hardcover 1st edition 2007 978-1-4039-9596-4

First published 2007 by
PALGRAVE MACMILLAN
Houndmills, Basingstoke, Hampshire RG21 6XS and
175 Fifth Avenue, New York, N.Y. 10010
Companies and representatives throughout the world

PALGRAVE MACMILLAN is the global academic imprint of the Palgrave Macmillan division of St. Martin's Press, LLC and of Palgrave Macmillan Ltd. Macmillan® is a registered trademark in the United States, United Kingdom and other countries. Palgrave is a registered trademark in the European Union and other countries.

ISBN 978-1-349-54491-2 ISBN 978-0-230-80131-8 (eBook)
DOI 10.1057/9780230801318

This book is printed on paper suitable for recycling and made from fully managed and sustained forest sources. Logging, pulping and manufacturing processes are expected to conform to the environmental regulations of the country of origin.

A catalogue record for this book is available from the British Library.

Library of Congress Cataloging-in-Publication Data

Suffrage outside suffragism : women's vote in Britain, 1880–1914 / edited by Myriam Boussahba-Bravard.
p. cm.
Includes bibliographical references and index.

1. Women—Suffrage—Great Britain—History. 2. Great Britain—History—Edward VII, 1901–1910. I. Boussahba-Bravard, Myriam, 1963–

JN979.S86 2007
324.6′230941—dc22 2006049294

10 9 8 7 6 5 4 3 2 1
16 15 14 13 12 11 10 09 08 07

Transferred to Digital Printing 2008

Contents

Acknowledgements

I wish to thank all the contributors for their participation in the book. Contributors who have been part since the beginning have shown patience. Contributors who have joined us at a later stage have been really good with the deadlines imposed by the editor. I would also like to thank Anne Besnault-Levita, Julia Bush, Georges-Claude Guilbert, June Hannam, Nathalie Vienne-Guerrin and Geraldine Vaughan for their helpful comments on the earlier drafts of the introduction. The final version is, of course, my sole responsibility.

Notes on Contributors

Myriam Boussahba-Bravard is Maître de conférences in British Studies, University of Rouen, France. Her research focuses on suffrage history and periodicals in the Edwardian period. Myriam's forthcoming publications in French academic journals and books include 'Le suffragisme ou le déni de la théorisation politique, 1900–1914', ed. Claire Charlot (Paris: Ophrys, 2007); 'Résistance passive et citoyenneté: la rébellion fiscale de la bourgeoise édouardienne' (Paris: Revue d'histoire moderne et contemporaine, forthcoming); 'L'argumentaire des "races" européennes dans les revues *Contemporary, Fortnighly* et *Nineteenth Century* 1900–1914' (Paris: L'Harmattan, collection Eugénisme et racisme, 2006); 'L'argumentaire eugéniste dans les revues *Contemporary, Fortnighly* et *Nineteenth Century* 1900–1914' (Presses Universitaires de Lille 3, 2007). She is currently writing a book-length biography of the feminist Teresa Billington-Greig (1877–1964).

Julia Bush is Senior Lecturer in History, University of Northampton, Northampton, UK. Her books include *Behind the Lines: East London Labour and World War I* (1984) and *Edwardian Ladies and Imperial Power* (2000), as well as contributions to oral history and community history publications and journal articles on labour history and women's history in *The London Journal, History Workshop Journal, Women's History Review, Women's Studies International Forum, Women's History Notebooks, Literature and History* and *History of Education.* Her current research focuses upon conservative women in the period 1880–1920, and a forthcoming book is titled *Women Against the Vote* (Oxford University Press, 2007).

Lucy Delap is Research Fellow of King's College, Cambridge, and the History Faculty, University of Cambridge, UK. She is completing a book, *The Feminist Avant-Garde: Transatlantic Encounters, c.1900–1920s*, which explores the intellectual history and cultural politics of feminism, set within Anglo-American transatlantic exchanges of the early twentieth century. She has co-edited with Maria DiCenzo and Leila Ryan a collection of primary sources, *Feminism and the Periodical Press, 1900–1918* (Routledge, 2005). She is an associate editor of *History and Policy*, and is currently working on domestic service and the idea of service in twentieth-century Britain.

June Hannam is Professor and Associate Dean, Humanities, Languages and Social Science Faculty, University of the West of England, Bristol, UK. She is the author of two books, *Isabella Ford, 1855–1924* (Blackwell, 1989) and (with K. Hunt) *Socialist Women, Britain c.1880 to 1920* (Routledge, 2002). She has written a number of articles on the Independent Labour Party and the 'woman question' and on the women's movement in Bristol. Her current research interest is in the politics of the emotions and Labour Party women MPs and candidates in the interwar years.

Lori Maguire received her doctorate at St Antony's College, Oxford and is currently Professor of British Studies at the University of Paris VIII, France. She is the author of two books *Anglo-American Policy towards the Free French* and *Conservative Women: a History of Women and the Conservative Party* and co-author of *La démocratie au 20e siècle*. She has published numerous articles in French and English.

Gillian Scott is Principal Lecturer in the School of Historical and Critical Studies at the University of Brighton, UK, where she has been in full-time employment since 1989. Her previous work experience included adult education and the British Consumers' Co-operative movement. The focus of her research is the relationship between feminist ideas and the organisation of working-class women in modern Britain. She has published several articles on different aspects of the history of the Women's Co-operative Guild, and a book, *Feminism and the Politics of Working Women* (UCL Press, 1998). She is the course leader of undergraduate programmes in the Humanities, and a member of the interdisciplinary 'Gender and Built Space' research grouping, at the University of Brighton.

Pat Thane (MA Oxford, PhD LSE) has been Professor of Contemporary British History, Institute of Historical Research, University of London, UK, since October 2002. She was Professor of Contemporary History at the University of Sussex, UK, from 1994–2002. Her main publications are: *The Foundations of the Welfare State* (Longman, 1982, 2nd edn 1996); *Women and Gender Policies: Women and the Rise of the European Welfare States, 1880s–1950s*, co-editor with Gisela Bock (Routledge, 1990); *Old Age from Antiquity to Post-Modernity*, co-editor with Paul Johnson (Routledge, 1998); *Old Age in England: Past Experiences, Present Issues* (Oxford University Press, May 2000); *Women and Ageing in Britain since 1500*, co-editor with Lynne Botelho (Longman, 2001); *Labour's First Century: the Labour Party 1900–2000*, co-editor with Duncan Tanner and Nick Tiratsoo (Cambridge University Press, 2000); *The Long History of Old Age*, editor (Thames and Hudson, Getty Museum, LA, 2005).

Susan Trouvé-Finding is Maître de conférences in British Studies, University of Poitiers, France. Her research interests include social policy, education policy, family policy in postwar Britain and the role of teachers in twentieth-century Britain and France. She has published extensively on these fields in French academic publications. A recent comparative article on women primary teachers appeared in *History of Education*, 2005, 5. She is currently preparing a book on contemporary British family policy.

Philippe Vervaecke is Maître de conférences in British Studies, University of Lille III, France. Philippe is an alumnus from the Ecole Normale Supérieure (ENS) de Fontenay-Saint-Cloud and from the London School of Economics, where he obtained an MA in International History. His PhD (2003) is entitled 'La Primrose League, 1883–2000: Culture et pratiques politiques d'un mouvement conservateur'. It covers the social and political history of the Primrose League from the days of its creation in 1883 to its recent demise in 2000. His research interests include popular conservatism in the nineteenth and twentieth centuries, Victorian and Edwardian political culture, women's involvement in politics and British political iconography, on which he has published articles in French academic journals.

Linda Walker is Research Fellow in the School of Nursing, University of Manchester, UK, currently working on the health of female shop workers in Britain, 1880–1930. Her wider research interests encompass the first wave of feminism and the formation of women's political associations in relation to the Victorian and Edwardian women's movement which was the subject of her doctoral dissertation at the University of Manchester (1984). Her publications include 'Party Political Women: a Comparative Study of Liberal Women and the Primrose League, 1890–1914', in Jane Rendall, ed., *Equal or Different: Women's Politics 1800–1914* (Basil Blackwell, 1987) and articles on Liberal women for the *Oxford Dictionary of National Biography* (2004). She has taught women's history and modern social and political history in universities since the 1970s.

1
Introduction

Myriam Boussahba-Bravard

'Suffragism' was a political field where non-party structures were set up to gain women's suffrage. The suffragist field outside 'suffragism' offered party and non-party structures that were not specifically suffragist although suffragists belonged to them. If 'the study of anti-suffragism is particularly important as an aid towards understanding suffragism',[1] then 'suffrage outside suffragism' should also be seen as a valid object of study that can offer meaningful perspectives for understanding 'suffragism'.

'Suffragism' has been studied through its organisations, whereas 'suffrage outside suffragism' has never been researched as a synchronic whole where various structures had to compromise with their suffragist activists. The aim of this book is to address how suffragists[2] outside 'suffragism' (hereafter 'outside suffragists') related to their original structures, what they targeted and how they fared, in a context where 'suffragism' as a separate field offered support and inclusion on an ad hoc basis. Such activists were thus suffragists with another (party or non-party) affiliation. The interaction between the two positions (suffragist and non-suffragist) must have been difficult to experience. The fact that most outside suffragist activists were women also emphasised the gendered reading of affiliations. For each individual, being a suffragist mostly coexisted with being a female activist, and both positions needed some acknowledgement. At the height of the suffrage campaign, in the Edwardian era, organised structures outside 'suffragism' found it difficult to integrate one or both of these issues, suffrage and female activism, and one or both types of activists, suffragists and females. The existence of 'suffragism' could hardly be ignored, especially as many outside suffragists also belonged to suffragist societies: double affiliations were common even if they were not always formalised through membership. How double affiliations were born but also how they affected the non-suffragist structures to which activists belonged, is discussed in this book. The fluidity and transfer of activists' affiliations – even if activists experienced contradictions – must have enriched both 'suffragism' and 'suffrage outside suffragism' (hereafter 'suffrage outside'): activists could compare political practices and structures, methods, back-up support and better assess how realistic their activists' expectancies were. Conversely, the structures outside 'suffragism' had to adapt to the pressure coming from their suffragist activists and gauge how realistic their expectancies (defined by the party or the group line) were in order to keep their suffragist members, that is, broadly speaking, their women members.

This book's focus on suffrage outside 'suffragism' should help us to understand both fields, 'suffragism' and 'suffrage outside', their interaction and how they related to the Edwardian social and political fabric. 'Suffragism' and 'suffrage' were an integral part of Edwardian politics. Studying 'suffrage outside suffragism' offers another reminder of the impossibility of disconnecting suffrage from mainstream politics; an understanding of their shared history is the aim of this book. This book's novelty lies in its broad scope: it looks at the importance of suffrage for a variety of groups at the same time. Research up to now has mostly focused on political parties and has tended to disregard other groups that were involved in pursuing reform. The party and non-party structures selected[3] for this book offer a reading of female activism from various perspectives, political and non-political, local and national, voluntary and union-wise, and from the avant-garde. Most women activists from these groups read their experiences as gendered but did not always perceive them as 'political'. They tended to restrict the definition of politics to formal party affiliations, whether they belonged to political parties or not. In the nine contributions to this book, the varied nature of the groups studied suggests that female activists shared characteristics and encountered common obstacles outside 'suffragism'. Examining (some of) the decor of suffrage outside 'suffragism' provides further insights into groups inside 'suffragism', what Andrew Chadwick has called the 'Suffragist Alliance'.[4]

In this introductory chapter, selected aspects of historiography are highlighted; the main concern is about categories of analysis when writing the history of suffrage taken as a whole, not the suffrage organisations which activists belonged to; in other words, neither Militants' nor constitutionalists' history[5] are within the scope of this book. Drawing the outlines of 'suffragism' suggests that it worked as a norm, a focal reference for contemporaries. Finding out about its nature, its architecture and its dynamics brings about the existence of a multi-layered milieu, both self-centred and outreaching. Once the picture of 'suffragism' as a milieu is clearer, it can be contrasted with suffrage outside 'suffragism'. Interestingly, despite all the variations shown in the contributions, convergence emerges. This must show that suffrage outside is also a field which takes its existence and definition through analogy and contrast. The nine contributions altogether outline an interpretative model of suffrage outside 'suffragism' with and beyond the particularities of these selected groups. All contributions are fully discussed in the last section of this introductory chapter.

The first part of this book is devoted to national parties and how they dealt with women's suffrage in the years preceding 1914. Pat Thane for the Labour Party, Linda Walker for the Liberal Party and Lori Maguire for the Conservative Party discuss the status and roles of women in them. They show the resistance of parties to women's agendas while integrating females to political work; they also depict how party women lobbied their executives and fought for political existence within their parties as well as outside them. National policies and executives represent parties more than they embody them. Indeed, a different image is projected when looking at activists' local involvement. Julia Bush and Gillian Scott describe women-only voluntary organisations, the National Union of Women Workers and the Women's Co-operative Guild. Both groups developed from their members' concerns and devised claims tailored to women recipients. One was mostly middle-class in outlook and approaches while the other was mainly working-class. In this case, class cannot be neutralised although both structures display a salutary concern for internal democracy. Class is also at the core of June Hannam's contribution on Bristol socialists and Philippe Vervaecke's chapter on the Primrose League. They also show how the relations between local and national levels could clash. However, both chapters suggest that the suffrage issue and more generally sexual politics proved more divisive than expected in political organisations, however hard they denied its relevance. The last section of the book is intended to discuss how female members viewed structure and tailored it to their needs as females beyond the suffrage issue. Although this section is a mere snapshot, Susan Trouvé-Finding explains how women teachers gradually controlled their union before 1914 but never managed to set equal pay, for instance, at the top of their agenda. Women teachers achieved control of their union but reluctantly listened to sexual politics and usually discarded such issues as outside the scope of their organisation. In the last chapter, Lucy Delap discusses the connection between 'suffragism' and feminism for avant-garde women who shared the ethos of the informal group participating in *The Freewoman*. Some of them came to despise suffragists and discard all formal structuring as obstacles against female emancipation.

Historiography

The Edwardian suffrage movement has received a great deal of attention from historians but, as Sandra Holton notes, there is still a great deal to be said about it. She signals new stories re-emerging which 'challenge existing frameworks or render uncertain the categories and concepts we apply, or suggest new lines of inquiry'.[6] The ambition of this book is to emphasise suffrage outside 'suffragism' as a meaningful choice made by individuals and executives of structures.

In the 1920s, the Suffragette Fellowship[7] created 'a master narrative of the Militant suffrage movement'.[8] Dominated by former participants, this is a fascinating instance of what the French call *le devoir de mémoire*. The Fellowship created its own archives and preserved valuable collections, but in the process emphasised only certain characteristics as representing the 'true suffragette spirit' and consequently seemed to deny the variety of suffragists inside and outside 'suffragism'. In the interwar years, such an endeavour simplified and obscured some of the interpreting options of prewar 'suffragism',[9] which obviously cannot be reduced to a campaign by one organisation nor be disconnected from the wider world outside 'suffragism'. 'This narrative has implications both for how historians have interpreted the suffrage movement, as well as for how former suffragettes constructed their political identities as feminists in the 1920s and after.'[10] To this should be added how (female) contemporaries perceived such a narrative; the postwar narrative also dwelt on women's share in the war effort, echoing wartime propaganda. Though these two instances of heroic posturing verge on edification, they have constituted powerful emotional narratives that recreate a façade of unity and exemplify efficient propaganda if they are not qualified and contextualised.[11] Such history-making borrowed heavily from a narrative of heroics that creates automatic distancing, and conveyed to the rank and file the idea that they could not participate because they were 'ordinary': creating heroines can be understood as an implicit dismissal of activism. Besides they were rooted in exceptional or extreme circumstances, which must have had little to do with day-to-day divided loyalties experienced by 'ordinary' women, then and now. Later in the decade, Ray Strachey's 1928 publication of *The Cause* and Sylvia Pankhurst's 1931 book, *The Suffragette Movement*, seemed to confirm that the campaign for women's emancipation had ended with their gaining of the vote on equal terms with men.[12] In any case the women's movement seemed to be over as the heroines of the war effort and of suffrage were no longer needed: these two facts alone may explain why younger women may have felt alienated from feminist politics after 1918.

'Reflecting on Suffrage History',[13] Sandra Holton suggests that from the 1970s to the late 1990s, the development of different research chronologies and the finding of new sources led 'to a significant shift in the interpretative frameworks shaping suffrage history in Britain, a shift that extended our understanding of the range and complexity of the internal politics of the suffrage movement'.[14] Suffrage history has gone through various stages, each time setting the canon and then revisiting it. New perspectives have reclaimed ideological layers of meanings and recast 'suffragism' as a consistent whole.[15] This has led to the development of a comprehensive approach rather than a segmented historiography that focuses on individual organisations. The purpose of this book is similar: suffrage outside 'suffragism' becomes a consistent object of study when a comprehensive approach is developed.

In an editorial of the *Women's History Review* in 2000, 'Borders and Frontiers in Women's History', Lynn Abrams and Karen Hunt state there is more often than not an ontological link between women's history, 'part of the mainstream but at the same time peripheral', and borders and frontiers as an object of study, where the frontier is not 'merely a place but also a process and an idea'.[16] 'Suffragism' can be defined in the same way. Women defined their own political space as 'suffragism' and thus challenged mainstream politics: such a process could not be neutral. While 'making and remaking borders'[17] to serve the suffrage cause, women explored undiscovered territories which were finally mapped by the 1930s.[18] In a subsequent editorial of the *Women's History Review* in 2002, June Hannam and Katherine Holden apply the 'Heartland and Periphery' concepts to women's history itself and stress the fluidity and interdependence of the inner geography of the field, by re-enacting 'the metaphor of heartland and periphery' which had been used by feminist historians 'to reclaim a place for women in history, and in so doing, challenged the view that women and their concerns were peripheral to mainstream historical inquiry'.[19] Such an ontological pattern is also at the centre of *Suffrage Outside Suffragism*.

'Suffrage' inspired late nineteenth-century and Edwardian propaganda-makers who made 'suffragism': not a political party yet a party of some sort; a political space where party politics was not the structuring force; a political platform from where (mostly) women activists published their views about women as one group or from various groups; a parallel public space where all the propaganda and debates were about 'women'; a modified echo of mainstream traditional public space but from the female perspective.[20] It was an excellent location from which producers and consumers of suffragist propaganda could test and echo that propaganda, staging it *as if it were* mainstream.

'Suffragism'

Outside suffragists played a part in 'the suffrage campaign' even if they were based outside 'suffragism'. They chose to remain in political parties or reforming groups whose concerns were not especially about 'suffrage'. This did not preclude these groups from opposing, supporting or caring for suffrage. Indeed, the three standpoints could be displayed within the same organisation. That is why 'suffrage outside' can be considered only by contrast with 'suffragism', it cannot be researched on its own. This book focuses on relations between suffragists and suffrage groups, on 'the relations between the sexes but also the relations within the sexes, not only those of women to men, and men to women, but also relations among women'.[21]

Suffragists have traditionally been defined according to the type of suffrage they favoured or prioritised. The traditional division of 'suffragism' into Militant and non-Militant organisations is not relevant to this study either, nor does it remain the consensual approach to 'suffragism' it used to be, even though differences in approach between organisations matter.[22] In this book, however, the real issue remains the difference between supporters of suffrage inside and outside 'suffragism'. If suffragists are on both sides of the boundary, what is relevant is the making of the boundary. The type of suffrage advocated (adult or women's) certainly contributed to its making. However, this choice often involved differences of priority rather than excluding one or the other type. It also took on different meanings according to the political or party platform from which it was voiced: women's suffrage could be read as the ultimate concession for Conservatives at an early point,[23] whereas it was only a first step for most inside 'suffragism' and a wrong step for the proponents of adult suffrage. Besides, individuals changed their views over time and events; political alliances fluctuated. For instance the 1912 Election Fighting Fund formalised an alliance between the National Union of Women's Suffrage Societies (NUWSS) and the Labour Party; it fundamentally changed the landscape of inside 'suffragism' and outside. Thus, the type of suffrage advocated (and even more so the reasons for its support) was not an absolute factor to determine the boundaries of 'suffragism'.

Proponents of Adult and Women's Suffrage did not exclude each other but devised different political strategies; in any case, all of them were suffragists of one type or the other, or of both types but with differing priorities at different times. 'Adult Suffrage', although it integrated women in the claim, seemed to be geared towards 'dependent men', males still deprived of formal citizenship, whereas 'suffragism' elaborated a discourse on females as an entirely disenfranchised group. The women's suffrage issue was a catalyst for other tensions (class, work and sex) and obviously informed mainstream politics. There were heated debates among Edwardian suffragists about the basis on which to make their demands – and historians have reflected these differences in their own debates about which factions had most influence on winning the vote. The collection of essays in this book, however, is more concerned with exploring the impact of women's suffrage on groups and their members outside 'suffragism'.

'Suffragism' implied a dividing line established by contemporary activists who knew on which side they stood. Boundaries were crossed in both directions, generating a dynamic exchange under various modes: partnership, confrontation, contrast or competition, between inside and outside suffragists. Suffragists' experiences stressed the political complexity of suffrage as an issue, a cause and a creed. Outside suffragists contributed to 'suffragism' through their conviction, their 'suffrag*ism*'. And many outside suffragists were insiders as well.[24]

'Suffragism' can be defined through suffragist political groupings that made up a political field with its own characteristics. That is why it deserves the –ism that is given to other political concepts: conservatism, socialism, labourism, liberalism, and radicalism – not all of them represented by political parties. As a network producing and distributing information and propaganda, 'suffragism' also gained the physical materiality of a space devoted to suffragist propaganda. Such propaganda fed inside and outside suffragist demands and proselytised outside to rally the indifferent and to silence (vocal) anti-suffragists. It is the outward dynamic that is perhaps more sophisticated than has been recognised as this outward drive addressed at the same time outside suffragists, those who were indifferent and anti-suffragists. The ins and outs of 'suffragism' have been examined for individuals and for one structure at a time, but it has been somewhat neglected as a pattern where a range of structures are involved.[25]

'Suffragism' covers three superimposed layers of meaning which do not fit perfectly; the boundaries of each layer fluctuated independently from the others, or at least their limits may not have been as clear-cut as is commonly acknowledged. The first defining layer is structuring: groups involved inside and outside were clearly different. Inside groups were set up to forward suffragist claims. In terms of organisations, there was hardly any doubt about which participated and which did not. These societies had affiliated members and supporters; they produced policies and propaganda, all geared towards establishing women's suffrage. The second layer involved their production of propaganda, a key activity for any political group. Arguments serving the suffrage cause were devised and deployed in all sorts of ways; supporters and members were their first targets and they in turn redeployed them for a wider public. As a mass movement in the Edwardian period, 'suffragism' could boast high numbers of activists and supporters and did draw contemporaries' attention through debates, meetings, press articles and traditional means of propaganda. Suffragist tours of the country and pageantry asserted the existence of the suffragist claim to everyone, whether supporters or not, and visually validated their petitioning to enter mainstream politics.[26] Outside suffragists associated themselves with or joined into propaganda making. The borderlines between outside and inside groups and outside and inside propaganda were neither similar nor static; they autonomously varied according to what was addressed. That is why outside suffragists must have experienced their activism as flexible, since they fluctuated between their 'suffragism' and their other affiliation(s). Tensions born out of 'divided loyalties' must have been stronger outside 'suffragism' than inside and must have affected the political texture of inside and outside 'suffragism'.

Thirdly, 'suffragism' connotes both a concept and a conception: it embodied a political reality in search of acknowledgement. As a concept, it encapsulated the comprehensive notion of a group made up of people and ideas. As a conception, it conceived its own processing and so asserted its objectives in dynamic terms. Such a process cannot be neutralised into a descriptive word: 'suffragism' was more than the reality of groups structured around the claim of suffrage; it was both the assertion of political existence and its self-validation. Such a multi-layered process saturated the issue (suffrage), globalised its virtues and colonised the outskirts of 'suffragism', targeting the far ends of the Edwardian political world. What is striking is its dynamics and ultimately its expansionist aims.

'Suffragism' does not equate to 'suffragists'. They can be defined through their group-belonging, the type of suffrage they supported, or the methods they advocated. 'Suffragism', on the other hand, was a category created by suffragists for whom suffrage was the priority and inclusion the strategy. 'Suffragism' meant to include one way or another all that was supportive of its claim. It would encompass all suffragists, and paradoxically even those outside, once they were artificially suspended from their main affiliation (parties, unions or other types of grouping). More than a narrowly defined locus of specific groups, which forms its usual definition, 'suffragism' embodied 'the suffragist norm' (the canon), stimulated debates outside and boosted the notion of suffrage throughout the Edwardian period. 'Suffragism' shaped 'a parallel public space'[27] where the claim for women's suffrage could be staged. Even if it was separate, its objective was to invade mainstream politics and to make mainstream public space suffragist. Such an inclusive dynamics fed inside as well as outside links, prospered from any endeavour and contribution that was serving the cause, through advocacy or through alienation. From this perspective, 'suffragism' has conquered and its disappearance is nothing but a triumph; far from being 'narrow-based', it has engulfed everything that is axiomatic to mainstream politics up to the present. 'Suffragism' is first the history of a conquest, not simply women's conquest of the vote, but more pervasively their right to be part of what used to be 'other', mainstream politics.

'Suffragism' was set as the centre, denying that it was peripheral to mainstream politics. As it was perforce self-centred, it projected inside and outside centrality and ambitions, and this was both politically and conceptually effective. It was the construction of a community inclusive of all that was marginalised about 'women', whether taken as female aggregated individuals or as a group sharing the same experience. This inclusive dynamic sprang from a clear sense of sex differences. Although born out of fragmentation,[28] 'suffragism' functioned on the inclusion principle: 'the other' was accepted and included into a flexible community whose borders were ever ready to fluctuate, open to anyone who shared the suffragist position. In the official exclusive (male) public space, citizenship had evolved from a pact of domination into a social contract where domination had to be consented to, where each and every member was equal to the other and so was guaranteed participation and expression.[29] Women set up their parallel public space, 'suffragism', in which they staged what they were denied: their political integration through formal citizenship. Citizenship was enacted at two levels. First, inside suffragists claimed suffrage as the result of their political practice, mostly inside 'suffragism', and as the accomplishment of their future political integration outside 'suffragism'. Secondly, as a sex group, they displayed common characteristics and identity, because they were already socially integrated (as wives, mothers, single women or even social activists). Excluded from the main public sphere, women had hijacked the margin and constructed the representation of their citizenship there. With 'suffragism', they targeted integration into mainstream politics while paradoxically organising separately; they aimed for individual aggregation (one day, each of them would be an individual citizen, in the liberal tradition) to the mainstream public space while as a sex group they campaigned collectively for their rights.

Jürgen Habermas's theory of competing public spheres [30] applied to 'suffragism' offers a stimulating reading of its setting up and development as a parallel public space, structured by suffragist periodicals and discourse. The original (male-dominated) public sphere had suspended emancipation whenever women were concerned: as a sex, women could never deserve the franchise whereas 'dependent men' (or voteless males) could. Inside suffragists made up a new public who consented to and self-validated their separate group: they organised separately and produced their own culture (including officialdom) that countered the mainstream public sphere where power and consent could only be male.[31] In the latter, women might be able to gain equality as individuals but never as 'women', the impossible 'other'. However, unlike this traditional (liberal mainstream) public sphere, 'suffragism' meant to include 'otherness', as long as it was suffragist.

Because their legitimacy as 'women' was not to be gained from mainstream society, legitimisation became suffragists' means and end instead. Hence, the all-inclusive and multifarious arguments that emphasised the injustice of women's exclusion from the liberal public sphere and served the cause of suffrage. Arguments were borrowed from all avenues and then developed consistently and coextensively: in the liberal version, women as competent individuals deserved the suffrage; in the natural rights version, women like all individuals were endowed with rights. Excluded from the traditional liberal public sphere as political citizens, women were praised as social actors for their work among the poor.[32] Since the 1860s, women had gradually seen how impossible it was for them to achieve political integration while the number of 'dependent men' declined. After 1867 and 1884, the increasing numbers of men who gained political integration pointed towards the introduction of manhood suffrage rather than a franchise based on 'competence' (the liberal tradition). In this renewed model, the origin of legitimacy came no longer from the competence of some individuals but from 'a public will' which resulted from information and debates, in fact the emerging pattern was mass democracy. If mass legitimisation was to replace validated exclusion (the liberal tradition), there would be less to gain from a public sphere where liberal influence and principles were declining, but more to gain from mass legitimisation: 'suffragism' was the place where womanhood in its diversity and future women-citizenry was already enacted and praised as a mass phenomenon, where debates, publications and demonstrations informed suffragists' awareness.

'Suffragism' was a parallel public sphere that was both identical and different. It both responded to and subverted the declining liberal model. Even before some women were enfranchised, mass democracy was characteristic of 'suffragism': pluralism, double affiliations, majority and difference had superseded the mainstream model of 'democratic universalism', based on one theoretical type of citizens that shared the same concerns and needs. By seceding from the mainstream public space, women signalled their disagreement and difference. They deployed 'general particularism'[33] as the foundation of 'suffragism'. Women were aware of their irreconcilable difference from the mainstream model (hence 'particularism') while they acknowledged their collective existence as a sex group (hence 'general'). Inside 'suffragism', women activists were heard and consulted as equals; debate was at the same time an instrument of propaganda and the validation of a shared ethic.[34] Emancipation, *raison d'être* of 'suffragism', generated an identical suffragist version of the public sphere along the traditional universal model. Emancipation of a sex group, the particular of 'suffragism', modified the parallel public sphere of 'suffragism' along the new lines of mass democracy. The example of education illustrates this well: if in the liberal public sphere, women could not be taught because they did not belong, in the traditional liberal version of 'suffragism', women should be educated so as to prove that they had the potential to serve and that they deserved the franchise. In the mass democratic version of 'suffragism', women should be taught to show that they could and did participate, a founding citizen's act.

The existence of 'suffragism' as a separate body of opinion and an alternative structuring strengthened activists and supporters' sense of identity, inside and outside. The dual mission of 'suffragism', the vote and female activism, enhanced the majority identity of the group as being female, the cause of their lack of franchise.[35] Suffragists built their community, 'suffragism', which could be easily apprehended through symbols and rituals.[36] The latter 'enable marginal communities to maintain solidarity, while also sending a message to the mainstream'.[37] Suffragist pageantry[38] both assimilated and dissented from mainstream rituals. Suffragists, notably the Militant groups,[39] also developed ritualised opposition to mainstream force. Ritualising was a characteristic way of shaping their own environment and of showing their potential power for the sake of inside cohesion and outside press reports, locally and nationally.

'Suffragism', as the basis of political alignment, implies the existence of a sex class, a category of analysis which subsumes others present in the field. There is this ontological link: 'about-women' questions interested mostly women. In addition, effective propaganda, it was believed, should stage females. Although 'women' – a topic and a 'spectacle'[40] – saturated the field, 'suffragism' still relied on the variety and heterogeneity that the sex class, women, could offer: common sex implied common claims but then all the rest could differ. And yet, 'suffragism' was more inclusive in discourse and propaganda than standard political parties or reforming groups. The latter generally insisted on preserving 'homogeneity', on rejecting 'divisive' issues, which allowed them to dismiss to some extent women's issues (or female 'otherness') or alternatively the 'suffrage' issue: exclusion became their ideological protection. Inclusion was the strength of 'suffragism' and because it was a deliberate process it was ideological. That such a space has been repeatedly presented as 'narrow-based' or 'single-issued' is denied by the fact that it constituted a parallel public sphere (in the sense devised by Habermas) where women's issues were validated. As a debating space for and about women, 'suffragism' was invaluable to their confidence-building and political practice, their acknowledgement of differences and democratic aspirations. Its inclusive dynamics and self-chosen fragmentation allowed for the voicing of new ideas; although it was a competing political space, it operated on the basis of collaboration. Propaganda-making and innovative posturing consequently provided a forum for creation and originality – which could horrify 'ordinary' activists.

Such a space modelled political practices for inside activists, outside suffragists and probably outside women. Because 'suffragism' had become their political norm, its operating modes became references. Outside women and suffragists set up platforms for women, women-only projects, or women's sections within their affiliated groups: an unparalleled self-structuring backed up by the knowledge of the existing practices of 'suffragism'. As many women (and some men) were both inside and outside suffragists, they were familiar with such approaches and effectively lobbied the executive and the members of their other affiliation.

As 'suffragism' was essentially political, it evolved and adapted to political and electoral changes, just as any traditional party would. None of the key suffragist organisations was ideologically committed to parties, although individual Liberal women activists must have been the most numerous. Double affiliations were common but remain difficult to investigate beyond biographies and group monographs. An activist was not likely to forget her (outside) affiliation once she put on her suffragist coat, just as a suffragist standpoint must have been difficult to muffle in a party or union branch meeting. 'Suffragism' did not support parties but was a political space; it answered and formulated political ideas which were vehicles of communication, within and without. Political ideas were also necessarily imported from outside with or without modifications. Political parties and other groups produced ideas that suffragists were keen to exploit for their own propaganda; outside suffragists who were also insiders brought in knowledge and mastered transfers of ideas and propaganda in and out.

Suffrage outside 'suffragism'

The operating mode between 'suffragism' and 'suffrage outside' was based on complex interactive connections, which allowed for divergence and convergence. The study of 'suffragism' (as a field) has been relatively neglected and has been distorted by an emphasis on specific structures or binary oppositions. For example, a binary opposition such as 'suffragists versus anti-suffragists' offers too simplistic a reading. Although pro- and anti-suffragist women had an obvious antithetical political positioning on suffrage, their operational modes and ideological positions were not systematically opposed so that the ways they processed ideas and advocated policies could be remarkably similar. On the other hand, male and female anti-suffragists may have had much less in common than is usually expected: neglecting the characteristics of female anti-suffragism – or making it inconsistent – cannot make anti-suffragism a coherent whole.[41] As Edwardian politics witnessed the rise of class-based politics,[42] it is worth asking where anti-suffragists stood in relation to 'suffragism'. Julia Bush suggests that anti-suffragists were divided into two groups, the positive and the negative ones, or the women's and the men's groups, and that 'it was also clear to many imperialist suffragists that only a fine line divided Violet [Markham]'s view from their own so far as gender difference and patriotic service were concerned'.[43] Female anti-suffragists could well have been near relations of some suffragist activists, inside and outside 'suffragism', while other Antis had political relevance only outside 'suffragism'. Obviously, 'suffrage' has to remain the conspicuous definition of the field; yet, because both female activism and politics participated in the making of the field ('suffragism'), because anti-suffragist women activists shared the characteristics involved in female activism, paradoxically and indirectly, they could have contributed to 'suffragism', the Edwardian norm for suffrage activism and female activism.

Protecting the centre: national parties and the control of women

From the Edwardian years onwards the political spectrum was modified through the rise of Labour politics, nationally and locally. Even though class increasingly competed with religion as the basis of political alignment, radical continuities and local diversity could still be seen.[44] That party workers should be deployed all over the political territory was an obvious necessity for the two main parties and their smaller competitor, Labour.[45] In this book, party women and suffrage are discussed by Pat Thane for Labour, Lori Maguire for the Conservative Party and Linda Walker for the Liberal Party. The Liberals and the Conservatives had enrolled female activists into support since the 1880s. Set up in 1883, the Conservative Primrose League admitted women the following year; the Women's Liberal Federation formalised Liberal women's activism at a national level in 1887 while the local Women's Liberal Associations had sprung up from the early 1880s.[46] Female activism had been encouraged on the basis of service to party, and to male members, while women were still excluded from membership. This was in keeping with a liberal public sphere where consent and participation could only be male. Thus, female activists were refused integration into parties;[47] they belonged to affiliated organisations or over time made up women's sections of parties. They were *separate* and the motivations and aspirations they had were not heard while they were expected to serve. Service and virtuous devotion recall the practice of female religious orders, except that women activists had not vowed to be silent.

The Women's Labour League (WLL) was established well into the Edwardian period; an all-female organisation, it was formed in 1906 as an autonomous 'organization of women to work for independent Labour representation of women in Parliament and in all local bodies' – implying a clear commitment to women's suffrage. Affiliated to the Labour Party in 1908 it got the right to attend and vote at party conferences despite coldness from the male leadership.[48] The WLL was almost the only gateway for women to access Labour Party officialdom; it dutifully adopted adult suffrage in 1911 to forward the aims of the party. Conservative women formed their suffragist group in 1908, the Conservative and Unionist Women's Franchise Association. 'Their goal, as their first president, Lady Knightley of Fawsley described it to *The Times* was "to have a large and representative body of Conservatives and Unionists pledged to assist their leaders and to influence the Conservative party to extend the franchise to duly-qualified women".'[49] Here service was foremost, and deserved its reward, the vote. The Women's Liberal Federation used the experience of its longer existence to defy the party and challenge its perception of female activism: 'their ideological and tactical mission to wrest control of party policy' ultimately failed. The suffrage issue 'helped to shape the identity and purpose of the Federation, and . . . led to serious divisions between members'.[50]

Socialist party orthodoxy negated the specificity of women as a sex, and, following Engels and Bebel, socialists extolled the sex/class analogy. Despite debates within the Social Democratic Federation, the woman question was not integrated in socialism itself as it was argued it could divide the working-class. This probably explained why the Women's Socialist Circles, the branches' separate women's organisations, were set up to encourage 'social aspects of branch life'.[51] That women should serve their party (itself serving the working-class) was also axiomatic for the socialist women from the Independent Labour Party; claiming the vote was reduced to a first step on the path to 'the overthrow of oppression'. In *Socialist Women,* June Hannam and Karen Hunt explore 'the diverse ways in which socialist women struggled to translate the tension between socialism and feminism into a creative political practice in the period from the mid 1880s to the 1920s'.[52] Socialist women from the Social Democratic Federation and the Independent Labour Party were full members of their parties; they expected a future society where 'sexual equality' – whatever it meant – was promised.[53]

All these parties integrated women as party workers but denied sex was a political issue or neutralised it into 'class'. Such a consistent approach whipped Edwardian suffragist societies into action away from traditional and new parties. The idea of party neutrality had been inherited from the first suffrage societies of the 1870s, which had then thought that it was more effective to be 'cross-party', especially as none of the main parties wished to take women's suffrage onboard. This issue, whether to remain outside formal politics or not, damaged and split the suffrage campaign in 1888.[54]

The common social experience of women did not mean uniform political responses. Class was one variable; ideas and social conditions strongly determined commitment but opinion was also mobilised by 'sentiments, interests and beliefs'.[55] As political parties allowed for some degree of divergence, intra-class differences could well be more significant than class-belonging[56] with sex being a major variable here. Sex difference, or a 'sex class', did provide common experiences and grievances within the same class or concurrently to class experience. If in the late nineteenth century, class-belonging became politically meaningful, sex-belonging could become so, too. Women as a sex class did exist and were concentrated in separate organisations or in women's sections of parties with little or no representation at the level of party executives; if they were insignificant as a political group within their own party, they could try to become significant and could look at what 'suffragism' offered.[57] Shifting their party loyalty to their sex group, they could easily swap to 'suffragism'; being non-party, it accommodated what was division and divergence elsewhere (for example the type of suffrage) while being consistent with sex loyalty. 'Suffragism' adopted sex as the basis of alignment. Its political agenda was about women's suffrage whether its activists and supporters were men or women. From the start, 'suffragism' did not replace party affiliations. It offered a parallel space where sex issues were taken for granted; party affiliations and sympathies then determined the suffragist course of action. Hence, the double affiliations that were more often than not the rule with female activists. 'Suffragism' was one possibility; other contemporary campaigns offered women potential involvement: temperance, free school meals, working-class housing, maternity benefit and child welfare are examples of campaigns in which female activists were involved.[58]

In 'suffragism', sexualised political agendas allowed male activists to participate even if female activists always prevailed numerically.[59] Women-only structures coexisted with all-male or mixed ones; if political and intellectual production had female and male authors, it was nonetheless entirely devoted to women's rights; it was all-female oriented even if activists were both men and women, if not couples.[60]

Adopting 'sex class' as one's first loyalty does not mean being without class-consciousness but it spelt out that women's issues had as much validity as class or party ones. Divided loyalties did not prevent prioritising. How suffragists established the validity of their perceptions, how they related to alternate choices, usually remains impossible to find out. What researchers can do though is grant suffragists, females and males, the consistency of their choice, inside or outside 'suffragism', and then try to account for it.

'Cross-party' was the Conservative Balfour's and the Liberal Gladstone's pretext to avoid the sex and suffrage issue; in both cases they thought women deserved the vote but wished 'to protect' their parties from further crises, fearing that suffrage would be damagingly 'divisive'. The new Labour Party claimed to represent the still disenfranchised males and the poorer disenfranchised females, and just like the two main parties was aware of party advantage and the constraints of representation.[61] That suffrage was 'cross-party', as claimed by contemporaries, illustrates what they saw as a fact; this cannot clarify much the object of study of this book. By contrast, 'suffragism' became the *other* space, the space where suffrage was essential and binding and structuring, generating loyalties about this issue. The 'cross-party' contention could mean delaying tactics against women's vote or classing suffrage low on the political agenda. Indeed, 'cross-party' seems to have stigmatised the issue as not very important. Mainstream politics refused to take it onboard, whereas women activists had already taken great pains to show its importance for them and society as a whole. Because women were not political subjects, their issues and enfranchisement were euphemistically connoted as 'sectional' and 'cross-party',[62] which manhood suffrage did not seem to have been. When in 1912, the Labour Party did commit itself on women's suffrage,[63] it rallied suffragists from inside and outside 'suffragism', and inflamed the feeling of divided loyalties for all except Labour women.[64] Over time, parties and activists changed or maintained the balance of their priorities between party affiliation and a suffragist stand while local involvement enabled many to experience both fully: 'Locally women retained a far greater commitment to party politics'.[65] Besides, according to regions, party politics could be stronger or particular just as interparty co-operation and/or 'suffragism' were likely to unite all local female activists into action.

In the hub of things: local activism and sexual politics

June Hannam has convincingly argued that 'local suffrage politics was not just about building support for a national movement – at particular times the local branches *were* the movement'. She reaches the conclusion that 'local studies transform our view of the nature and meaning of "suffragism" *for the participants*' (my italics).[66] Local 'suffragism' had 'a life of its own'. If local and national perspectives had a complex relationship, the neat labelling and differentiation between suffragist groups could lose meaning locally.[67] When competing for members, labelling was vital, less so when groups were collaborating; when organisations, and not activists, are the focus of propaganda or research, labelling remains useful. However, the history of structures[68] does not always mirror the affiliating choices and loyalties of people involved. Ideology, inner organisation and decision-making do play an important role but community loyalties, family history and perception of arguments can supersede or qualify ideology, class or sex interests. Local studies seem to offer a better perspective to examine individual activists and their rationale;[69] formal recruitment and informal companionship are aspects which could also be better assessed at the local level. With 'suffragism' as a linguistic and political space loosely federating the local branches of groups, non-affiliated women as well found an informative and debating space for their suffragist conviction. 'Suffragism' could also merge with the scene of local party politics if party activists were suffragists or if their networks were identical. The reception of national propaganda by the rank and file activists, their local knowledge and propaganda-making, 'the political loafers' waiting to be included, are elements that can enrich or qualify the national pattern. The relation between regions and the capital allowed for singularity and fluctuation. The national perspective was structure-centred; it liaised with Parliament, government or executives of political parties, emphasising its own importance. The local perspective relied on activists, their numbers, personal constraints and local interaction. Because local networks and pressure groups differed in scope and manner from national ones does not mean that they were in a subservient relation; local and national levels can show convergence and divergence if not contradiction.[70]

In this book, Julia Bush, for the middle-class National Union of Women Workers (NUWW), and Gillian Scott, for the working-class Women's Cooperative Guild (WCG) write about two non-party organisations and the suffrage issue. The NUWW was 'an "umbrella" organisation [which] depended upon mutual respect among women of varying beliefs and varied social, political and religious background. The desired ethos of gender solidarity in support of gendered social service' of the NUWW paralleled 'the self-styled "trade union of married women" ', the WCG, that brought 'this previously unrepresented constituency into public life, broadcasting their needs and views on a range of social and political questions which were by no means limited to suffrage'.[71] Both were national women's organisations with affiliated local groups. Both expected members to voice social needs and produce social answers: these bottom-up structures ensured that democratic procedures and aspirations took place. From the local scene, both groups claimed social legislation should serve women's needs as mothers and wives, even if the WCG women were more likely to be recipients. While they expected political reform from Parliament, they could not ignore the value of the parliamentary vote. They did not differ from party women: the WLL women claimed social reform and action in a partnership with the state; in a more traditional liberal tradition, the Conservative and Liberal women stressed the need for moral reform as instrumental to social reform. Non-party and party women defended the same, or a similar, agenda of social action. Locally they collaborated with each other or were identical groups of women activists. What was locally true of party and non-party women matched the reality of the way women were involved outside and inside 'suffragism'. Their various hats ensured that local female activism was identified with women whose affiliations represented a cross-section of the female Edwardian political fabric, suffrage included.

Local activism tells the story of groups and individuals but also of shared means of propaganda: all party and non-party women groups emphasised political teaching and individual empowerment,[72] altruistic interests and denunciation of sexual injustice. They participated whenever they could in local government and encouraged their members to contribute to local social action, stressing their apolitical or party view, depending from which platform they talked. Their local involvement was founded on the idea they had of female representation and delegation; it gradually became synonymous with electioneering, and this could only lead to suffrage being acknowledged as a vital tool in the process. Besides, local activists, even when they wished their organisations to remain noncommittal on the issue, were often suffragists themselves: they simply thought it would be a mistake to have their group officially endorse women's suffrage. Just as formal parties claimed that suffrage was 'divisive', many groups outside 'suffragism' thought that adopting suffrage would foster division; they feared that they would experience antagonism in the same way as party politics did (although the latter did not since suffrage was deemed to be 'cross-party'): a remarkably contradictory version of 'cross-party'. This non-party official stand seems to have been stronger among middle-class groups such as the NUWW where party affiliations, mostly Conservative or Liberal, may have been more contentious. The non-party NUWW, however, showed how the integration of political language contradicted the (self-staged) isolation fantasy that women were above politics, lobbying for new social legislation while accepting their political exclusion from mainstream politics.[73]

By contrast the active female citizenship of the more (politically) homogeneous WCG activists developed on pragmatic lines; they were working-class suffragists and women whose urgent priorities and lack of free time did not accommodate infighting well, compared with such contests as Fawcett vs. Ward in the NUWW. WCG members testified in favour of the divorce law reform (1909), argued for provision for women in the national insurance scheme as mothers and home workers, and supported municipal schemes of maternal care. They served their sex interests but these could hardly be divorced from their class or social experience: as married women at home, they had been formerly cut off from any form of group support, parties, unions or social organisations.[74] Acknowledging their sex and class identity, they 'naturally' claimed suffrage as another empowering tool.

Women of the NUWW had been assertive about social issues, exerting their class privilege. Yet as a sex group, they had to be content with 'advisory if need be', a secondary status that clashed with their middle-class identity. Through the NUWW, they discovered their numbers and variety. Repeatedly class was empowering, sex was disabling. The suffrage contest between Fawcett and Ward within the NUWW can be read as the sex versus class debate: how the defining priority made a movement avowedly suffragist (women should unite because of their sex) or socially homogeneous (women from the same class should unite). In a way, the NUWW was a site where two different public spheres competed for supremacy and although 'suffragism' won, reluctance to discard the class strategy, which granted middle-class women a fair sample of class advantages, still informed the NUWW shared vision of sex reformism.

The same tensions were experienced in local socialism and Conservatism where the top-down approach of national structures made local activists rebel in a number of instances. In this book, June Hannam shows how Bristol socialist women, Philippe Vervaecke how Primrose League women, contested national policies for the sake of their consistency as local activists. Women's suffrage could become the test question to assess how far their national organisation cared for their women supporters. 'Many socialist women, and some men, became involved in the suffrage campaign itself as well as using the issue to raise questions about the commitment of socialist groups to working for women's emancipation as a key part of the project of constructing a new society'.[75] The answer for Primrose League women was even clearer as 'the lesson they were taught constituted a caveat against the male complacency and female subservience which characterised the League's gender-integrative approach that was gradually repudiated by female activists within the party.'[76] In both cases, the WSPU was the suffrage organisation which could compete with the original affiliation, probably because the National Union of Women's Suffrage Society (NUWSS) may have looked even more Liberal locally than nationally, a sure reminder that party politics mattered within 'suffragism' as well as without. The description of the Bristol NUWSS as the 'Liberal Primrose Leaguers' by a WSPU supporter[77] connotes not only the monolithic perception of Liberal influence in local 'suffragism' but also shows how political rivalry within 'suffragism' took to the standard phrasing of party politics. When Kensington Primrose Leaguers suggested alliance with the WSPU to obtain women's suffrage (against the official neutrality policy of the League), they showed how acceptable the WSPU could be while Grand Council sternly repulsed the more dangerous NUWSS attempts to contact Primrose League female local activists. A number of local rebels had already made the Primrose League second to their suffragist commitment, risking expulsion, when in 1910 Betty Balfour, President of Ladies' Grand Council, informed *The Times*'s readers why she could not support her local anti-suffragist Conservative MP.[78] Conversely, the establishment of the national WSPU (1903) was analysed as potential poaching of socialist women and encouraged socialist organisations to set up their own women's groups. Locally, socialist women could be employed as NUWSS organisers to deflate class hostility and approach working-class potential supporters of 'suffragism'. Class could also be powerfully divisive within 'suffragism'. The example of socialist women from the East Bristol WSS showed how precarious a suffragist affiliation could be versus class loyalty at the time of a parliamentary election.[79]

At times of local elections, female activism was both promoted and circumscribed by political organisations and parties. Female activism according to the Primrose League could be channelled into 'temperance, public morality, charity and religion', 'women's traditional public duties', while women's suffrage was deemed irrelevant.[80] Liberal women had a similar definition of women's citizenship except that a majority of them made women's suffrage a decisive commitment via the Women's Liberal Federation. In any case, Primrose League women were effective canvassers and political instructors in the localities and provided they remembered that 'women's suffrage was a question of opinion and not of principle', Grand Council could hope to save them from politics and safeguard their moral principles.[81] Such a definition of the political and of the proper involvement of women did not prevent them from participating in local government where the ideal of service and womanly public duties prevailed. Socialist women were involved in the same local duties: like their Conservative and Liberal counterparts, they were actors and targets of political education; they were both political workers and candidates for local elected positions. As social event organisers, these women were usually responsible for catering and recreational facilities. Such activities can be seen as politically inferior (many contemporaries must have thought so), but they were geared to consolidate local activism. Sharing activities and celebrating events kept local groups together and helped recruit new members, especially women. At the local level, women's groups outside 'suffragism' involved women in 'women's tasks' whose political importance became increasingly difficult to deny: the expansionist labour and suffrage movements competed for women members while the Primrose League tried to shut them out from suffrage and sex issues.

Domestic ideology was inherent to socialist discourse, denying women's individual claims except as wives and mothers of socialist men. Unsurprisingly it was also part of the Primrose League which called women's suffrage 'a subsidiary question' (1910) and had always denied female representation at the head of the movement. Parallel to this, the League painstakingly (and in a somewhat suicidal manner) emphasised the men's share in popular Conservatism and encouraged male-only bodies within the League while losing women to other women-only Conservative bodies.[82] Domestic ideology was dominant within 'suffragism' as well. But as a forum 'about women', 'suffragism' allowed for a variety of discourses: a discourse which strengthened female occupational and paid work issues; an avant-garde discourse which could be trying to female 'modesty' because of its explicit discussion of sexuality. In suffrage outside 'suffragism', the unionised female teachers and the avant-garde women echoed or initiated these discourses.

Beyond the structure: mastering and discarding organisations

In the Edwardian years, 'suffrage' became one vested point to define the political. If suffrage was the priority, 'suffragism' was the answer. Outside 'suffragism', political parties defined suffrage as 'cross-party', that is as 'non-party', and conveniently discarded it along with women's issues. Women's groups pursuing social reform were more or less reluctant to adopt it for fear of entering the political field. Yet their 'social' participation in local government, supposedly divorced from any political standpoint, could not make the fiction last, especially as they saw how political parties carved out local responsibilities among their successful candidates. Activists experienced the political differently from their structures, differently locally and nationally; they had to struggle to have their viewpoints considered. In this book, Susan Trouvé-Finding examines the National Union of Teachers (NUT) which claimed they could not adopt 'suffrage' as it was 'too political' and that as a professional union, occupational issues were their main concern. Conversely, Lucy Delap shows how avant-garde women disclaimed 'suffrage' as 'just political' and too narrow a basis for feminists who discussed the personal. In both cases, individual activism, with men and women involved, was compatible with occupation alignment (teaching) and individualistic concerns (creative activities). What is striking is the feeling of triumph that women as a sex group could not but feel when they became executives of their teaching associations (1910s),[83] a triumph that avant-garde women could safely deride now that some of them had left the teaching profession.

Even though they did not manage to turn the NUT into a suffragist organisation, the unionised women teachers (as well as their non-unionised colleagues) represented independent working women whose dignified professional roles pervaded schools and neighbourhoods as well as their unions: 'by 1899 three-quarters of the 82 000 elementary teachers were women . . . By 1904 57.7 per cent of certificated women teachers (97.5 per cent of their male colleagues) were members of the union.'[84] As unionised labour, their subscriptions were used to return male MPs who did not even need to be suffragist while women were 'specifically excluded from the benevolent fund's top category'.[85] Equal pay and career promotion were standing claims across the period. Suffrage was added to the list of demands from the 1911 annual conference onwards but to no avail. Despite the NUT Executive becoming favourable to women's suffrage, the rank and file never gave it a majority. In fact, equal pay, though 'a domestic issue', proved more 'divisive' a topic than suffrage. Inside the NUT the National Federation of Women Teachers (NFWT) welcomed all women teachers (even if unqualified) and promoted both equal pay and suffrage, two issues which showed women teachers how sex played against their interests, even though they had then reached the decision-making levels of their union. Despite moderate female leaders and a majority of female members, their union remained deaf to women teachers' concerns. This led to the setting up of the (moderate) National Union of Women Teachers (1920): it opposed the marriage bar and promoted equal pay, two objectives that the NUT still refused to support. Whatever their qualifications and their professional competence, women would still be paid less in the 1920s, just as on the basis of sex, they had been excluded from the parliamentary franchise before the First World War. Whatever their record, work achievements and ethics, it was as a sex group that they were victimised in their career prospects and pay; although women were more numerous in their union, suffrage (up to the 1910s) as well as equal pay remained officially 'sectional' and 'divisive' issues. As educated self-confident women, female teachers knew this was an effective lesson in sexual politics; unsurprisingly quite a number of them joined suffragist groups and political parties before 1914.

As an increasingly numerous work group whose expertise was acknowledged, as educated lower middle-class women, teachers represented a valuable input to 'suffragism' and politics as a whole. Assertive and financially independent, these women probably brought their own devised vision of ordinary 'new women', neither the exploited working-class worker and mother nor the leisured philanthropic middle-class woman. They competed with the young educated middle-class girls for jobs in journalism and 'suffragism'. Aware of their social origins and subsequent social promotion, they had little to lose. Mary Gawthorpe, Dora Marsden and Teresa Billington-Greig[86] claimed equal pay within the NUT, went through suffragist (Militant) politics before entering the new stage of *The Freewoman*. 'Many of the "advanced" or "vanguard" women who came to describe themselves as feminists were motivated by their former experience as suffragists.'[87] They claimed that true emancipation was undermined by suffragist discipline and competition for power. Having abandoned the official male public space where women were denied as a category at work and lacked influence on the union scene, these vanguard women invested in 'suffragism' as organisers or prominent activists. Some then abandoned this 'corrupt and inept'[88] parallel public sphere in order to set up a new space centred on the periodical *The Freewoman*. There men and women produced and spread ideas for the 'uncommitted, progressive, and younger group' who were not shocked by sexual explicitness and permanent polemics[89] and above all who saw 'suffragism' for what it was – whatever that was. Away from inclusive 'suffragism', they generated the elite profile of the vanguard feminists for whom 'feminism was not understood in these early stages as a democratic and egalitarian movement ... Elitism span[ned] Fabian, new liberal and avant-garde feminist political discourses.'[90] Avant-garde women could be seen as an end-product of 'suffragism': they had experienced participation in a mass movement, even if, as they said, it was 'narrow-based' because geared only towards one cause. They next ventured into individual assertiveness and voiced arguments with no cause but the (female) individuality they knew they had, a long way from suffrage inside and outside 'suffragism'.

Thus even though 'suffragism' did eventually disappear as a cause, its political teaching may have had a more lasting influence than the Edwardian period on both women and structures. Women had already proved themselves valuable members – even if they needed to be controlled to be instrumental to the party – and once enfranchised they would also provide votes. For female activists, 'suffragism' must have sustained their political apprenticeship outside, offering not only traditional back-up but also showing the efficiency of political separatism: above all it displayed what women could do when they were not ostracised. To political parties and reforming groups, 'suffragism' could be seen as a threat, competing with them for female activists and defining loyalty in terms of neither party politics nor common social action. That women flocked into social and political structures at that period showed that women were ready to invest the public sphere whilst political parties still found it difficult to accept and integrate women as 'women'. On the other hand, middle-class women's reforming groups could still be tempted by 'genteel womanly' influence as a proven method instead of straightforward political lobbying.

Political parties had a stake in women as party workers and potential voters despite the fact that in the Edwardian period most of them did what they could not to enfranchise them. Non-political structures such as the National Union of Women Workers or the Women's Co-operative Guild, managed by and for women's interest, had sprung from the 1880s onward to voice women's views on women's issues as if neither of them was political; they lost the monopoly of women's issues (basically social reforms affecting children and the family), once party women developed their social agenda inside parties. Reforming groups continued to be relevant but they had to build alliances and accept the idea that the social was also political. Such a transition was not as brutal as it sounds because most Edwardian women activists possessed a culture of double affiliations and of collaboration on the basis of sex. Their chameleon-like political positioning can be said to reflect what they were used to experiencing in ordinary life as well. As wives, mothers and daughters, they invested roles they were expected to play. Practically, in 'ordinary' life as well as in political life, being female still meant subordination so that sex solidarity as exemplified in 'suffragism' remained a powerful attraction and an incentive to reform structures and objectives. Outside suffragists fought against the acknowledgement of female political and social subordination as 'natural' and made a breakthrough on the battlefield. It meant forcing on political parties social agendas geared towards women's needs; in reforming groups it meant acknowledging that political emancipation should be at the origin of social action and not a side issue.

Empowerment came from the practices and the model that 'suffragism' advocated inside and exported outside, the more diligently so as a number of suffragists were also outside political or social activists. Ideas and individuals left 'suffragism' and mushroomed outside, sometimes against the original model. The flux in and out demonstrated that subordination out there was not final: political emancipation would open the gates of elected office and decision-making, adding up to what women had already painstakingly achieved. To insiders and outsiders, 'suffragism' not only denounced the characteristic wrongs women suffered from but also publicised women's potential outside their traditional roles.

Notes

1. B. Harrison, *Separate Spheres: the Opposition to Women's Suffrage in Britain* (London: Croom Helm, 1978), p. 17.
2. Such suffragists could be members of suffragist organisations or not. In this introduction 'suffragists' means individuals who were committed to women's suffrage whatever their affiliations. Whether suffragists belonged to Militant or constitutionalist organisations is outside the scope of this book; the differences between suffrage organisations and their methods have already been abundantly researched.

3. There is no attempt to be exhaustive in this book. For women's suffrage and temperance groups, see M. Barlow, 'Teetotal Feminists: Temperance Leadership and the Campaign for Women's Suffrage', in C. Eustance, J. Ryan and L. Ugolini, *A Suffrage Reader: Charting Directions in British Suffrage History* (London, Leicester University Press, 2000), pp. 69–89; M. Smitley, '"Inebriates", "Heathens", Templars and Suffragists: Scotland and Imperial Feminism, c. 1870–1914', *Women's History Review*, 11, 3 (2002), pp. 455–80. For the Social Democratic Federation, see K. Hunt, *Equivocal Feminists, the Social Democratic Federation and the Woman Question 1884–1911* (Cambridge: Cambridge University Press, 1996). For local women's organisations, see K. Cowman, *Mrs Brown is a Man and a Brother: Women in Merseyside's Political Organisations 1890–1920* (Liverpool: Liverpool University Press, 2004).
4. A. Chadwick, *Augmenting Democracy, Political Movements and Constitutional Reform During the Rise of Labour 1900–1924* (Aldershot: Ashgate, 1999), especially 'Constructing a Suffragist Alliance', pp. 104–41.
5. The constitutionalists advocated legal methods and were represented by the powerful National Union of Women's Suffrage Societies. The Militant societies, the Women's Social and Political Union and the Women's Freedom League, adopted illegal means to forward their cause.
6. S. S. Holton, *Suffrage Days: Stories from the Women's Suffrage Movement* (London: Routledge, 1996), p. 244.
7. E. Crawford, 'The Suffragette Fellowship', *The Women's Suffrage Movement: a Reference Guide 1866–1928* (London: Routledge, 2001), pp. 663–4. The 'Votes for Women' fellowship set up by the Pethick-Lawrences in 1912 published as one of its objects: 'To tell the true story of the Movement, both in its constitutional and Militant development, and also to show the causes that have produced and are still fomenting the present revolt', an insert in E. Pethick-Lawrence, *In Women's Shoes* (Letchworth: Garden City Press, 1913). However, the Pethick-Lawrences were announcing a somewhat larger scope than what was basically financial support for their suffragist paper: 'As may be surmised from the name of the organization, it was built around the weekly suffrage paper, *Votes for Women*', E. Crawford, 'Votes for Women Fellowship', *The Women's Suffrage Movement*, p. 698.
8. L. N. Mayhall, 'Creating the Suffragette Spirit', *Women's History Review*, 4, 3 (1995), pp. 319–44, pp. 332–3.
9. Laura Mayhall's analysis could be applied to most suffrage organisations even though the Suffragette Fellowship only gathered former Militant activists' testimonies from the Women's Social and Political Union and the Women's Freedom League. Prewar suffragist contemporaries published books in the 1910s to position their suffrage societies either in historic continuity or in rupture. What was at stake was the justification or criticism of methods towards gaining women's vote which they thought was imminent. For continuity B. Mason, *The Story of the Women's Suffrage Movement* (London: Sherrat & Hughes, 1912); M. G. Fawcett, *Women's Suffrage: a Short History of a Great Movement* (London: T. C. & E. C. Jack, 1912). For rupture, T. Billington-Greig, *The Militant Suffrage Movement: Emancipation in a Hurry* (London: Franck Palmer, 1911); E. S. Pankhurst, *The Suffragette: the History of the Women's Militant Suffrage Movement 1905–1910* (London: Sturgis & Walton, 1911).

10. Mayhall, 'Creating the Suffragette Spirit', pp. 332–3. The year equal suffrage was won, Ray Strachey (a 'constitutionalist') published *'The Cause': a Short History of the Women's Movement in Great Britain* (London: Bell, 1928). It was not only a contribution to history-making but also a tribute to M. G. Fawcett (1847–1929) whose biography she published in 1931, R. Strachey, *Millicent Garrett Fawcett* (London: Murray, 1931).
11. Mayhall, 'Creating the Suffragette Spirit', pp. 334–5.
12. R. Strachey, *'The Cause'*; E. S. Pankhurst, *The Suffragette Movement: an Intimate Account of Persons and Ideals* (London: Longmans, 1931).
13. S. S. Holton, 'Reflecting on Suffrage History', in Eustance et al., *A Suffrage Reader*, pp. 23–36; Holton, *Suffrage Days*, pp. 244, 249.
14. Holton, 'Reflecting on Suffrage History', p. 25.
15. 'There is equally a contradiction in the way masculinist history criticises the suffrage movement for being one-dimensional in its pursuit of a single issue, while dismissing concerns with the sexual exploitation of women as pathological. The suffrage movement can be interpreted as narrow or disordered in approach only by an almost wanton blindness to the sexual politics intrinsic to the suffrage campaign. Masculinist histories also consistently underrate the symbolic and cultural force, both of the winning of the vote, and of women's militancy. Similarly it is difficult to understand why the political achievements of the suffrage movement are either denied or diminished in masculinist accounts', S. S. Holton, 'The Making of Suffrage History', in J. Purvis and S. S. Holton (eds), *Votes for Women* (London: Routledge, 2000), p. 28.
16. Lynn Abrams and Karen Hunt, 'Borders and Frontiers in Women's History' (editorial), *Women's History Review*, 9, 2 (2000), pp. 191–200, p. 191.
17. Ibid., p. 197.
18. C. Beaumont, 'Citizens, Not Feminists: the Boundary Negotiated between Citizenship and Feminism by Mainstream Women's Organisations in England 1928–1939', *Women's History Review*, 9, 2 (2000), pp. 411–29.
19. J. Hannam and K. Holden, 'Heartland and Periphery: Local, National and Global Perspectives on Women's History' (editorial), *Women's History Review*, 11, 3 (2002), pp. 341–8, pp. 341–2.
20. This similarity to and contrast with the mainstream political field recalls, through analogy, what Gisela Bock wrote about the relation between women's history and the history of men, 'Women's History and Gender History: Aspects of an International Debate', *Gender & History*, 1, 1 (Spring 1989), pp. 8–9.
21. Ibid., pp. 15–16.
22. 'By the second half of the 1980s, then, there had been a significant shift in the interpretative frameworks shaping suffrage history in Britain, a shift that had extended our understanding of the range and complexity of the internal politics of the suffrage movement, that challenged absolute distinction between Militants and constitutionalists, and that increasingly recognised the importance of local movements and provincial suffrage societies', Holton, 'Reflecting on Suffrage History', p. 25.
23. Lori Maguire, Chapter 3 below, p. 81: in the Conservative Party, women's suffrage was seen as a protection against manhood suffrage (John Buchan's argument); for the suffragist Conservative Betty Balfour, women's suffrage should not lead to womanhood suffrage either.

24. Suffragists who were both insiders and outsiders would select one or the other identity according to situations. In this introduction they will be artificially considered as one or the other.
25. The chapters below offer a number of examples of this.
26. L. Tickner, *The Spectacle of Women: Imagery of the Suffrage Campaign 1907–1914* (London: Chatto & Windus, 1987); M. Boussahba-Bravard, 'Vision et visibilité: la rhétorique visuelle des suffragistes et suffragettes 1907–1914', LISA e-journal, 1, 1 (2003), pp. 42–54.
27. S. Herbst, *Politics at the Margin: Historical Studies of Public Expression Outside the Mainstream* (Cambridge: Cambridge University Press, 1994), p. 4: 'What I call parallel public space – the arenas that marginal groups develop in order to voice their opinions.'
28. Jürgen Habermas, *L'intégration républicaine. Essais de théorie politique* (Paris: Fayard, 1998), pp. 5–6.
29. Ibid., pp. 73, 76.
30. Jürgen Habermas, *L'espace public,* new 'Introduction' (Paris: Payot, 1992).
31. Carol Pateman demonstrates that the modernisation of the social contract is limited to the 'fraternal' type and excludes the 'female' type, Carol Pateman, 'The Fraternal Social Contract', in J. Keane (ed.), *Civil Society and the State* (London: University of Westminster Press, 1988), p. 105, quoted in Habermas, *L'espace public,* 'Introduction', p. 9.
32. P. Hollis, *Ladies Elect: Women in English Local Government, 1865–1914* (Oxford: Clarendon, 1987); J. Lewis, *Women and Social Action in Victorian and Edwardian England* (Aldershot: Edward Edgar, 1991); P. Thane, 'Labour and Local Politics: Radicalism, Democracy and Social Reform, 1880–1914', in E. Biagini and A. Reid (eds), *Currents of Radicalism: Popular Radicalism, Organised Labour and Party Politics in Britain 1850–1914* (Cambridge: Cambridge University Press, 1991), pp. 244–70, pp. 259–61.
33. Habermas, *L'espace public,* 'Introduction', p. 21.
34. Ibid., pp. 24, 26.
35. S. Holton, 'Manliness and Militancy: the Political Protests of Male Suffragists and the Gendering of the "Suffragette" Identity', in A. John and C. Eustance (eds), *The Men's Share? Masculinities, Male Support and Women's Suffrage in Britain 1890–1920* (London: Routledge, 1997), pp. 110–34.
36. E. Yeo and S. Yeo, 'On the Uses of "Community": from Owenism to the Present', in Stephen Yeo (ed.), *New Views of Co-operation* (London: Routledge, 1988), pp. 229–41; C. Eustance, J. Ryan and L. Ugolini, 'Introduction: Writing Suffrage Histories: the "British" Experience', in Eustance et al. (eds), *A Suffrage Reader*, p. 10.
37. Herbst, *Politics at the Margin,* p. 24.
38. 'A nation-wide production, *A Pageant of Great Women* which she [Edith Craig] devised with Cecily Hamilton, made front page news in the *Daily Mirror* [12 November 1909]', Katharine Cockin, *Edith Craig (1869–1947): Dramatic Lives* (London: Cassell, 1998), pp. 83, 95. Edith Craig also organised women's suffrage processions; she was the general director of the procession set up by the Women's Freedom League on 18 June 1910, 'Women's Suffrage Procession', *The Vote*, 28 May 1910, p. 56. I am grateful to Katharine Cockin for drawing my attention to Edith Craig's role.

39. The Women's Social and Political Union and the Women's Freedom League.
40. For instance, the discussions about 'the woman question' adopt the perspective of 'women as a topic'. For 'women as a spectacle', see Tickner, *The Spectacle of Women*; Boussahba-Bravard, 'Vision et visibilité: la rhétorique visuelle des suffragistes'.
41. Julia Bush, 'British Women's Anti-suffragism and the Forward Policy, 1908–1914', *Women's History Review*, 11, 3 (2002), pp. 431–54, p. 440.
42. For instance Duncan Tanner, *Political Change and the Labour Party 1900–1918* (Cambridge: Cambridge University Press, 1990), p. 1.
43. Julia Bush, *Edwardian Ladies and Imperial Power* (London: Leicester University Press, 2000), p. 173.
44. L. Barrow and I. Bullock (eds), *Democratic Ideas and the British Labour Movement* (Cambridge: Cambridge University Press, 1996); E. F. Biagini, *Liberty, Retrenchment, and Reform: Popular Liberalism in the Age of Gladstone, 1860–1880* (Cambridge: Cambridge University Press, 1992); Biagini and Reid (eds), *Currents of Radicalism;* A. J. A. Morris (ed.), *Edwardian Radicalism 1900–1914: Some Aspects of British Radicalism* (London: Routledge, 1974); Tanner, *Political Change and the Labour Party.*
45. Thane, 'Labour and Local Politics: Radicalism, Democracy and Social Reform, 1880–1914'; K. Young, *Local Politics and the Rise of Party, the London Municipal Society and the Conservative Intervention in Local Elections 1894–1963* (London: Leicester University Press, 1975).
46. L. Walker, 'Party Political Women: a Comparative Study of Liberal Women and the Primrose League 1890–1914', in J. Rendall (ed.), *Equal or Different: Women's Politics 1800–1914* (Oxford: Blackwell, 1987).
47. Socialist women were full members of the Independent Labour Party and the Social Democratic Federation, J. Hannam and K. Hunt, *Socialist Women, Britain 1880s to 1920s* (London: Routledge, 2002).
48. See Pat Thane, Chapter 2 below, pp. 36, 40.
49. Lori Maguire, Chapter 3 below, p. 54.
50. Linda Walker, Chapter 4 below, p. 78.
51. Hunt, *Equivocal Feminists*, pp. 24–5, 53, 55, 16; Hannam and Hunt, *Socialist Women,* pp. 79–104, p. 91.
52. Hannam and Hunt, *Socialist Women*, p. 2.
53. 'There would be sexual equality, although there was less certainty as to what exactly that would mean in everyday life and how such aspirations ought to influence the political practice of socialists in the meantime', ibid., p. 2.
54. See Walker, Chapter 4 below, p. 78.
55. Tanner, *Political Change,* p. 12.
56. Ibid., pp. 11–15.
57. Chapters 2, 3, 4 below.
58. Chapters 2, 3, 4 below for women involved in party politics. See Julia Bush, Chapter 5 below and Gillian Scott, Chapter 6 below for voluntary action and moral reform combined.
59. John and Eustance (eds), *The Men's Share?* In the main the selected case studies deal with male suffragists inside 'suffragism' with the exception of Carolyn Spring's contribution, 'The Political Platform and the Language of Support

for Women's Suffrage 1890–1920', pp. 158–81; S. Strauss, *'Traitors to the Masculine Cause': the Men's Campaigns for Women's Rights* (Westport: Greenwood Press, 1982).

60. J. Baldshaw, 'Sharing the Burden: the Pethick-Lawrences and Women's Suffrage', in John and Eustance (eds), *The Men's Share?*, pp. 135–57. Other famous suffragist couples abound: the Fawcetts, the Pankhursts. 'Ordinary' and famous suffragist couples become invasive when looking at certain episodes of suffrage history, such as the Edwardian wives' fiscal rebellion: the Wilks, the Housmans (brother and sister), the Sprosons; see Myriam Boussahba-Bravard, 'Résistance passive et citoyenneté: la rébellion fiscale des suffragistes édouardiennes' (Paris, *Revue d'histoire moderne et contemporaine*, forthcoming).
61. Walker, Chapter 4 below, pp. 88, 95–6; Maguire, Chapter 3 below, p. 63; Thane, Chapter 2 below, p. 36.
62. Walker, Chapter 4 below, pp. 87–8.
63. It was already committed to Adult Suffrage.
64. Maguire, Chapter 3 below, p. 71: 'In what is there much point in a Conservative Suffrage Society which is afraid to avow its Conservatism?'; Walker, Chapter 4 below, pp. 96–7; Thane, Chapter 2 below, p. 42.
65. J. Hannam, ' "I had not been to London', Women's Suffrage – a View from the Regions', in Purvis and Holton (eds), *Votes for Women*, p. 233.
66. Hannam, 'A View from the Regions', p. 242.
67. June Hannam has stressed that local and national profiles did not always match and that 'local studies do reveal continuing connections between suffrage groups which are often seen as separate in standard accounts', Hannam, ibid., p. 238. In 1912, M. G. Fawcett had already underlined that 'however acute were the differences between the heads of the different societies, the general mass of suffragists throughout the country were loyal to the cause by whomsoever it was represented', Fawcett, *Women's Suffrage*, pp. 61–2.
68. For example, Duncan Tanner, 'Ideological Debate in Edwardian Labour Politics: Radicalism, Revisionism and Socialism', in Biagini and Reid (eds), *Currents of Radicalism*, p. 283.
69. Hannam, 'A View from the Regions', p. 228.
70. Ibid., pp. 231, 238.
71. Julia Bush, Chapter 5 below, p. 106; Gillian Scott, Chapter 6 below, p. 132.
72. For party women, Chapters 2, 3 and 4 below. For non-party women, Chapters 4 and 5 below.
73. Bush, Chapter 5 below, p. 106: 'the Parliament of Women'. This name adopted by the NUWW shows that before the WSPU version of 'the Women's Parliament', the NUWW accepted seeing itself as a public space parallel to the parliamentary politics they so prudishly refused. Imitation forcefully demonstrates how women could only be self-contradictory in a mainstream public sphere which excluded them but whose values they had integrated.
74. Scott, Chapter 6 below, pp. 136, 141.
75. June Hannam, Chapter 7 below, p. 158.
76. Philippe Vervaecke, Chapter 8 below, p. 182.
77. Hannam, Chapter 7 below, p. 161.
78. Vervaecke, Chapter 8 below p. 189.
79. Hannam, Chapter 7 below, pp. 161, 164.

80. Vervaecke, Chapter 7 below, p. 183. On suffrage and temperance, see Barlow, 'Teetotal Feminists'; M. Smitley, '"Inebriates", "Heathens", Templars and Suffragists'.
81. Vervaecke, Chapter 8 below, p. 189.
82. Ibid., pp. 190–2.
83. Susan Trouvé-Finding, Chapter 9 below, p. 205.
84. Trouvé-Finding, Chapter 9 below, pp. 208, 210.
85. Ibid., p. 212.
86. Ibid., p. 206.
87. Delap, Chapter 10 below, p. 231.
88. L. Delap, '"Philosophical Vacuity and Political Ineptitude": the Freewoman's Critique of the Suffrage Movement', *Women's History Review*, 11, 4 (2002), pp. 613–30.
89. Delap, Chapter 10 below, p. 234.
90. Ibid., p. 242.

Part I

Protecting the Centre: National Parties and the Control of Women

2
Women in the Labour Party and Women's Suffrage

Pat Thane

One would expect women who chose to be active in a political party whose aim was to gain representation in Parliament to be committed to women's suffrage. This was true of women who supported the fledgling Labour Party before 1918, though they were mostly equally committed to gaining the vote for all men. The Labour Party was founded in 1900 as the Labour Representation Committee (LRC), to fight for greater representation of working people in Parliament, yet at this time only about 60 per cent of men, and, of course, no women had the parliamentary vote. Not all of the disenfranchised men were working-class, significant numbers of unmarried middle-class men were also disenfranchised,[1] but very many, especially poorer, working-class men lacked the vote for a variety of reasons under complex voter registration rules.

The LRC was formed not of individual members but of 'affiliated organisations', that is, pre-existing associations that shared the commitment to working-class political representation. These included many trade unions and political organisations, including the moderate, intellectual Fabian Society, the more socialist Independent Labour Party (ILP) and the quasi-Marxist Social Democratic Federation (SDF). Ideologically the LRC embraced a spectrum of views from just left-of-centre liberalism to socialism, though not of a revolutionary kind. Consequently, the SDF ceased its affiliation shortly after the formation of the LRC. Nevertheless, there were always tensions, which continue to the present day, between the more liberal and the more socialist tendencies in the party.

The LRC took the name Labour Party following the general election of 1906, in which for the first time it gained a significant number of seats in the House of Commons – thirty. It is never easy for a third political party to achieve prominence in the British political system, which has traditionally been dominated by just two parties, a situation reinforced and perpetuated by the 'first-past-the-post' electoral system. It was particularly difficult for a working-class party before 1918 because, as we have seen above, not only all working-class women but also a high proportion of working-class men were disenfranchised.

Hence, for many working-class women and men the goal was not only women's suffrage but the full adult franchise, for women and men. This created some tension between Labour women and other suffragists in the leading suffrage organisations, the Women's Social and Political Union (WSPU) and, to a lesser and over time diminishing extent, the National Union of Women's Suffrage Societies (NUWSS). These organisations campaigned, as a first step, for enfranchisement for women on the same terms as men, arguing, mistakenly as it turned out, that this was more readily attainable than a less restricted franchise. Given the essentially property-based nature of the existing franchise qualification, this would disproportionately have enfranchised better-off women and potentially weighted voting, in a largely class-based political system, still more strongly against a nascent working-class political party such as Labour and, it was believed, against the interests of working-class people who were the majority of the population.

An all-female organisation, the Women's Labour League (WLL), was formed in 1906 as an autonomous 'organization of women to work for independent Labour representation of women in Parliament and in all local bodies'[2] – implying a clear commitment to women's suffrage. The aim was to draw into active Labour politics women who were not in unionised trades or political organisations or who might be workers at home with limited opportunities for political involvement. The WLL became an 'affiliated organisation' in 1908, which carried with it a right to attend and to vote in proportion to the size of its membership at the party's annual conference.[3] Its membership by 1914 was 5000. After most women over the age of 30 gained the vote in 1918, membership shot up to reach over 250 000 by 1927.[4]

This was also true of the other major political parties. The Women's Unionist Association (the women's division of the Conservative and Unionist Party) had one million members by 1928.[5] Even the Women's National Liberal Federation, despite disillusionment with the attitude of the party leadership towards women's suffrage and the wartime split in the party, had 100 000 members in 1928.[6] This was partly a response to efforts by the Labour and Conservative Parties, and, more tardily, the Liberals, to integrate the new female voters into their party organisations. The Labour Party granted women four places on its ruling National Executive Committee, and appointed a Chief Woman Officer and regional women's organisers – permanent, paid officials whose role was to encourage women's membership and activism. The WLL was wound up, but women could and did continue to meet in separate women's branches of constituency organisations as well as joining mixed-sex branch meetings.

Party membership should also be seen as evidence of the determination of many women to make use of their new civil rights. A similar determination can be seen in the proliferation of women's organisations active in the 1920s which were not identified with any political party – indeed they refused such identification – but were committed to, among other things, achieving changes in the law to promote gender equality. Organisations old and new, such as the National Union of Societies for Equal Citizenship (as NUWSS renamed itself in 1918), the Women's Institutes (founded by suffragists in 1915 to increase political awareness among countrywomen[7]) and the National Council for the Unmarried Mother and her Child (founded 1918) worked together and separately on a range of campaigns. By 1928, at least 23 new items of legislation, mostly connected with the law concerning children or the family, passed into law, for which women's organisations had lobbied and manoeuvred through Parliament with the assistance of male parliamentarians.[8]

The membership of the prewar WLL may have been more middle-class than the larger interwar female membership of the Labour Party and than the bulk of male members of affiliated organisations. The WLL was established by middle-class female socialists, including Margaret MacDonald, the wife of James Ramsay MacDonald, the party chairman from 1911–14 (when he resigned due to his opposition to the party's support for Britain's involvement in World War One), and again from 1922–1931, when he became Britain's first Labour Prime Minister in 1924. But the WLL's main strength was in working-class industrial areas of northern England, south Wales and in Scotland, around Glasgow. It was weak in the south of England.[9]

An organisation committed to the interests both of women and of the working class as a whole faced different challenges from those experienced by exclusively women's organisations. Although very many women found no conflict between membership of WLL and of WSPU or NUWSS, or, at least, in demonstrating alongside them, increasing numbers of WLL members came to find the WSPU's militant tactics unappealing, a view reciprocated by Christabel Pankhurst. Many Labour-supporting women believed that attaining any of the aims of any of these organisations would be progress. However, they were divided. Ethel Snowden, married to a leading member of the Labour Party but a notably independent feminist, resigned from WLL early on, as did Selina Cooper, the working-class

Lancashire socialist,[10] because it did not give primacy to women's suffrage, while Charlotte Despard (founder of the breakaway group from the WSPU, the Women's Freedom League), Ada Nield Chew (the northern factory worker, trade unionist and suffragist) and others, remained members of WLL whilst continuing to argue for women's suffrage.[11] Other individuals and local branches reached their own accommodations with these conflicts and the leadership accepted such differences as essential in a democratic organisation. However, the official position of the WLL moved by 1911 towards the belief that anything short of full adult suffrage was futile and contrary to the aims of the party.

Women had been very active in some of the affiliated organisations from their inception, notably the ILP[12] and the Fabian Society, though the SDF was less receptive to women asserting the distinctive objectives of women. Women were poorly represented in the affiliated trade unions in view of the strong gender division of labour and the concentration of women in low-paid, non-unionised employment. There were only 357 956 female trade unionists in 1914.[13] An exception was the predominantly female shop assistants' union which, with 7000 members, was one of the first unions to affiliate to the LRC in 1900, represented by Margaret Bondfield, who was later, in 1929, to become the first woman cabinet minister.[14] However, there were no women members of the executive committee of the Labour Party on its foundation and few women attended its early conferences.

The WLL was committed to improving all aspects of the living and working conditions of all women, children and men. Essential to achieving such improvements, they believed, was that women should be active in public debate and public affairs, including as voters. Long before 1906, some women already had the vote in local government elections and could stand for election to certain local authorities. Voting in most elections was restricted to women who were independent local rate (tax) payers, who were mainly unmarried or widowed women. There were about one million female local voters at the beginning of the twentieth century, by no means all of them middle class.

> The Labour Party calculated from the returns of fifty towns in 1905 that 82 per cent of women local voters were working-class, as were 95 per cent of the women in Nelson (Lancashire), 90 per cent in Bolton (also a Lancashire cotton town) and 60 per cent in St Pancras, in central London. In two wards in Leeds 532 of 536 and 1,100 of 1,190 women on the local register were regarded as working-class. Clara Collett's more detailed study in 1908 estimated that 51 per cent of women ratepayers

> were in gainful employment (shop-keeping, clothing, medicine and education); 38 per cent were housewives without servants; 5 per cent had one servant; and just 6 per cent had two servants or more.[15]

Such calculations, of course, complicated the debate between adult and women's suffragists, since they suggested that many working-class women would have been enfranchised by the WSPU's proposals to grant the vote to women on equal terms with men.

The structure of English local government at the beginning of the twentieth century was complicated (the situation was different in Scotland and Ireland). From 1834, when the administration of the Poor Law was substantially overhauled, women ratepayers could vote for the Boards of Guardians who administered the Poor Law at local level. From 1870, after a struggle, they could also be elected to these Boards. There were 15 546 female Guardians by 1914. Women who had one year's residence in a municipal corporation could vote for municipal councillors from 1869, but could not stand for election before 1907. They could vote for and be elected to school boards that administered education at the local level from 1870. These were abolished in 1902 in England and Wales, though not in Scotland and Ireland, but, after complaints from women, it was ordained that at least two women should be co-opted to each of the new English and Welsh local education authorities, appointed by municipal and county councils, which replaced them. There were about 270 elected female members of school boards in 1900 in England and Wales; 679 were co-opted by 1914. When county councils were established in 1888, women ratepayers were empowered to vote but after two women stood for election, following a legal challenge, they were banned retrospectively. The ban was lifted in 1907, which owed much to campaigning by the Women's Local Government Society, supported by the executive of WLL, among others. In 1914, there were 48 elected women county or municipal councillors. Parish and district councils, with restricted and highly localised powers, were created in 1894 and women ratepayers had the right both to vote and to stand for election to these; 215 women had been elected by 1914.

Women gained the vote and the right to stand for election first in those areas of public life deemed to be within the 'female sphere': poor relief, education and local, small-scale community issues.[16] However, the fact that women could vote and be elected at local level both gave them experience and confidence when operating in the political world and made their exclusion from national political participation increasingly absurd. The WLL was active in working to extend women's local political rights and in encouraging women to use them. Working in local elections and encouraging women to vote and to stand for election, wherever this was open to them, was a central activity of local WLL branches from their foundation. Some WLL members were already Guardians or parish or district councillors before the League was formed. Soon after its foundation in 1906, the Leicester branch ran 16 female candidates in the local Board of Guardians election; 15 were successful. The League conference report of 1912 listed 19 members elected as Guardians; in 1913, 28 were elected. The League encouraged women to believe that through such work they could put their skills of household management and experience of caring to use in the public sphere, though they did not believe that this should be the full extent of women's political involvement.[17] Between 1907 and 1914, some prominent members of the WLL were elected to county and borough councils, among them Edith Kerrison in West Ham, Ada Salter in Bermondsey, Marion Phillips and Ethel Bentham in Kensington, all in London. Ellen Wilkinson, later an MP and Minister of Education between 1945 and her death in 1947, was elected to Manchester City Council.[18] All too often, they encountered resistance and hostility from men and other women, voters and non-voters, both as they campaigned and after election. Lack of funding also hampered the election campaigns of the majority of women candidates who were not trade union backed due to the low level of female unionisation previously discussed.

The WLL's main objective at the outset was defined as 'to work for independent Labour representation in connection with the Labour Party'. At its first conference in 1906, Emmeline Pethick-Lawrence, seconded by Isabella Ford, moved an amendment to widen the aims to include a commitment to seek 'full rights of citizenship for all women and men and to work for the immediate removal of sex disability'. This implied support for women's suffrage on the same, restricted terms as then existed for men. It was defeated by 28 votes to 18. Isabella Ford then moved that the objectives should include the words 'to obtain direct representation of women in parliament and on local bodies'. This was less controversial since it did not imply commitment to a limited franchise and it passed,[19] with general support from the women present.[20] Isabella Ford was a supporter of the ILP and committed to women's suffrage even, as a first step, on the limited terms of the existing male franchise. She played no further part in the League, committing herself instead to the WSPU and the ILP.

The League aimed to encourage and to assist women to use the civil rights they had by voting, seeking election, co-option or appointment to the growing number of bodies open to them and by speaking out at political meetings. Margaret MacDonald told the 1907 conference that:

> At their meetings many women had shown powers of organizing and speaking which they had not shown when attending meetings where men took part and they were able to express their opinions as women on matters of which they had a special knowledge.

The WLL aimed to encourage and enable women to use these skills equally effectively in mixed-sex meetings. This was its central *raison d'être*. It sought to provide a supportive environment in which women could learn about political ideas, Labour policies, and learn the skills of political campaigning, at a time when the large, often open-air, public meeting was central to any campaign. As described in 1908, 'the branches of the League usually hold meetings for educating their members on political subjects and training them to speak and express their thoughts clearly'.[21] Some of its members complained, not always justly, that women in suffrage organisations had become so absorbed in the struggle for the national vote that they were not assisting women to use the civil rights they already had. The WLL did not work for Labour Party candidates who opposed women's enfranchisement.

The male leadership of the Labour Party did not immediately welcome the formation of an autonomous women's organisation, outside its direct control, despite the involvement of Margaret MacDonald. The affiliation of WLL was agreed only in 1908 after it had proved its value to the party by working in local elections.[22] From 1911, the party gave financial assistance to the WLL. The male leaders, however, were more supportive of women's suffrage than the leaders of other British political parties. From 1912, it was the only party committed to women's suffrage, provided, of course that it was a component of full adult suffrage rather than a continuation of the existing restrictive suffrage. Keir Hardie, the first chairman of the party, and close friend of Sylvia Pankhurst, was an uncompromising supporter of women's suffrage. George Lansbury, a future leader of the Labour Party and close to the Pankhursts, became increasingly enraged at the refusal of the Labour leadership to oppose the Liberals more strongly on women's suffrage. In 1912, he resigned his parliamentary seat in East London and fought a by-election on the issue of 'Votes for Women'. He was supported by WSPU, NUWSS and the Women's Freedom League, but not by the Labour Party since he had resigned and risked one of Labour's few parliamentary seats without consulting the party. He was narrowly defeated by the Conservative candidate, a Mr Blair.[23]

In 1911, following the sudden and untimely deaths of Margaret MacDonald and of Mary Middleton, another key figure in the foundation of WLL, Margaret Bondfield, took on the role of organising secretary, until she too fell ill and the role, half-time and poorly paid, passed, initially temporarily, to Marion Phillips. Phillips was an Australian graduate who remained a leading figure in the Labour Party for the rest of her life, until she also died, at too early an age, in 1932. There is a sad, but much needed story yet to be written of the way that a succession of women – Margaret MacDonald, Mary Middleton, Marion Phillips and Ellen Wilkinson among them – literally worked themselves to death in the service of the Labour Party. Marion Phillips had been secretary to NUWSS but had come to oppose limited women's suffrage and now favoured full adult suffrage. Nevertheless, she gave more time to the campaign for women's suffrage than other WLL leaders, after some tension over the permanency of her succession to Margaret Bondfield. Marion Phillips held growing power and influence in the WLL and the Labour Party thereafter. She negotiated the terms on which the WLL was incorporated into the reconstituted Labour Party in 1918 and became the party's first Chief Woman Officer. She was a Labour MP from 1929–31, by which time she was already suffering from the cancer that caused her death.

Phillips's change of view in 1911 was perhaps stimulated by the introduction into Parliament in 1911, by the Liberal Prime Minister H. H. Asquith, of a manhood suffrage Bill which did not include women, and by his obvious lack of enthusiasm for women's suffrage. This Bill went too far even for a male-dominated Labour Party conference, which in 1912 resolved that no franchise reform was acceptable unless women were included. This removed one source of tension between the WLL and the Labour Party.

Asquith's move propelled a group of Liberal women in NUWSS to form the Election Fighting Fund (EFF) to support Labour candidates in elections in constituencies in which there was no candidate committed to women's suffrage. WLL members and other Labour-supporting women were active in these campaigns, though the WLL was not formally involved. In by-elections between 1911 and 1914, they succeeded in helping to reduce the Liberal vote, but without managing to elect any Labour MPs. The WLL became increasingly active in suffrage campaigning, taking part in the Women's Freedom League's national conference in December 1912 and deciding in March 1913 to send resolutions to the Prime Minister, David Lloyd George (Chancellor of the Exchequer), the People's Suffrage Federation and the Labour Party, demanding the immediate introduction of a government Bill to enfranchise women. It was impelled both by the failure of the Liberal leadership to move forward on women's suffrage and by the treatment in the law courts and the prisons of WSPU protesters, with whom there was considerable sympathy in the WLL even among women who disapproved of WSPU tactics.[24]

The WLL, meanwhile, campaigned, sometimes more successfully, on other issues, such as school meals and school medical inspections, and they played an essential part in building grass-roots support for the new party through their local activism. By these means they demonstrated the capacities of women in politics and hence that they merited the vote. They seem often to have been more willing than men in the Labour Party to work among and for the poorest people. For example, in Wolverhampton women of the WLL and the Women's Co-operative Guild (WCG) were willing to work among 'slum dwellers' where some Labour men were not, demanding the introduction of free maternity and child welfare clinics and free school meals and urging the party leadership to take more account of the needs of very poor people.[25] The WCG was the largest working-class women's organisation in Britain, founded in 1884. It was not affiliated to the Labour Party until after World War One, though it sent delegates regularly to WLL annual conferences. It had 30 000 members by 1914.[26]

Such activities were a large part of the function of the WLL. They enabled it to place social welfare more firmly on the Labour Party agenda and reinforced the commitment of many Labour women to suffragism. They argued – as did many non-Labour supporting women who were active in philanthropy – that only when women had the vote would there be serious attempts to banish appalling levels of poverty that a male-dominated polity had tolerated for too long. The demand for the vote often arose out of and was intimately bound up with women's other preoccupations.

In consequence, Labour women developed imaginative plans for improved working-class housing, which they believed was fundamental to improving the lives of the whole class, especially the women. The home was the workplace of large numbers of women and it was as important to improve the working conditions and hours of women as it was for the trade union movement to improve those of men; and improved housing would come only by political means, with government effort and taxpayer subsidy. Labour women saw better housing as not merely good in itself, contributing to better health and greater comfort for families, and hence to the productivity of working men, but also as having the potential to liberate women from full-time commitment to domesticity by making their domestic tasks easier, for example by improving the design of kitchens. This would free women to devote more time to activities outside the home, including politics if they chose; above all it would give them a choice, which very many working-class women lacked, as to how to spend a portion of their time. The British government became more receptive to such demands during and after World War One. Labour and other women kept up the demands through the war. After the war, there was a notable expansion of subsidised house-building.

The WLL, along with the Women's Co-operative Guild, was also strongly committed to improved maternity and child welfare services. This was part of a wider, international, movement, which was especially strong from the early years of the twentieth century, to reduce high infant mortality rates and to improve the health of children and hence of future generations of adults. Such pressures, in some quarters, had imperialist and nationalist origins.[27] The WLL and WCG seized the opportunity presented by the imperialist discourse that followed the revelation of the poor health of volunteers for the armed services during the Boer War (1899–1902). Their aim was to improve the lives of poor women and children, though they were all too well aware that even not-so-poor women, including Margaret MacDonald, lost children in infancy. They also placed more emphasis on the personal needs of women for health care than nationalist groups who focused more upon children as embodying the future of the 'race'.

In 1913, to promote such care, the WLL established a mother and baby clinic in Notting Hill, then a poor district of London, using voluntary funds and voluntary effort. Although increasing numbers of voluntary clinics existed at this time, almost certainly this was the first clinic to be run and fully controlled by a national women's organisation, open daily to all pre-school children who needed advice or medical care, without the recommendation from a philanthropic organisation or individual often required by voluntary institutions. A resident nurse was appointed and there were doctors in attendance; one of them, Dr Ethel Bentham, was a prominent member of the WLL. A dentist's surgery was held once a month and a dispensing pharmacist was available. The League raised funds and believed that poor mothers needed and wanted advice and material help when bearing and rearing children and that this should be provided by the state out of taxation paid by the better-off. But, they argued, until this could be achieved, voluntary effort was necessary to alleviate the immediate need, provided that it was not delivered in such a way as to patronise poor women. One role of voluntary action was to expose need and show the way forward for state action and indeed many of the social welfare measures of the British state in the first half of the twentieth century, and later, were modelled upon voluntary initiatives. As the journal of the Labour women expressed it some years later:

> It was not a question of superior people trying to go in and teach the mother her job, she had the right to every kind of knowledge and the

> working mothers were asking for teaching in all the subjects that affected them in the life of their children.[28]

They recognised that voluntary action could be marred by middle- and upper-class patronage of poorer women, but also that state action could become excessively centralised and bureaucratic. The WLL aimed to avoid both. Not that working-class women were necessarily easy to patronise. An article in *Labour Woman* in 1918 commented:

> The mother of a healthy baby of some six months old told the present writer that she had studied with great care the latest book of advice for the bringing up of babies and she had come to the conclusion that she did a number of things that were wrong according to the book and yet definitely helped the well-being of her household. She felt that no doctor or nurse knew the whole story and she began to wonder how many mothers with three or four children, all of them healthy, actually kept to the rules to which they listened so politely.[29]

The League campaigned for state-funded local authority clinics on the model initiated in Notting Hill to be established everywhere. This became possible from 1918, after the passage of the Maternity and Child Welfare Act, which owed much to campaigning by the WLL and WCG.

Concerning state action, the WLL advocated maximum decentralisation through elected local authorities responsible to local communities and they encouraged women to play a full part in these communities as voters, elected representatives and campaigners. As in the case of housing, it was only during and after World War One that substantial state funding was put into improved maternity and child welfare facilities. One motive of the wartime coalition government was to improve morale and to build a healthy population to replace men killed in the war, but the prewar work of the Labour and Co-operative women, and of other men and women, provided the models for state action. Labour women demanded the involvement of women in the administration of the new services, ideally to be incorporated into a comprehensive state maternity service. From July 1914, the government inched towards this goal by giving grants to local authorities to establish child and maternal welfare services. It was left to local authorities to decide whether to take them up, but they came under determined pressure from women at local level, especially those of the WLL and WCG, to do so. The government funding gradually increased as the war went on, culminating in the 1918 Maternity and Child Welfare Act, which enabled local authorities to establish Maternity and Child Welfare Committees which were required to include at least two women and were empowered to provide a range of services subsidised by the state. These included hospital services for children under the age of five, maternity hospitals, 'home helps' to take over the housework of the mother after childbirth (free of charge for necessitous women), food for expectant and nursing mothers and children under the age of five, crèches and day nurseries. As was normal at this time in Britain, social legislation was left to the discretion of local authorities as to whether or not to make use of the powers granted to them by the law. In the following years, Labour and other women campaigned hard and with some success at local level for implementation of these powers.[30]

Less successful was the campaign for family allowances. The WLL conference of 1907 passed a resolution unanimously:

> Whereby necessitous mothers shall receive monetary assistance at the time of the birth of their children and whereby mothers with children dependent upon them shall receive continued adequate support to enable them to attend to the children without having to work for wages.

Margaret MacDonald believed that a wife without children also deserved 'endowment' for the work she performed in the home. As she put it, 'public opinion should be changed in the direction of recognizing the wife's full share of her husband's earnings, and whatever reforms are proposed should be in the direction of increasing the responsibility of both parents for their children.'[31] The belief that a woman's domestic labour should be recognised as work and as an essential contribution to her husband's performance in the labour market remained a central belief of the Labour women through the interwar years.

On these, as on other matters, there were differences of opinion within the Labour movement. A working-class woman trade unionist at the 1907 conference argued that the central cause of family poverty was the inadequacy of wages, male and female. To guarantee wives a fixed proportion of the miserable sums entering working-class homes would not increase household income and might increase tension between husband and wife in already difficult circumstances. In her view, women should fight not for family allowances but for adequate pay for all, alongside the trade union movement.[32] There were also fears expressed that family allowances would unintentionally reinforce the notion that woman's place was only in the home and that parenting was her responsibility alone and not that of the father.[33] In 1917, the executive of the WLL passed a resolution in favour of 'pensions for mothers', urging that 'widows with children or women whose breadwinners are incapacitated should receive pensions for their children sufficient to ensure their upbringing in a suitable and comfortable manner'. This proposition would arouse less opposition than family allowances for women with working husbands and would provide for especially needy families. Widows' pensions had been an objective of other women's organisations, such as NUWSS, for some time. For WLL at this point the proposal was intended as an attainable first step towards family allowances at a time of heightened consciousness of the plight of widows due to the war. War widows themselves were granted state pensions for the first time during World War One but other widows had no welfare recourse but the Poor Law. Widows' pensions became official Labour Party policy from 1918.

In 1919, 'dependants' allowances' were introduced for the wives and children of insured, unemployed men who received 'out of work' relief. Modest state pensions for widows and orphans were introduced in 1925, with the support of a wide range of women's organisations. The campaign for family allowances was a major one in the interwar women's movement. The Labour women continued to support it and to keep it on the Labour Party agenda, despite differences among themselves over aspects of the proposals and with the party due to trade union opposition to a proposal which it feared would undermine pay demands.[34] Small family allowances were finally introduced by a Labour government in 1945.

Before World War One, women supporters of the LRC/Labour Party were active campaigners for free schools meals for needy schoolchildren. One prominent campaigner was Mary Gawthorpe, the schoolteacher who helped form the first Leeds branch of the WLL and became a founder-member of the national executive committee of WLL at the age of 25. With Margaret MacDonald, she advised the Minister of Education on the drafting of the legislation that introduced free school meals in 1906. Like other women, Mary Gawthorpe was torn between her commitment to the WSPU, for whom she became, also in 1906, a local organiser, later national organiser and a very effective speaker, and to the Labour Party, a tension which became all the greater as Christabel and Emmeline Pankhurst became increasingly antagonistic to Labour. As WSPU took over her time and the activities of the two organisations became increasingly incompatible, Mary Gawthorpe drifted away from the WLL. Given the differences between the WLL and WSPU such conflicts were unavoidable, as we have seen, and the WLL appears to have accepted that women would handle them in varied ways. Other early supporters both of WSPU and of Labour, such as Hannah Mitchell, became more critical of

WSPU as it became more militant and adopted the policy of attacking the leaders of all political parties:

> I did not agree with this. I thought it was wrong to attack men like Keir Hardie and George Lansbury. Neither of these great souls ever wavered in their support for our cause. We should have made splendid exceptions for our friends in any party. They were few enough, God knows, in any party.[35]

Many, perhaps most, Labour women, like women in other organisations, were active on many fronts. Margaret MacDonald worked herself to death, campaigning for school meals, state registration of nurses, better conditions for women in paid work as well as for the Labour Party, while bringing up six children and presiding over a chaotic household (without servants, unusually for someone of her background). She also made a major financial contribution to the WLL in its early days.

The League produced leaflets on various subjects, including the need for pit-head baths, medical inspection of schoolchildren, and advice on the work of a Poor Law Guardian. The WLL joined the Fabian women and the Women's Industrial Council in the campaign which led to the Trade Boards Act 1909, which effectively established a minimum wage for women in a number of low-paid trades, despite divisions in the WLL as to whether legislation was the most appropriate solution to the problem.

The biggest WLL campaign of the prewar years was to enforce the adoption by local authorities of the permissive Education (Provision of Meals) Act 1906. Branches lobbied local councils, attended council meetings en masse, held public meetings, and organised petitions. They were driven by concern about the high levels of ill health among children, due to poverty and malnutrition, which hindered their education. They also pointed out and sought to remedy the facts that local provision was haphazard in organisation and quality and often delivered in ways that stigmatised the children receiving free meals.[36]

The numbers and activities of Labour women varied from place to place and they have not been comprehensively studied. The Glasgow branch lobbied locally in 1909 for work to be provided for unemployed women. The local authority routinely provided it for unemployed men, usually road-building or heavy digging. The Labour women demanded practical training for women in domestic work and elementary nursing and achieved some concessions. On Merseyside, women found it difficult to attain leadership positions in any socialist or labour organisation or even to win Labour Party support in local elections. A women's section of the Labour Party became firmly established only after World War One.[37]

However, in this as in other organisations of the left, disputes at the level of the national leadership did not prevent co-operation at local level, as in Leeds where most members of the local WLL were members simultaneously of WSPU, WCG and ILP and were active on more issues than the vote.[38] Many League branches worked with local trade unionists, though they had to tread carefully. Independent-minded women trade unionists did not always need or value their assistance. Among other events, in 1911 the Wigan WLL was reported as organising pit-brow girls to join the Miner's Federation. When Hull seamen and dockers went on strike, also in 1911, WLL women set up a relief committee to help strikers and their families. During the same strike wave, Margaret Bondfield and members of the Cardiff WLL advised young girls employed in cigar-making, bottling and laundry work on strike tactics, so successfully that the employers 'came to terms'.[39]

It was hard for the London-based national leadership to keep close control of distant local branches even if they had wished to do so. The executive committee itself was often divided on the issue of adult versus women's suffrage. Membership of and co-operation among the different progressive women's organisations was often fluid, with much ad hoc personal contact and collaboration, especially in smaller towns where the number of female activists in any organisation might be few. Many women could not afford to pay dues to more than one organisation, though they might support and work with more than one. In consequence, support for an organisation such as the WLL might well have been larger than the formal membership.

The war disrupted the WLL's central organisation but not its local activities. The executive committee instructed branches to ensure that the wives of servicemen received their state separation allowances or pensions and to support those who did not. Branches were to campaign for improved working conditions for women war workers, above all for equal pay and a living wage, for support for unemployed women,[40] improved housing, free meals for schoolchildren, support for 'illegitimate' babies and their mothers whose numbers increased during the war, aid for refugees, opposition to attacks on the properties of 'aliens' (often Jewish immigrants) and others identified with the Germans, and for a negotiated peace and support for women in other countries, including those on the other side in the war.

By the end of 1918, women were more closely integrated into the Labour Party than before. They were no more, but also no less, influential within it than before. In addition, the vote had been extended to all men aged 21 and above and most women over the age of 30, not the full adult franchise that many Labour women had fought for, but more than the WSPU had sought before the war. The WLL, which like much of the Labour Party contained many critics and outright opponents of the war, had continued to support this goal throughout the war, siding with the campaigns of NUWSS, when WSPU gave up and swung to support of the war. The WLL continued to support the campaign for the equal franchise that came, at last, in 1928. For all the tensions between Labour women and other suffrage campaigners, the Labour women contributed to both the gaining and the using of the vote by women in Britain. On its side, the suffrage campaign contributed to the growing strength of the Labour Party. Although activities of the WSPU created some divisions, Labour won support among women after 1912 as the only major political party to support women's suffrage and gained in particular from the alienation of Liberal women from Asquith and the formation by NUWSS members of the Election Fighting Fund to support Labour candidates.

Notes

1. Duncan Tanner, *Political Change and the Labour Party, 1900–1918* (Cambridge: Cambridge University Press, 1990).
2. *Report of the First Conference of the Women's Labour League*, 1906, p. 4.
3. C. Collette, *For Labour and for Women: the Women's Labour League, 1906–18* (Manchester: Manchester University Press, 1989) is the best study of the League.
4. *Annual Report*, National Conference of Labour Women, 1927. Pat Thane, 'The Women of the British Labour Party and Feminism', in H. L. Smith (ed.), *British Feminism in the Twentieth Century* (Aldershot: Edward Elgar, 1990), p. 125.
5. M. Pugh, *Women and the Women's Movement in Britain, 1914–1999* (London: Macmillan, 2000), p. 125.
6. P. Thane, 'Women, Liberalism and Citizenship', in E. Biagini (ed.), *Citizenship and Community. Liberals, Radicals and Collective Identities in the British Isles, 1865–1931* (Cambridge: Cambridge University Press, 1996), p. 68.
7. Maggie Andrews, *The Acceptable Face of Feminism: the Women's Institute as a Social Movement* (London: Lawrence and Wishart, 1997).
8. P. Thane, 'What Difference did the Vote Make? Women in British Politics since 1918', in A. Vickery (ed.), *Women, Privilege and Power* (Stanford: Stanford University Press, 2001), pp. 253–88.
9. Collette, *For Labour and for Women*, pp. 60–1.
10. J. Liddington, *The Life and Times of a Respectable Rebel: Selina Cooper, 1864–1946* (London: Virago, 1984).
11. J. Liddington and J. Norris, *One Hand Tied Behind Us: the Rise of the Women's Suffrage Movement* (London: Virago, 1978), p. 236.
12. J. Hannam, *Isabella Ford* (Oxford: Blackwell, 1989); J. Hannam, 'In the Comradeship of the Sexes lies the Hope of Progress and Social Regeneration', in Jane Rendall (ed.), *Equal but Different* (Oxford: Blackwell, 1987).

13. B. Drake, *Women in Trade Unions* (London, 1920).
14. Collette, *For Labour and for Women*, p. 28.
15. P. Hollis, *Ladies Elect: Women in English Local Government, 1865–1914* (Oxford: Oxford University Press, 1987), p. 32.
16. Ibid.
17. Collette, *For Labour and for Women*, pp. 94, 96.
18. Ibid., pp. 98–9.
19. Hannam, *Isabella Ford*, pp. 117–18.
20. Collette, *For Labour and for Women*, p. 35.
21. Ibid., p. 108.
22. Ibid., pp. 30–8.
23. J. Schneer, *George Lansbury* (Manchester: Manchester University Press, 1990), pp. 68–129.
24. Ibid., p. 148.
25. Ibid., pp. 71–5; M. Francis, 'Labour and Gender', in D. Tanner, P. Thane and N. Tiratsoo (eds), *Labour's First Century* (Cambridge: Cambridge University Press, 2000), p. 202.
26. J. Gaffin and D. Thoms, *Caring and Sharing: the Centenary History of the Co-operative Women's Guild* (Manchester: The Co-operative Union, 1983).
27. A. Davin, 'Imperialism and Motherhood', *History Workshop*, 5 (Spring 1978), pp. 9–66.
28. *Labour Woman*, July 1925.
29. Ibid., September 1918.
30. E. Peretz, 'Maternal and Child Welfare in England and Wales between the Wars', PhD thesis, Middlesex University, 1992.
31. *National Conference of the Women's Labour League*, 1909, pp. 28–30.
32. *Labour Woman*, November 1913.
33. *The League Leaflet*, December 1913.
34. G. Bock and P. Thane, *Maternity and Gender Politics: Women and the Rise of the European Welfare States, 1880–1950s* (London: Routledge, 1991), pp. 111–14.
35. H. Mitchell, *The Hard Way Up: the Autobiography of Hannah Mitchell, Suffragette and Rebel* (London: Virago, 1977), p. 177.
36. Collette, *For Labour and for Women*, pp. 120–6.
37. K. Cowman, *'Mrs Brown is a Man and a Brother': Women in Merseyside's Political Organizations, 1890–1920* (Liverpool: Liverpool University Press, 2004).
38. Hannam, *Isabella Ford*, pp. 125, 154.
39. Collette, *For Labour and for Women*, p. 66.
40. C. Law, *Suffrage and Power: the Women's Movement, 1818–28* (London: I.B. Tauris, 1997), p. 24.

3
The Conservative Party and Women's Suffrage

Lori Maguire

Traditionally, the Conservative Party has been represented as possessing a negative attitude on the question of women's suffrage, with a few exceptions. But the reality is far more complicated, for the party's attitude on the question was decidedly ambivalent. While it is undoubtedly true that the vast majority of diehards opposed to enfranchising women were Tories, the party contained many ardent supporters and played a major role in its achievement. They were the first party to organise large numbers of women for political work through the Primrose League, an affiliated organisation, and depended on them during campaigns. Thanks to the Primrose League, the Conservatives possessed the largest body of politicised women in the nation. Furthermore, a significant proportion of both male and female Conservatives were actively engaged in the suffrage movement. The party's leaders, from Disraeli on, had spoken in favour of at least limited female enfranchisement at one time or another – although, it must be admitted, until 1918, none of them did anything about it. Most importantly, it was a coalition government, to which the Conservatives belonged, that voted the Representation of the People Act of 1918 giving most women over the age of 30 the right to vote, and a purely Conservative government that, in 1928, enfranchised women on the same terms as men. In spite of the existence of a significant anti-suffrage rearguard, the party made numerous, very positive contributions to the 'Cause'.

Our analysis will consider several aspects of the question. First, we will examine the suffragists and the suffrage movement within the Conservative Party, notably the Conservative and Unionist Women's Franchise Association (CUWFA).[1] They sought to convince their fellow party members of the rightness of a cause that many associated with the left. To do so, they had to develop their own specific battery of arguments, some of which belong to the long history of Conservative thought and can trace their ancestry to Burke and other leading theorists of the right. After this, we must turn to the party leadership and their generally nuanced position, as well as their reasons for seeking to avoid the issue. Finally, we will scrutinise the effect of the party's ambivalence on Conservative women suffragists and its position on the Reform Acts of 1918 and 1928.

While, as a number of historians have pointed out, much of the intellectual basis for the suffrage movement and many of its early male supporters came from the Liberals – most notably John Stuart Mill – many women feminists, such as Frances Power Cobbe, Lydia Becker and Emily Davies, among others, were actually Conservatives.[2] All these women obviously wanted society to change so women could have greater opportunities, but they made no fundamental re-examination of women's role in society. In fact, they frequently claimed that they accepted the status quo and agreed with it: women were different from men and these differences could not and should not be overcome. These feminists asserted, though, that there was no real conflict between traditional femininity and an improved status for women. Furthermore, most of them used fundamentally Conservative means to promote their cause. Barbara Caine has explained how Emily Davies organised her strategy to encourage reform:

> For her, as for Frances Cobbe, the appropriate way to begin campaigning for any measure was not to call a public meeting, but to organise a committee composed of respectable and well-known individuals. It was not popular support that she sought, but rather the quiet support of prominent people.[3]

Emmeline and Christabel Pankhurst, who leaned towards Conservatism from a certain point, are the obvious exceptions to this rule, although many aristocrats and respectable middle-class women joined their group.

The presence of aristocrats, usually in highly visible leadership roles, and the middle class, is an obvious characteristic of Conservative suffragism and was paralleled in the party at large.[4] Because of intermarriage among aristocrats, Conservative suffragism often gives the impression of having been a family affair. First, the Cecils stand out. One of the most illustrious families in English history, they descended from Elizabeth I's chief adviser and had been given the title of Earl of Salisbury (later marquess) by James I. From 1880 to 1914, the Cecils dominated the Tory Party, providing two prime ministers (Lord Salisbury and his nephew Arthur Balfour) and a number of other influential politicians. This same ascendancy can be observed in the suffrage movement during the same period. Salisbury's daughter, Maud, was a leading member of the CUWFA and its second president. Her husband, Lord Selborne, and her brother, Lord Robert Cecil, were two of the most important advocates of the 'Cause' in Parliament. Lord Robert, in particular, and his wife Lady Eleanor, worked tirelessly for women's suffrage, giving speeches, writing articles and working in various ways to bring it to public attention. Another of Salisbury's sons, Lord Hugh Cecil, also championed the 'Cause'. Lady Frances Balfour, a cousin by marriage and sister-in-law of Arthur Balfour, was a major figure in the suffrage movement from 1889. A founder of the National Union of Women's Suffrage Societies (NUWSS) and leading personage in the London Society for Women's Suffrage (LSWS), Millicent Fawcett considered Balfour one of her chief lieutenants. Lady Betty Balfour, another of Arthur Balfour's sisters-in-law, also played an enthusiastic role, although not to the extent of her sister, Lady Constance Lytton. Lady Constance belonged to the Pankhursts' Militant Women's Social and Political Union (WSPU), was imprisoned, went on hunger strike, suffered forced feeding and wrote a moving book about this experience. Finally, two of Arthur Balfour's sisters supported women's suffrage: Lady Rayleigh and Eleanor Sidgwick, wife of Henry Sidgwick and Principal of Newnham College, Cambridge. As well as their public activities, they and others constantly lobbied their powerful friends and relations on the question.

Conservatives joined the suffrage societies from the very start but did not form their own organisation until 1908. It began with two separate initiatives by untitled Conservative sympathisers. The two groups met at an NUWSS procession in that year and decided to establish an association with its headquarters in London.[5] The foundation of the CUWFA at this time was no accident: it coincided with the creation of the predominantly Conservative Men's and Ladies' Leagues for Opposing Women's Suffrage. These groups obviously constituted a threat to the progress of suffragist opinion within the party, which already counted many opponents in its ranks. Millicent Fawcett, president of the NUWSS and a Liberal Unionist herself, and others felt that an opposing group should exist within the party to counter the Antis' propaganda, present their views, and provide visible evidence that Conservatism and suffragism went together. The year 1908 was also significant because the WSPU began its Militant campaign then; undoubtedly this pushed Conservative women to establish their own organisation to show that suffragism was essentially respectable.

Their goal, as their first president, Lady Knightley of Fawsley described it to *The Times*, was 'to have a large and representative body of Conservatives and Unionists pledged to assist their leaders and to influence the Conservative Party to extend the franchise to duly-qualified women'.[6]

The term 'Unionist' here refers to those Liberals who had broken with Gladstone in 1886 over Irish home rule. They formed their own women's organisation, the Women's Liberal Unionist Association in 1888. By 1893, Kate Courtney, one of its leading figures, was worried about the future of, what was in effect, a one-issue group, for, as she put it, it had no 'sufficient collective creed on other questions'.[7] Over the following years, the Unionists gradually collapsed into the Conservative Party until they were amalgamated in 1911. The two organisations worked closely together and both referred to themselves as Unionists. Note that while the CUWFA specifically includes Unionists in its title, its vocation is stated as being to work in the Conservative Party – it is assumed that no separate Unionist party exists. In fact, few of the original Liberal Unionists appear to have joined the CUWFA although several of their suffragists, notably Millicent Fawcett, played an important role in the formation of the NUWSS. Certainly some women found that the acknowledged existence of the Unionists made their own politics easier. Frances Balfour, for example, came from one of the great Whig families, being the daughter of the Duke of Argyll. Marrying the nephew of Lord Salisbury placed her in a difficult position that Unionism allowed her to reconcile – at least to some extent. To a lesser extent, the same observation holds true for Lady Knightley who was a Liberal by inclination but married to a Conservative politician. She loyally supported him, becoming an active member of the Primrose League and an enthusiastic imperialist but, once again, Liberal Unionism may have helped her resolve her political views. Jane Maria, Lady Strachey became a vice-president of the CUWFA although she had been a disciple of Mill. She had a long and distinguished history of suffragism as did her daughter Philippa and her daughter-in-law Ray. She also appears to have been attracted to Liberal Unionism and eventually Conservatism.

Like the Antis, the CUWFA came up with an impressive list of aristocratic officers and supporters. First, almost the entire Cecil family was involved in one way or another. Maud Selborne replaced Lady Knightley as the group's second president in 1910. The CUWFA always had a large number of vice-presidents at any one time and an examination of these women can lead to interesting insights. Among them were Eleanor Sidgwick, Lady Rayleigh, Lady Betty Balfour and Lady Robert Cecil – all connected to the Cecil family. Other aristocratic vice-presidents included the Countess of Meath, Lady Edward Spencer Churchill, Edith, Viscountess Castlereagh and Viscountess Middleton. But aristocracy is not the whole story, for members came from two other major groups (which overlapped with each other and with the aristocrats): educationalists and philanthropists. Both these activities were considered acceptable areas for women – an extension of their role in the home – and almost all upper- and middle-class women participated in philanthropic work. The inclusion of representatives of these groups emphasised the essentially respectable image the CUWFA was trying to project. Margaret Tuke, Principal of Bedford College, London, transformed that college by raising academic standards and doubling the number of students. Constance Jones was the Head of Girton College, Cambridge, Henrietta Jex-Blake Head of Lady Margaret Hall, Oxford, and Eleanor Sidgwick, Principal of Newnham College, Cambridge. Louisa Twining, of the famous tea family, was an outstanding philanthropist who had worked for workhouse and prison reform, among other causes. She also laboured for greater political representation for women, becoming in 1904, at the age of 84, President of the Women's Local Government Society. Another vice-president, Lady Chance, saw an important moral dimension to the women's movement and argued that women needed the vote in order to end the evils of male sexual exploitation. In a NUWSS pamphlet, she insisted that:

> Immorality is almost always accounted a sin of the worst description in a woman, while in a man it is a slight offence easily forgotten and forgiven. Now we Suffragists want to change that false view. We want to make everybody feel that it is equally wrong for both sexes to transgress the moral law. I say especially we Suffragists, because our desire to win direct political power is founded upon our belief that in that way only shall we become possessed of the power and the weapons necessary to fight this terrible evil.[8]

The list of notable women was long. In keeping with their eminent respectability, the CUWFA subscribed to constitutional methods and sought to clearly distinguish themselves from the WSPU. Therefore, their tactics consisted mainly of verbal persuasion and distribution of literature, although they did organise classes to educate women on political questions. Of course, their high level of contacts ensured that their efforts reached leading political figures. To provide a forum for their ideas, they created *The Conservative and Unionist Women's Franchise Review*. While they lacked the excitement of the Pankhursts, they did serve two major purposes. First, they provided an important counterbalance to the Antis and prevented them from presenting Conservatism as naturally anti-suffrage. Furthermore, being frequently active in local party politics through the Primrose League, they also helped convince many undecided people, many of whom were MPs or party agents, that women could responsibly exercise the vote and that their demand was a perfectly reputable one.

The obvious comparison here was with the suffragette militancy of the WSPU, and Antis often tried to use these disturbances to discredit the suffragist cause in the party and in the nation. Most of the prominent Conservative suffragists realised this danger and deplored the aggressive tactics of the WSPU. This does not mean, however, that there was real hostility between the two groups for relations with the WSPU were never simple. When the CUWFA leadership sought a public denunciation of their activities, they found that many women in their organisation were not only reluctant to condemn the suffragettes but actually supported them. Lady Constance Lytton was only the best known of them. Some Conservative women actually belonged to the WSPU, others contributed to them, some sought an alliance with them, while still more sympathised quietly and refused all attempts at condemnation. Lady Eleanor Cecil, who wished to dissociate her movement from the WSPU, wrote to Maud Selborne to lament the attitude of others:

> Many [in the Conservative Suffragist Society] don't approve of the Militants but they are afraid of offending them, hope to profit by their deeds, and have a sentimental sympathy for certain individuals, consequently they won't commit themselves to a definite public protest – extraordinarily silly and short-sighted, I think.[9]

Eleanor Cecil feared that the suffragettes were creating a negative opinion in many people's minds, providing arguments for the Antis, and producing an atmosphere in which politicians felt they could not give women the vote without a loss of face. In fact, Liberal Antis frequently presented the WSPU as a Tory plot to embarrass the Liberal government. Their targeting of Liberal cabinet ministers, even those who were anti-suffrage, and ignoring the Conservative front bench, again even those who were anti-suffrage, lent credence to this idea.[10] Lord Robert Cecil was so alarmed by the situation that he actually introduced the Public Meetings Bill in the House of Commons in 1908 to try to control the activities of the WSPU. In doing so, he sought to make a public statement that the suffrage movement as a whole was perfectly respectable and did not support lawbreaking.

But too much should not be made of this hostility towards the WSPU, for it did not prevent Conservative suffragists from being in contact with the Pankhursts and even, at certain times, co-ordinating policy with them. After Christabel Pankhurst suspended militancy in June 1911, following the Liberal Prime Minister's promise of a Reform Bill, Lord Robert advised his sister, Maud Selborne, to work with her. Christabel certainly seemed quite anxious to work with the Conservatives. Lord Robert was even somewhat surprised by her moderation and evident desire to limit the scope of the proposed Reform Bill:

> Christabel is evidently anxious that the Bill should not be extended. Whether this is due to hostility to Lloyd George or to a desire to keep the Bill as it is I do not know. But she wishes us to strengthen her hands in her negotiations with the Radical Suffragists by saying that we are strongly opposed to any extension of the Bill. I feel a little difficulty myself in saying that I would not support an extended Bill, but I think that is what she would really like us to say.[11]

Christabel's retreat from radicalism is clearly shown here. She wanted to use the Conservatives to put pressure on the Liberals to limit as much as possible any franchise extension to the lower class. It is certainly extraordinary to find the Militant suffragette and former Labour sympathiser pushing the son of Lord Salisbury to take a more Conservative stand on the question than was his inclination. But it does show that, whatever their rhetoric, Conservative suffragist leaders were willing, at times, to work with the Pankhursts – even if they waited until Militant activities had been suspended.

There is no denying the rightward movement of Emmeline and Christabel Pankhurst. It is well known that Emmeline finished her life as a Conservative candidate for Parliament and that, after her death, the Conservative Prime Minister, Stanley Baldwin, unveiled her statue at Westminster. As early as 1907, Christabel had warned Balfour that people within both the NUWSS and the WSPU wanted to ally the suffrage movement with Labour. Christabel insisted that she was opposed to such a course:

> I am very anxious that the whole women's suffrage movement (and not our society alone) shall remain independent of the Labour party, because I am far from being persuaded that the Labour party can or will take effective action upon this pledge.[12]

Emmeline and Christabel's hostility to such a development led to the departure from the WSPU of mainly left-wing members in that year. Partly, Christabel's stance can be explained by rivalries between herself and her sister, Sylvia, a socialist close to James Keir Hardie, the Independent Labour

Party leader. It also represents a suspicion of Labour, and especially of trade unionist, attitudes towards women. In 1905, Emmeline had hoped that the Labour Party Annual Conference would endorse a bill giving limited enfranchisement to women. Instead, it had voted against it from the belief that it would increase 'the political power of the propertied classes'.[13] The Annual Conference maintained the need for full adult suffrage and stated that any other bill should not be supported by Labour MPs. While the party's position is not difficult to understand, it certainly pushed Emmeline and Christabel towards both the Conservatives and Militancy.

Christabel, in particular, felt that there was a fundamental antagonism between feminism and the trade unions. Writing to Balfour, she condemned the attitude of trade union officials:

> These men are very ready to propose restrictions on working women's labour. There are some who advocate the entire exclusion of women, whether married or single, from certain industries. There are those who desire to close wage earning occupations to married women.[14]

Christabel's observations were fundamentally correct. The overwhelmingly male trade unionists viewed women as unfair job competition since they were paid less than men were and obviously wanted to end this. In most cases, however, their proposed solution was not equal pay but the limitation of women's work. Christabel, unlike her sister Sylvia, was first a feminist. She realised that the labour movement's fundamental interest was in universal male suffrage and that female suffrage was only a secondary consideration. Since the Liberals were in power and showed little desire to grant women the vote, that left only the Conservatives. Her inclination was also reinforced by the large number of Conservatives in the NUWSS and in her own organisation – the latter receiving a great deal of its funding from certain wealthy Conservative supporters, like Lady Constance Lytton.

Conservative women also played a major role in the NUWSS and its subsidiary groups. Conservatives dominated the LSWS, whose president for much of the period was Lady Frances Balfour. From 1907, tension grew between the northern, left-leaning suffrage groups, on the one side, and the LSWS and the NUWSS executive on the other. Many provincial societies were unhappy with the powerful positions occupied by Conservative women, mainly from the LSWS, on the executive. This eventually led to the introduction of a more decentralised structure in 1910, in spite of objections from the executive and the LSWS. In particular, there is some controversy over Millicent Fawcett's position in all this and of the extent of her conservatism, if it existed. Although starting as a Liberal, she became a Liberal Unionist over home rule. She left the Liberal Unionists in 1903 because of her support for free trade. A number of scholars have noted Conservative elements in her thought. To the dismay of many left-leaning members of the NUWSS, she did not espouse adult suffrage, from the belief that it would make reform more difficult. Although she never belonged to the Conservative Party, she referred to Burke's ideas in her writings. Fawcett also strongly defended British involvement in the Boer War in spite of her role in the commission on the concentration camps.[15] Her biographer, David Rubinstein, described her as 'Unionist-leaning' even after 1903.[16] It has to be said, though, that she approved the later electoral pact with Labour even if she felt uncomfortable with it and ended it at the start of World War One.

But, to return to the Conservative Party, the principal Conservative suffragists wanted to show that they were not Militants and were not making radical demands. Women's enfranchisement, they argued, would benefit the party. For example, many contended that women were naturally more conservative than men so that enfranchising at least some of them would actually act as a brake on the growth of radicalism and socialism. Lord Salisbury even gave some support to this idea in a speech in 1886:

> I am now speaking for myself only, but I do earnestly hope that the day is not far distant when women also will bear their share in voting for Members of Parliament . . . and in determining the policy of the country. I can conceive of no argument by which they are excluded. It is obvious that they are abundantly as well fitted as many who now possess the suffrage, by knowledge, by training, and by character, and that influence is likely to weigh in a direction which, in an age so material as ours, is exceedingly valuable – namely in the direction of morality and religion.[17]

Salisbury was here claiming that women were more likely to vote Conservative and he did this by placing them squarely within the theory of 'separate spheres' – the belief common at that time that men and women were supposed to operate in different areas: men in the public world, women in the home. Being cut off from the outside world, women were supposed to be more ethereal than men – more concerned with 'morality and religion'. This was a typical Conservative argument, for there was no basic questioning of the differing roles of men and women. They were not seeking a revolution in women's status but were simply trying to allow the nation to benefit from woman's particular characteristics. Lady Castlereagh even asserted that: 'Politics have so invaded the home that it is an anomaly to urge women to abstain from politics, when politics follows them everywhere.'[18] It was politics that had aggressively entered the realm of women, not the reverse, and so political involvement no longer conflicted with domesticity but was necessary to preserve it. Edith Castlereagh argued that because of the vote, women's 'home influence [would] be greater and better'.

Salisbury conceived the vote not as a right but as a privilege exercised by an elite. If a woman belonged to that elite then there was no reason why she should not vote. In fact, many people (and not just Christabel Pankhurst) supported a limited franchise for women – obviously for richer women – on these grounds. Lady Knightley in her letter to *The Times* stated that the CUWFA was working for the enfranchisement of 'duly-qualified women' – an evident elitist conception. The CUWFA clearly stated in its journal that:

> The Conservative and Unionist Women's Franchise Association is opposed to the demand of a vote for every woman; they only ask that sex should cease to be a disqualification, and that women who fulfil the same conditions as men should enjoy the same political rights and privileges.[19]

The Reform Acts had given the vote to many poorly educated men without property and, to them, it seemed anomalous that educated, tax-paying, property-owning women should not have a voice. Why should responsible women with a stake in society be excluded? Indeed, they would provide a counterbalance to the lower classes. The writer John Buchan used anti-democratic arguments to justify his support for limited women's suffrage:

> We [Conservatives] hold that the franchise depends upon citizenship, and we define citizenship as the bearing of certain civic burdens . . . Now, it is incumbent upon Conservatives who accept the 'citizenship' doctrine to admit no irrelevant tests; whether the citizens are men or women is as immaterial as the colour of their hair . . . if the vote be denied to an educated and capable woman, who is a real asset to the State and takes a share in its burdens, not because she is not a citizen, but because, unfortunately, she is not a man, you are on the edge of a very dangerous doctrine. You are very near the position that male sex is the sole and sufficient ground for the Franchise, and once you get there, you will be compelled to grant the vote to every shred

> and wisp of male humanity, however debased and degenerate; indeed, I do not know how you can deny the vote to the male pauper, the male lunatic or the male criminal.[20]

Buchan believed that citizenship was linked to class and the possession of enough wealth to pay taxes. He dismissed universal male suffrage as granting the vote to 'every shred and wisp of male humanity'; he listed paupers first among those deemed unworthy to have the franchise.

Conservative suffragists, thus, were not generally interested in *all* women getting the right to vote. The feminist leader, Emily Davies, a pioneer in women's education, campaigned for female suffrage but of a very limited kind: only for unmarried women with means.[21] Lady Betty Balfour, in *The Standard* of August 1912, quoted an anti-suffragist as saying that the party leader, Bonar Law, was against 'adding ten millions of women to the register'. Her comment: 'So, I can assure him, am I.'[22] Lady Betty's emphasis on the moderation of Conservative suffrage demands was undoubtedly also a response to the electoral pact between the NUWSS and the Labour Party announced in the same year. She wanted to divorce herself from the latter's support for adult suffrage and reassure those within the party who feared such an eventuality. Conservative suffragists sought to show that granting their demands would not lead to social revolution but simply give a voice to those who were already part of society. In fact, it would help *prevent* revolution. Maud Selborne insisted to Austen Chamberlain in 1910 that a limited form of women's suffrage would favour the Conservatives. She believed that they should try 'to enlist the naturally conservative force of property-owning women on the Unionist side'.[23] The main expression of these ideas can be found in *The Conservative and Unionist Women's Franchise Review*, the journal of the CUWFA. It repeatedly argued that granting the vote to certain 'qualified' women would not only help the party but also postpone the arrival of universal male suffrage that might, as one contributor put it, 'bring civil war in its train'.[24]

Of course, not all Conservatives were so fearful on the subject. Some looked back to Disraeli and the Second Reform Act. They insisted that a rational expansion of the electorate was in line with Conservative traditions. Lord Lytton asserted that the House of Commons should be 'representative of all interests in the country which would be affected by the laws that Parliament passed'.[25] Lord Selborne went even further, using the word 'democracy':

> We believe in Democracy because we are convinced that, for our country at any rate, it has advantages which will preponderate over

> its disadvantages. One of those disadvantages is this: that A, B, and C are classes enjoying the franchise; they may be trusted on the whole to do complete justice to class D so long as there is no clash of interest between those of A, B, and C and of unenfranchised D. Directly there is such a clash of interest; it is inevitable, in a democratic system, that the unrepresented class does not get its full and fair share of consideration.[26]

He used this argument specifically in relation to women's suffrage but he certainly did not exclude further extensions of the franchise to the lower classes – in fact the use of the word 'class' and the lack of gendered language points in that direction. Later in the speech, he went even further:

> We know perfectly well that there are many thousands of men who enjoy the Franchise who are not fit. We know there are very many thousands of electors who take very little interest or who understand very little about politics, and we accept that as part of Democracy. We want to get the general opinion of the average man in the street, even if he be not the best, the wisest, or the most intelligent.

He thus dismissed the elitist arguments and presented a very inclusive view of the franchise.

All of these activities and arguments of Conservative suffragists, however, failed to convince the political leaders to commit the party on the issue. There were a number of reasons for this hesitation. First, the question was extremely divisive and potentially threatened party unity. While Conservative opposition may have been exaggerated in the past, many Conservatives did figure on the lists of the anti-suffrage movement and hostility to the Acts of 1918 and 1928 was overwhelmingly located within the Tory Party.[27] In 1907, the party leader, Arthur Balfour, told Christabel Pankhurst that he supported women's suffrage in theory. Logically, he admitted, 'the "rights" of one sex are the "rights" also of the other', but confessed that he was in no hurry to deal with the question.[28] In 1909, he candidly explained to a female friend that:

> Of course, one of the great difficulties in dealing with the question is that, while opinion is deeply divided on the subject, the division does not follow party lines – a party leader, therefore, could hardly take it up seriously, in the present state of public feeling, without risking the destruction of his party.[29]

Balfour had experienced first-hand how disagreement could decimate a party. He had witnessed the battle over Irish home rule which had split the Liberal Party at the end of the nineteenth century. More importantly, he had presided over an internecine struggle in his own party over tariff reform. In 1903, Joseph Chamberlain had nearly split the Conservatives over his proposal to introduce 'imperial preference' or 'tariff reform', which would have ended free trade with countries outside the Empire. Tariffs would not have been imposed within the Empire in order to link its diverse peoples closer to the mother country. Both Conservative men and women fought over this. Balfour only succeeded in reuniting the party after the tragic collapse of Chamberlain's health in 1906. He certainly was not going to risk reopening division by taking a strong stand on an issue as controversial as women's suffrage.

By this time, different camps had formed within the party, trying to recruit members and publicly expressing their differences. The Antis also had powerful friends and many of them were quite vocal on the question. One of the leading figures in the National Society for Opposing Women's Suffrage was Lord Curzon, a major personage in the Conservative Party and future cabinet minister. Austen Chamberlain, party leader briefly after World War One, was strongly hostile to the question, exclaiming at one point, 'Lord! How I do dislike the suffragists en masse.'[30] Austen Chamberlain was the son of Joseph Chamberlain who had already divided the party over tariff reform. To make matters worse, from Balfour's point of view, his leadership was constantly under attack and he finally resigned in 1911. Although intellectually he supported women's suffrage, he felt unable to do anything about it.

Undoubtedly, the health of the Primrose League played a large role in Balfour's calculations. Founded in 1883 to honour Disraeli's memory (whose favourite flower was supposed to have been the primrose), the League was, in the late nineteenth and early twentieth centuries, effectively the women's branch of the Conservative Party and was extremely powerful. In particular, it provided a large proportion of the money and the volunteers the party needed for its campaigns. Originally created as a ploy by Lord Randolph Churchill, Winston's father, to increase his power within the party by establishing a rival group, it became an immense success – even though Churchill soon faded away – because it fulfilled an immense need. Gladstone's Electoral Corrupt Practices Act of 1883 had severely restricted the number of paid political helpers that a candidate could have in an election. Added to this, the Third Reform Act of the following year had greatly increased the number of voters while the Redistribution Act that followed had completely redrawn the constituencies of Britain. The party organisations were thrown into chaos and the establishment of an unpaid system of volunteers became vital. The Primrose League provided this source from an unexpected area. From the very beginning, women had been admitted to the League and they soon outnumbered the men. They provided the volunteers the Conservatives needed and their work was generally credited as a major element in Salisbury's victory of 1885. The Primrose League certainly was not an organisation committed to women's suffrage – although some of its members were deeply involved – but as the largest women's political grouping in the nation, its success illustrated the important potential force of women in politics. Its work had certainly convinced many Conservatives that women were politically responsible adults and could be trusted with the franchise. It had also forced those opposed to women's suffrage to find increasingly outlandish reasons to justify their position. Lastly, and perhaps most importantly, it had brought home to many women the injustice of their situation. Lady Knightley, the first president of the CUWFA, is a case in point. She had never particularly felt the need for the vote until she became involved in her husband's campaigns. In 1885, she accompanied him when he went to vote and underwent an awakening: 'I felt – for the first time personally – the utter anomaly of my not having the vote.'[31] Others came to feel like her.

Some, however, within the League, continued to oppose suffrage and the potential for schism was real. The League had already suffered greatly during the tariff reform debate. Because most of the Primrose League had remained loyal to free trade, Chamberlain had founded another group, the Tariff Reform League, which had its own organisation for women. Chamberlain's supporters fought a kind of civil war with the Primrose League, which greatly weakened the latter group and precipitated its decline. In any battle over women's suffrage, the Primrose League, by its very nature, would have been in the frontline. Indeed, the Liberal women's organisation had actually split over the question in 1892 and the existence of rival women's groups greatly hindered the effectiveness of their work. Balfour, therefore, felt he could not risk any more damage to such an important association.

Of course, over time, opinion within the party did evolve. An examination of the voting records of MPs also yields interesting information. We can see three distinct phases: from 1867 to 1883, from 1884 to 1908 and before World War One.[32] In the first period, Conservative MPs voted by margins of three or four to one against franchise bills. Afterwards, from 1884 to 1908, the trend reversed itself with a majority for suffrage on all but one occasion. On occasion, the Conservatives used the issue to score political points off the Liberals and to disrupt the extension of the franchise to more men. In 1884, for example, 95 Conservatives voted in favour and 28 against a women's suffrage amendment to Gladstone's Reform Bill. Thus, the Liberals defeated it. In 1906, the Liberals introduced a bill to end plural voting which had always worked strongly in favour of the Conservatives. Robert Cecil proposed an amendment that stated the Act would only come into force after the next election unless women's suffrage had first been introduced. This was an obvious attempt to seduce the Liberal and Labour suffragists to vote against the government and did not work.[33] In 1913, the tactic was used again. One Conservative, Robert Sandars, explained his reasoning for such a course:

> I have been rather busy over the Franchise Bill. The general idea is that it will have a most disastrous effect on our party if it goes through. I am trying hard to get our people to support the women's vote in some form; it seems to me if we get the two questions mixed up together there must be an appeal to the country before the Bill becomes law.[34]

His goal, then, was not to achieve women's suffrage but to force a general election in the hope that the Tories would win. Far more than a commitment to the Cause, it shows a willingness to cynically manipulate the question for party advantage – but the Conservatives were not the only guilty party.[35]

But it was not all cynicism for opinions were changing. Surveys conducted by some regional groupings of the NUWSS in 1912 showed that in the localities under consideration a majority of Tory activists were willing to sign pro-suffrage petitions.[36] Furthermore, the National Union, the central organisation for all Conservative societies, approved suffrage resolutions at annual conferences in 1887, 1889, 1891, 1894, 1907, 1908 and 1910 and even invited Millicent Fawcett to speak in 1891.[37] These were conference decisions that did not bind the party, but they show that the rank and file members were much more favourable than has often been realised. Those party members who came to conferences were usually heavily involved in the party's local branches and witnessed first-hand the valuable work that women were doing.

In the third period, from 1908 to the start of the war, it becomes even more difficult to situate Conservative opinion on the subject for the whole issue became enmeshed with other questions relating to the growth of democracy. One of the most important of these was the powers of the House of Lords for all bills still needed its approval to become law. In the years from 1906 to 1910, Balfour used the Lords, with its enormous

Conservative majority, to block Liberal legislation. The Liberals felt increasingly frustrated by the repeated vetoes of a profoundly undemocratic house. Matters reached a head in 1909 when the Lords violated centuries of tradition and vetoed the budget. The constitutional crisis that followed finally ended in a reduction of the Lords' power by the Parliament Act of 1911 so that they could only delay bills for two years. Furthermore, the House of Lords was not only Conservative but highly reactionary and, at least until the 1911 Parliament Act, constituted an impassable blockade. Opinion was certainly evolving at a faster rate at the party grassroots than in that august institution. Before the war, even if Balfour had ordered them to vote for women's suffrage, they would not have done it.

Another reason the Conservative leadership avoided the issue was from fear of reawakening the debate on it. Many Conservatives saw a limited female franchise as beneficial to the party and as a protection against the propertyless. From 1905 to 1915, a Liberal government was in power and many Conservatives felt that any attempt to reopen the Pandora's Box of a franchise debate would inevitably lead to a bill for universal manhood suffrage which certainly would not help the party – and many of the more extreme feared it might even lead to revolution. No less a figure than Lady Salisbury argued that, if the Conservatives gave some women the right to vote, no matter how few, it 'must lead to manhood suffrage the moment the other side comes in again. That is the worst of a Conservative majority passing Liberal measures.'[38] There was undoubtedly a great fear of democracy and of the increasing political power of the working class.

It would take the First World War to break the logjam. The existence of a coalition government and the formation of an all-party conference helped to divorce the question from pure party interests. Many people at the time asserted that the contribution of women to the war effort had made them change their opinions, but women's suffrage did not figure greatly in the parliamentary debates on the Representation of the People Act of 1918.[39] Most MPs focused on the non-enfranchised *men*. It seems that the real evolution was in the attitude of the political elite, especially within the Conservative Party, to universal male suffrage. The suffering and deaths of hundreds of thousands of men in fighting caused a feeling of guilt and ended much of the fear of democracy. Most politicians felt they had to give the vote to servicemen. Once a consensus had been reached on this, women's suffrage followed without too much difficulty or controversy – although, it has to be said, in only a limited form. In the decision to limit the vote to women over the age of 30, most politicians showed they did not want women to be a majority of voters when men had sacrificed so much in the war. As late as 1924, the Conservative MP, the Duchess of Atholl, rejected an equal franchise bill on the grounds that:

> No one will dispute that the proposal means that women will be in the majority on the Parliamentary register. When I reach that point I cannot forget that that preponderance, whatever the exact figure may be, will have been largely due to, or at least greatly increased by, the fact that we lost 740,000 precious lives of men in the great war, and that War is still taking its toll among the ex-service men. Therefore, I cannot help thinking that I see that to propose a great extension of this kind looks like taking advantage of the heroic sacrifices of these men.[40]

Once universal male suffrage had been agreed, it was clearly to the Conservatives' advantage to enfranchise at least some women. Conservative constituency agents, who knew the localities better than anyone, favoured it by a margin of two to one.[41] Many believed that women over the age of 30 were more likely to vote Conservative than younger persons so that their enfranchisement would counteract the left-wing tilt of universal male suffrage.

It is perhaps surprising, then, that a Conservative government finally granted the younger women the vote on the same terms as men in 1928. Certainly the party leader, Stanley Baldwin, played a large role in this decision for he had committed the party to 'equal political rights for men and women' during the campaign of 1924 and promised that an all-party conference would be established to do so.[42] After Baldwin's victory, a committee of leading party members was formed to examine the question, although, interestingly, no woman was included. In spite of the active work of feminist groups, much of the country as well as the Conservative Party appeared apathetic to the question. J. C. C. Davidson, party chairman from 1926 to 1930, had actively worked to increase the role and visibility of women in the party but his comments at this time showed that this was not primarily because of his feminist ideas but because he believed it worked to the party's advantage:

> It must I suppose be accepted as certain that the Government are committed to the introduction of a Bill to equalise the franchise for men and women. If this is not so, and there is still room for argument on the political question, we are decidedly of opinion that the reduction of the franchise age in the case of women to 21 would have a detrimental effect on the fortunes of the Party. In the agricultural districts

> it is not considered that such a reduction would make any difference – in fact it might be favourable; but in the industrial areas, particularly in those districts where women work in the mills, it is believed that such a measure would bring on to the electoral rolls a large majority of votes for the Labour Party, by reason of their being under the influence of the Trade Union officials. This, at any rate, is the general view of our constituency Agents in the industrial areas whenever they might have been consulted.

Leading Conservatives suggested a number of ways in which the government could technically fulfil its pledge without doing too much damage to the party's electoral fortunes. Some thought that both men and women should be given the vote only at the age of 25 – although the proposal was quickly dropped since it went against an ancient tradition and would have undoubtedly caused uproar in the country. Another Conservative recommended that men and women should have the vote at the age of 21 if they had an occupation qualification but only at 25 with a residence qualification.[43] This would clearly have helped the Conservative Party but was felt to be a step backward – a return to a past of fancy franchises and limited voting rights. It certainly went against the image that Baldwin was trying to promote of a moderate, open, *democratic* party. He had, after all, presented himself as the champion of democracy and the people during the General Strike of 1926, arguing that it was anti-democratic for the minority to try to impose its will on the majority. He could hardly then attempt an obviously cynical manipulation of the franchise.

Thus, the decision was made, with strong support from Baldwin, to respect the campaign promise. The male and female franchises were equalised at the age of 21. The most complicated question was that of the business premises qualification. At that time, men who owned businesses could have two votes: one in their constituency of residency and one where their business was located. This obviously worked in favour of the Conservatives and they had no wish to drop it.[44] They could simply have given a second vote to those women who actually owned businesses – a very small number. They finally decided to give a second vote not only to such women but also to those whose husbands owned businesses. This both pleased the feminists and clearly helped the Conservatives. Party advantage was never very far from politicians' thoughts.

The story thus ended well, but, in the years before 1918, the party's failure to do more for women's suffrage inevitably caused disillusionment. Lady Betty Balfour actually resigned her position as Dame President of a

Primrose League habitation to protest about a speech by her MP against the enfranchisement of women. She explained that: 'To continue to work for a Member holding such views seems to me an absurdity.'[45] Her sister-in-law, Lady Frances, revealed a sense of bitterness in her comments:

> Lady Betty advanced rapidly in the ranks of constitutional work; she set herself the hardest of all tasks, attacking one by one the Conservative leaders. Let anyone try to convert 'a fossil' and they will know what she met with from a stiff-necked and perverse generation of Tories.[46]

Here we have the stereotypical portrayal of the reactionary Conservative 'fossil', although she clearly stated it to be a phenomenon of one generation that had failed to move with the times. The Balfour sisters-in-law were not alone in their feelings. Conservative suffragists felt impatient at the lack of progress on the question within their own party. Robert Cecil confessed to his sister in 1911 that he was tempted to participate in the creation of an 'independent party'.[47]

The situation became particularly complicated after the foundation of the Labour Representation Committee in 1900, which became known as the Labour Party in 1906, for it took a more progressive stance on the question that led to closer ties to the suffrage movement. Many Conservatives feared that this would affect women's voting patterns when they were eventually enfranchised. Indeed, women's resentment of Liberal policy on the issue may well have played a role in the decline of that party after 1918. Christabel Pankhurst had warned Balfour about just such a possibility as early as 1907.[48] Her fears came true in 1912 when an electoral pact was negotiated between the NUWSS and the Labour Party. The NUWSS agreed to campaign for Labour candidates because of their support for women's suffrage and started an Election Fighting Fund to help them. Certainly, the Labour Party, always short of funds, got an excellent economic return on their policy. However, this placed prominent Conservative members of the group like Lady Selborne and Lady Betty Balfour in the embarrassing position of aiding the political enemies of both their party and their men folk. Their dilemma became almost unbearable. Lady Eleanor Cecil wrote in distress to Maud Selborne:

> It seems to me we shall soon have to make up our minds between our Conservative followers (if they exist!) and our radical allies. We can't hope to make a really effective appeal to Conservative women who are at all keen about our party (and it's just these women we ought to get) if we are never to say anything which may offend Common Cause. This

> policy would also – and does in fact – leave us at the mercy of the Antis who say we are all Socialists. In what is there much point in a Conservative Suffrage Society which is afraid to avow its Conservatism?[49]

There is a clear expression of anguish here: Eleanor Cecil felt torn between her commitment to the suffrage movement and her loyalty to her political party. She even felt betrayed by both groups. The NUWSS, through its electoral pact, had allied the movement with the left. Eleanor Cecil lamented this development for several reasons. First, of course, because it went against her own personal political beliefs, but, more importantly, she feared that such a situation would ultimately divide the suffrage movement. She felt frustrated because the use of specifically Conservative rhetoric and criticism of the left was frowned upon by other suffragists as a violation of the pact. This state of affairs gave more ammunition to the Antis who could increase their influence within the party. But she was also distressed by the lack of progress against the indifference and even hostility to the 'Cause' exhibited by many Conservatives. Her final question reveals her inability to reconcile the two causes.

Indeed, we might go further and assert that there was a general disillusionment with politics and with all political parties for their failure to listen and act. Many women felt they were being ignored and even mocked by the political elite. Once again, Eleanor Cecil expressed this feeling well:

> I'm afraid a defeat on a 'free' vote wouldn't settle any grievance and I am not at all an extreme suffragist. A free vote as I understand it means no party pressure for or against. But how many really important reforms would get through the House on a free vote – adopted – as of course it always would be – because the existing government refused to back the particular Bill proposed. Party considerations it seems to me must always be present whatever the form of the bill and without some form of party pressure we have no real prospect of succeeding. That's one reason why I am very much in favour of my poor husband jeopardising his so-called career if necessary. It might or might not make much difference to his party. But the women would at least feel that someone was staking something on their cause. At present when the women are defeated absolutely nothing happens to government – independent ministers, or even the private member at his next election.[50]

The overwhelming impression here is one of powerlessness. Women had tried numerous methods to get the vote: persuasion, electoral funding, militancy and peaceful demonstrations. They had shown their political sense and worthiness through the women's organisations and made significant contributions to all the parties. Yet, politicians still felt free to ignore them and their demands. As she summarised it in another letter: 'The paradox that women will never get the vote till they have the vote expressed the root difficulty and cause of grievance.'[51] This sentiment of helplessness and hopelessness was bringing some suffragists near to despair. Certainly, it was fostering a strong sense of injustice, as Cecil's use of the word 'grievance' shows: the political class was treating women unfairly.

Women, of course, were not as politically powerless as Cecil worried – and this was especially true in the Conservative Party. They provided most of the volunteers needed for elections and they raised large sums of money. It is no coincidence that the development of a structured suffrage movement matched the arrival of large numbers of women in political organisations. Politics became a fashionable pastime for middle- and upper-class women and, as they became more politicised, they began to ask for political rights. This holds true for the Conservative Party as much as for any of the others.

Overall, in spite of Eleanor Cecil's fears, the Conservative Party certainly had a positive effect on women's achievement of political equality. There was no inherent conflict between Conservatism and suffragism as the party's support for the 1918 and 1928 Reform Bills shows. Conservative does not mean reactionary, although there were reactionary elements within the party. Even if the standard argument offered by Conservatives was that limited women's enfranchisement would help block the effects of universal male suffrage, they still came to accept overwhelmingly full democracy after World War One. In all honesty, most Tories did not have strong views on women's suffrage and primarily considered it from the angle of party advantage. In this, they hardly differed from the other parties. By the Edwardian period, few people still believed that women were incapable of making intelligent political decisions – women's party organisations, especially the Primrose League, had been too effective to allow such an attitude to continue. The real sticking point was universal male suffrage: when the majority of Conservatives accepted this, their opposition to votes for at least some women evaporated.

Most of the suffragist leaders were older people and thus did not play a major role in the party after women achieved the vote. Maud Selborne became a J.P. for Hampshire but her political influence, like that of the Cecil family, declined after the war. Frances Balfour continued on the National Council of Women of Great Britain and Ireland, holding the office of president from 1921 to 1923 and was one of its vice-presidents from 1923 until her death in 1931. She also wrote five biographies, her autobiography and received honorary degrees from Durham in 1919 and Edinburgh in 1921. Edith, Viscountess of Castlereagh, became Lady Londonderry in 1915. She was heavily involved in the Women's Legion during World War One and later became the most important political hostess of the interwar period. Her close friendship with and supposed influence on the Labour Prime Minister Ramsay MacDonald made her infamous in left-wing circles as did her husband's visits and hers to Nazi Germany. Throughout her life, she remained involved in public affairs, notably as a magistrate. Of those Conservative suffragists who continued to work for feminist causes, the most popular was that of women's employment – extending opportunities and gaining equal pay – but they generally worked in the background. Robert Cecil was the major exception to the rule. Government minister in World War One, he became a leader of the peace movement between the wars, a champion of the League of Nations and winner of the Nobel Peace Prize in 1937.

Overall, real power in the party moved to a new generation of women who had had little involvement in the suffrage movement or had even been hostile to it. In 1919, the American-born Nancy Astor became the first woman MP and an international celebrity. Although she had shown little interest in the suffrage question before, Astor became a champion of extending the vote to women on the same terms as men. She also supported then controversial issues like birth control, equal pay, employment of married women and nursery schools, although she remained convinced that a woman's place was in the home with her children. Ray Strachey acted as an unpaid parliamentary adviser to Astor, thus ensuring some continuity with the suffrage movement.[52] The second Conservative woman to enter Parliament and the first to hold ministerial position, the Duchess of Atholl had actually opposed women's suffrage. She progressed gradually towards the left, though, and, in 1929, she allied with Eleanor Rathbone to bring the problem of female circumcision before the House. She earned the nickname of the 'Red' Duchess during the Spanish Civil War because of her opposition to Franco and the Nationalists. She eventually lost her seat because of her opposition to appeasement.

In the story of the achievement of political rights for women, the party had both heroes and villains within its ranks. The contributions of Conservative women may not have been as exciting as those of the Pankhursts were (although it may be argued that after 1907 the Pankhursts, except for Sylvia, were Conservatives): heated discussions at dinner parties, letter writing, peaceful marches and newspaper articles can hardly be qualified as dramatic, but they did contribute to the evolution of male politicians' ideas and ultimately to the achievement of equal voting rights.

Notes

1. It is also sometimes called the Conservative and Unionist Women's Suffrage Association (CUWSA).
2. See, for example, M. Pugh, *The March of the Women* (Oxford: Oxford University Press, 2000), p. 102.
3. Barbara Caine, *Victorian Feminists* (Oxford: Oxford University Press, 1992), p. 86.
4. This was especially true for the period under study for most of the aristocracy left the Liberal Party during the split over Irish home rule in 1886 and eventually joined the Conservatives.
5. *Conservative and Unionist Franchise Review*, November 1910, p. 60.
6. Lady Knightley, letter to *The Times*, 9 November 1908, p. 16.
7. Kate Courtney, quoted in P. Jalland, *Women, Marriage and Politics* (Oxford: Clarendon Press, 1986), p. 219.
8. Lady Chance, *Women's Suffrage and Morality: an Address to Married Women*, NUWSS Pamphlet 1912. *Collected Pamphlets of the NUWSS*, vol. 7.1.v (London: Women's Library).
9. Eleanor Cecil to Maud Selborne, 3 November 1909, MS.Eng.Lett.d.424, Countess of Selborne Papers, Bodleian Library, Oxford.
10. And, indeed, the fundamental Conservatism of Emmeline and Christabel Pankhurst at the time of their militant activities cannot be denied. For more on this see Pugh, *The March of the Women*. The WSPU were not the only ones to have Conservative leanings: Lydia Becker and Millicent Fawcett also had links.
11. Robert Cecil to Maud Selborne, 29 June 1911, MS.Eng.Lett.d.427, Countess of Selborne Papers.
12. Christabel Pankhurst to Arthur Balfour, 6 October 1907, Add. 49793, Balfour Papers, British Library.
13. See D. Morgan, *Suffragists and Liberals: the Politics of Woman Suffrage in Britain* (Oxford: Oxford University Press, 1975), p. 34.
14. Christabel Pankhurst to Arthur Balfour, 28 October 1907, Add. 49793, Balfour Papers.
15. See, for example, Caine, *Victorian Feminists*, p. 213.
16. D. Rubinstein, *A Different World for Women: the Life of Millicent Garrett Fawcett* (London: Harvester Wheatsheaf, 1991), p. 183.
17. *Primrose League Gazette*, 15 December 1886, p. 3.
18. *Conservative and Unionist Women's Franchise Review*, February 1910, p. 14.
19. Ibid., May 1910, p. 25.
20. 'Women's Suffrage: a Logical Outcome of Conservative Faith', *The Conservative and Unionist Women's Franchise Review*, January 1911, pp. 84–5.
21. Caine, *Victorian Feminists*, p. 85.
22. *The Standard*, August 1912, in the Bonar Law Papers, Box 2711, House of Lords Record Office.
23. Quoted in Morgan, *Suffragists and Liberals*, p. 69.

24. *The Conservative and Unionist Women's Franchise Review*, November 1910.
25. Lord Lytton, 'Votes for Women', 1909, quoted in Pugh, *The March of the Women*, p. 106.
26. Lord Selborne from a speech given on 9 March 1911, ibid., p. 104.
27. Only twelve MPs voted against the 1928 Act and all were from the Conservative Party.
28. Arthur Balfour to Christabel Pankhurst, 23 October 1907, Add. 49793, Balfour Papers.
29. Arthur Balfour to Mrs Templeton, 29 October 1909, Add. 49793, Balfour Papers.
30. Austen Chamberlain to Mary Chamberlain, 26 March 1909, in Austen Chamberlain, *Politics from Inside: an Epistolary Chronicle 1906–1914* (London: Cassell, 1936), p. 169.
31. Quoted in M. Pugh, *The Tories and the People* (Oxford: Blackwell, 1985), p. 57.
32. The data comes from B. Harrison, *Separate Spheres: the Opposition to Women's Suffrage in Britain* (London, 1978), pp. 28–9. See also Pugh, *The Tories and the People*, pp. 60–1, and G. E. Maguire, *Conservative Women: a History of Women and the Conservative Party* (Basingstoke: Macmillan, 1998), p. 62.
33. The bill was defeated in the House of Lords.
34. Entry for 19 January 1913 in John Ramsden (ed.), *Real Old Tory Politics: the Political Diaries of Sir Robert Sandars, Lord Bayford, 1910–1935* (London: Historians' Press, 1984), p. 59.
35. In any case, these tactics may have had one result: convincing Christabel Pankhurst that she could work more easily with the Conservatives than with the Liberals.
36. For more on this see Pugh, *The March of the Women*, p. 114.
37. In fact, Fawcett became a frequent speaker at Conservative and Unionist functions in the 1890s.
38. Lady Salisbury to Lady Frances Balfour, 11 February 1897 in Lady Frances Balfour, *Ne Obliviscaris: Dinna Forget* (London: Hodder & Stoughton, 1930), vol. 2, p. 48.
39. Lord Balfour of Burleigh, who opposed women's suffrage, commented: 'I think what happened was that the War gave a very good excuse to a large number of excellent people, who had up to that time been on the wrong side, to change their minds.' Quoted in Harrison, *Separate Spheres*, p. 204.
40. Duchess of Atholl, 29 February 1924, *Parliamentary Debates*, 5th series, vol. 170, col. 866.
41. John Ramsden, *The Age of Balfour and Baldwin* (London: Longman, 1975), p. 120.
42. Appendix II of 'Minutes of Equal Franchise Committee of Cabinet', 21 December 1927, HO 45/13020, part 1, Public Record Office, Kew (henceforth cited as PRO). All references on this subject in this paragraph come from this document, unless otherwise noted.
43. Memorandum by Home Office, some time in 1926, HO 45/13020, part 1, PRO.
44. It was only after World War Two that the Attlee government introduced the principle of 'one man, one vote'. Until then qualified voters could vote twice, in their residency and in either their university or the constituency of their business.
45. *Primrose League Gazette*, 1 September 1910, p. 12.
46. Lady Frances Balfour, *Ne Obliviscaris: Dinna Forget*, vol. 2, p. 163.

47. Robert Cecil to Maud Selborne, 13 June 1911, MS.Eng.Lett.d.427, Countess of Selborne Papers.
48. Christabel Pankhurst to Arthur Balfour, 6 October 1907, Add. 49793, Balfour Papers.
49. Eleanor Cecil to Maud, Countess of Selborne, 6 February 1914, MS.Eng. Lett.d.424, Countess of Selborne Papers.
50. Ibid., 28 May 1914.
51. Ibid., 6 June 1914.
52. Ray Strachey had been active in the women's suffrage movement from the early twentieth century, working closely with her sister-in-law, Philippa Strachey, and Millicent Fawcett. During World War One, she served as parliamentary secretary of the NUWSS.

4

Gender, Suffrage and Party: Liberal Women's Organisations, 1880–1914

Linda Walker

Liberalism and suffrage shared a long, if somewhat troubled, history over the course of the nineteenth century. The forces that shaped the political discourse of growing democracy and the enfranchisement of citizens brought about the development of a movement that sought to couple the Enlightenment doctrine of individual rights to the position of women. From Mary Wollstonecraft to John Stuart Mill came a lineage of ideas that underpinned the Victorian campaigns for suffrage and women's rights. It was a movement that inspired many women to political and social activism and which was largely successful in its broader aims. By 1914, many goals had been achieved, but the parliamentary franchise, arguably the most coveted of these, was not. For women in the Liberal Party this was not only a tremendous disappointment; the failure of a Liberal government to embrace women's suffrage was a source of great chagrin to those who had pinned their hopes on it. The emergence of a women's wing within the Liberal Party from 1887 had opened up the tantalising prospect of a cadre of committed suffragists exerting influence on the government of the day. From a privileged and powerful position as party workers whose electioneering efforts became essential to the fortunes of aspiring MPs, the Women's Liberal Federation and Associations sought to gain the ultimate goal: the full commitment of the Liberal Party and a Liberal government to the franchise for women. The contribution of women to the party had been acknowledged by all, and in asserting the primacy of suffrage within their own organisation, Liberal women had seen deep divisions within their ranks and many divided loyalties. Yet they were denied what many felt was their due reward. While the vote was eventually won, the failure to obtain the franchise before World War One had profound consequences. By 1914, the Women's Liberal Federation (WLF) and Associations (WLAs) had seen a haemorrhage of members, many of whom were the stalwarts of the party, and although the rift with the Women's National Liberal Association (WNLA) was bridged with the creation of a new organisation in 1919, the loss was severe. This chapter will explore the initial success and ultimate failure of their ideological and tactical mission to wrest control of party policy. It will examine the ways in which the suffrage issue helped to shape the identity and purpose of the Federation, and how it led to serious divisions between members. Finally, it will explore the legacy of an organisation that tried to put women's rights before party loyalty, and why its 'muscular feminism' demonstrated a model of political engagement that, although it did not ultimately succeed, helped to galvanise the late Victorian movement and its Edwardian successor.

The roll call of Liberal women who were active in the suffrage campaigns of the 1870s and 1880s was indicative of the links between party and cause. Most were Radicals rather than Gladstonian in allegiance and they helped to shape the identity of the suffrage societies that had taken root in Bristol, Manchester, Birmingham, Nottingham, Edinburgh and elsewhere after 1867. Upper middle-class and often Nonconformist in religion, they formed an interlocking network of suffrage activists, bound by ties of kin, friendship and party.[1] Many were married or otherwise related to MPs who promoted a raft of progressive policies, including suffrage and women's rights. Sandra Stanley Holton and Rosamund Billington have pointed to the tensions between the different factions within the early suffrage movement in which Radicals played a part.[2] Despite having Liberal sympathies, Lydia Becker had been the chief architect of the policy of party neutrality. She firmly believed that not only should suffragists work with MPs of all parties on what should be a cross-party issue – a strategy that was pursued throughout the 1870s – but that given the large number of Liberal women within the National Society for Women's Suffrage, any form of political affiliation would result in it becoming an adjunct of the Liberal Party. The growth of party associations for women in the 1880s made affiliation a highly contentious issue and threatened Becker's strategy of careful neutrality.[3] Divisions over this question and what kind of suffrage measure to support culminated in the splitting of the suffrage campaign in 1888 and the emergence of three distinct groups: the Central Committee for Women's Suffrage, the Central National Society and the Women's Franchise League. Many suffragists in this period experienced frustration caused by the failure of the Liberal government to include a woman suffrage amendment in the Reform Act of 1884; they were keen to develop new ways of working and to pursue the tactical benefits of exerting political leverage wherever it could be found.

The links between the suffrage issue and the Liberal Party began a new chapter in the 1880s when women began to move towards formal association with party politics. The winds of change brought about a significant shift in the ways in which women could be politically active. The Corrupt Practices Act of 1883, which forbade the payment of canvassers, encouraged party organisers to reconsider their electoral strategies and to enlist the support of women and party workers as unpaid volunteers. Women were admitted to the Primrose League in 1884, a year after its foundation; the Women's Liberal Federation was established in 1887, and the Women's Liberal Unionist Association in 1888, following the split in the Liberal Party over the vexatious and highly emotive issue of home rule for Ireland.[4] As the main political parties excluded women from formal membership, the new structures offered the wives, sisters and daughters of party members a novel opportunity to engage with politics in a more direct way and to give assistance in the constituencies to local MPs. Although the reasons for harnessing women's energies as party workers were therefore mainly pragmatic, the suffrage question nonetheless played a part in the formation of some Women's Liberal Associations in the early 1880s. Helen Blackburn, editor of the *Englishwoman's Review* and a key member of the WLA in West Bristol, wrote that the new political organisations had a lively appeal for suffrage workers for whom the 'rigid neutrality in regard to party' which characterised the suffrage societies 'might easily seem dull and tame to the ardent party enthusiasts'; many threw their energies by preference into the WLAs.[5] An example was Anna Priestman, who with her sisters had been active at the national and local level, but who found the suffrage societies, including her own in Bristol, not just tame but disgracefully inert. Holton cites her growing disillusion with the Liberal Party in pressing forward the suffrage issue in Parliament and with the more moderate members of the movement such as Becker.[6] Priestman and her sisters were typical of those who saw the embryonic associations as a more promising vehicle for their efforts. Blackburn, on the other hand, worked with equal emphasis in both. Initially based in London, she had helped to promote the suffrage demonstrations of 1880, after which her activities became centred in Bristol, working with Priestman in the WLA and as secretary of the Bristol and West of England Society for Women's Suffrage.[7] Billington has noted the importance and practice of such cross-fertilisation in Hull and elsewhere, especially in the Edwardian years, to the extent that in some localities the suffrage societies and WLAs were virtually synonymous, with implications for electoral strategy and in particular the 'test question' on suffrage.[8]

The Bristol association, one of the earliest, began in 1881. While Holton is right to point to the emergence of similar associations in areas where Radicalism held sway, her argument that they were formed largely out of disillusion with suffrage politics and with a desire to energise a truly popular campaign for the vote needs considerable qualification.[9] There were other forces and influences at work, as in Wales where the first associations were formed not only to provide electoral assistance but also to engage with Welsh politics and rising nationalism. Issues relating to religion, land and language were central to this movement, as Ursula Masson has argued. The emergence of new associations in Denbigh (1883), Bala (1886), Caernarfon and Bangor (1889–90) appears to have been linked to elections that saw the demise of Tory landholding dynasties and the rise of Welsh Liberal politicians such as David Lloyd George and Thomas Edward Ellis. Of the earliest Welsh associations, according to Masson, only Newport and South Monmouthshire WLA (1888) was overtly suffragist.[10] We also have to remember the philanthropic impetus that underpinned much of the women's movement in the public sphere in the second half of the nineteenth century. The desire for the franchise emanated as much from a perception of what could be achieved with the vote as from the doctrine of political rights. There were those with a particular moral and social vision who sought to bring about concomitant reform, and many of the new political workers were also engaged in philanthropy and social activism. The notion of a woman's mission to improve the world, and to care especially for the young, the old, the sick and the poor, underscored the public work of many middle-class women, many of them Nonconformists, and this strand of thought and action is a well-documented part of the development of Victorian feminism and the broader women's movement.[11] The concept of moral and social progress was therefore as much a part of Liberal women's liberalism as was their belief in equality and rights. It was to feature very prominently in the discourse and conference agendas of the 1890s, and the formation of associations in the preceding decade should therefore be seen as part of this reforming zeal.

Eliza Orme's biography of Sophia Fry (1837–97), the architect of the Federation, frames her life and public work very much within such a context of social action.[12] Fry's early life in Darlington and Bristol, her Quaker faith and philanthropic good work before and after her marriage established a platform for the later political activities that brought her on to the national stage.[13] Her religious, charitable and educational activities were typical for a woman of her background and time: from setting up mothers' meetings and savings clubs at the Hopetown mission, raising funds for a general hospital, to the development of education for girls and young women, including the Darlington High School for Girls attended by her daughters and a college to train mistresses for elementary schools. Many of the Liberal women who came into the associations in the 1880s were similarly engaged in philanthropic and religious work and were appealed to on this basis. Gladstone had spoken to the moral conscience of women during the Midlothian campaign of 1879, with its theme of oppression in Eastern Europe and Ireland; he had called upon them to 'bear your own part in a political crisis like this', with the result that many who had held themselves aloof from party politics took an active part in the general election activity of 1879–80.[14] In keeping with a long tradition of women working informally in politics, Sophia Fry campaigned for her husband Theodore who became Liberal MP for Darlington. This appears to have been the catalyst for the formation of the Darlington WLA, which along with York and Bristol became one of the pioneers of the movement. By the spring of 1886, there were 17 associations in the north, Midlands and southern counties, with some 6000 members. Their purpose was clear, as Hannah Cheetham told the Southport association at its inaugural meeting in 1886 in words which signalled the primacy of gender: 'We mean to work, and to work hard, for the political education of women', and stressed their womanly influence which would lift the entire nation to a 'higher level of moral greatness'.[15] However, not all were agreed as to where the emphasis of their efforts should lie, and the question of divided loyalties that Cheetham's speech hinted at was to disturb the identity and purpose of Liberal women in the decades ahead.

Fry came to realise that better communication between local associations would greatly improve their efforts, and it was to this end that she and others began a process of discussion that culminated in the establishment of a national organisation, the Women's Liberal Federation, in 1887. By that time, there were already some 40 associations, which were socially mixed and which reflected the preoccupations of the liberal middle-classes. Some were active in local government as Poor Law Guardians and on school boards; others were engaged in philanthropic work in the Charity Organisation Society, in temperance and church societies and were precisely the sort of public spirited women whom Fry thought would be suitable to fill the associations.[16] As Eliza Orme, Fry's biographer and colleague in the Federation, made clear, it was understood that suffragists would also be welcomed, but Fry wished to restrain their influence. This was not anti-suffragism, for although she never spoke about it in public Fry supported women's suffrage and thought the franchise would eventually come. Her main concern was to keep the Federation a broad church and to make the associations welcoming to those without political experience. She hoped to attract women of all social classes, including the wives of those working-class men who had the vote: 'to have the full sympathy of the wives in the work our committees can undertake'.[17] It was a vision that was shared by the Federation's first president, Catherine Gladstone, who was rarely more than a figurehead and who brought with her, inevitably, the strong views of her husband and a reminder of why they were there. Fry clearly believed that the main aim of any organisation of Liberal women was to secure the election of Liberal politicians; party loyalty in this respect could not be challenged. According to Orme, she thought that the new venture ought not to be used for the promotion of reforms about which Liberals were in disagreement and that were not part of an accepted party programme.[18] These were the views which she took with her into the Women's National Liberal Association after the break-up of the Federation in 1892.

Over the next five years, the membership grew rapidly so that by 1892 there were 360 associations and 75 000 members.[19] Instrumental in its growth was the issue of home rule for Ireland, the political crisis that galvanised many Liberals and split the party. The tales of outrage that accompanied the Coercion and Crimes Acts especially moved Liberal women and there were numerous meetings held and pamphlets published. It seems that many associations in England and Scotland were inaugurated during this period, as the political sympathies of women were awakened. Josephine Butler and the Countess of Aberdeen, a president of the WLF, were amongst those whose oratory had a stirring effect upon their audiences, attracting thousands of women to the fold. Speaking to the Birmingham Women's Liberal Association in 1889, Mrs Osler claimed that 'The Irish question has done more in the last two or three years to settle the long-contested question of women's mission and women's place in politics than the patient and laborious efforts of twenty years past.'[20] It rallied those who were already immersed in public life, like Butler, and those who were novices.

The period from 1887 to 1892 was therefore one of organisational growth but it also witnessed a struggle for the soul of the Federation and associations, and it was this perhaps which worried the founders of the WLF. Highly politicised and divisive issues such as suffrage and home rule were being pushed by their respective supporters, and a broader social feminist agenda of temperance, education and labour laws reform was taking shape in the background. The appeal to wives and mothers to take an interest in politics was often linked to the idea that there were many worthy causes which needed their attention, and while often couched in the language of separate spheres, the clear implication was that Liberal women had a moral duty to concern themselves with public affairs.[21] As Leonora Wynford Philipps told the members of the Westminster association and the wider readership of her pamphlet, *An Appeal to Women*, they had a 'double duty': to their own families first, and then to the 'little children . . . growing up uncared for, untaught, unthought of, in slums and alleys or the streets of our great cities'.[22] However, Wynford Philipps was also a committed suffragist and a Radical with a wide-ranging agenda of social reform, and her appeal to women to become involved in politics had these objectives in mind. She urged them to claim the vote for themselves and for the good that they then could do.

Her views were echoed in a number of pamphlets and leaflets published by individual associations, exhorting their members and the wider constituency of women to join the crusade – for this was the tenor of the message and the rhetoric. Politics was the new religion, as the Reverend Tuckwell reminded them in a leaflet printed by the Warwick and Leamington association: 'Religion is not more important to our spiritual wants than politics to our material wants.' He asked: 'why are social happiness and legislative reform and political struggle to be confined to men's capacity?'; women had to take up their rightful place alongside men and to imprint their womanly influence on the laws of the land.[23] Tuckwell's concerns were linked to social matters such as labour reform; Gertrude Tuckwell, secretary of the Women's Trade Union League was his niece.

On the other hand, Mrs Broadley Reid's pamphlet on *The Protection of Child Life* prepared on behalf of the Federation was precisely the sort of issue which conformed to the image that Fry and her colleagues wished to project and which they believed would be most successful in attracting women to the party.[24] There was a general understanding that many of the women who came into their ranks were politically inexperienced, and while this was true for all women's political organisations in this period, it was one of the arguments that the moderates of the Federation put forward in order to restrain the suffragists from promoting their cause. They especially doubted the wisdom and expediency of pressing their claim for suffrage at a time when the Liberal government was embroiled in difficulties over the Irish question; nor did they feel that their new associates should be rushed into supporting the vote.[25] This was probably a correct assessment of the indifference or ignorance which many members felt towards one of the most passionately fought issues of the day. Even Kate Ryley, a suffragist and member of Southport WLA, voiced the following lament in a paper given to the annual conference in

Birmingham in 1889: 'The Liberal women of England are not unanimous, they are apathetic, they are indifferent in the matter, which of all others concerns them most vitally.' She noted that at the recent annual meeting in London only a small proportion of affiliated associations professed any real desire for the vote.[26] A year earlier, Annie Bayley had found an 'absolute want of political knowledge amongst many women in these remote country districts' while setting up a WLA in Chesterfield.[27] Many shared the view that the political education of their members should be their first priority.

The suffragists were, at this early stage, in a minority on the executive of the Federation, and held sway in only a few associations such as Bristol, Manchester, Southport, South Kensington and Edinburgh. However, they were a vocal minority who put the enfranchisement of women before that of campaigning for the Liberal Party. As Wynford Philipps told the delegates to the annual council meeting in May 1891: 'It was impossible for them to be Liberals first and Suffragists afterwards. They must be Suffragists before they could be good Liberals.'[28] Their standpoint was first and foremost one of principle, and a much cherished Liberal principle, namely the enfranchisement of the whole community: 'if we are Liberals at all, we should be everything that springs out of Liberalism . . . I am a strong Suffragist because I am a strong Liberal . . . and I say that we women want the keystone of the vote as men did.'[29]

This was a theme taken up by Bristol WLA in a broadside to the Federation in 1891: 'a Federation of Women which puts Women Suffrage to one side does not represent Liberalism'.[30] Its authors included Anna Priestman who had long queried the inconsistency of working for MPs who would not grant them the franchise ever since the association's foundation in 1881; she was one of the first to suggest that they should withhold their labour in elections from candidates who would not support them.[31] Eva McLaren, who served as honorary treasurer of the English Federation from 1897 to 1914 and honorary secretary of the Welsh Union of Women's Liberal Associations from 1894, remembered these early years as a period when the original aims of the organisation which did not give any prominence to suffrage or include it in the formal programme came to be questioned. The founders' initial stance was not surprising, she suggests, as it had always been regarded as a non-party issue. However, this view began to change as suffragists within the associations grew in number, and 'it became evident that the legitimate demands of women for political justice could not be ignored'.[32] They argued that if women were to co-operate with the Liberal Party it must be on the basis of franchise equality and recognition of the need for just legislation in other matters. In spite of her own part in the feuding, McLaren underplays, perhaps understandably, the rancour and strong feelings that surfaced as the Federation hierarchy repulsed the encroachment of those who wished to push the suffrage question to the fore of Liberal politics.

The suffragists were vocal from the outset, introducing amendments at the first annual council meeting in 1887 and in every subsequent year. Although initially few in number and at first unsuccessful in their main objective, their support in the associations increased, aided by the decentralised structure of the organisation which allowed associations to decide their own policy and activities. In addition to an executive committee, there was a national council of affiliated associations which had the power to elect the officers of the Federation and which met regularly. The annual conference and the various publications that the Federation produced enabled considerable airing of a range of issues germane to Liberal politics and, especially, to those women's issues which were the focus of the late Victorian women's movement. Further decentralisation followed the formation of the Scottish Women's Liberal Federation in 1891, along with the Welsh Union of Women's Liberal Associations and other similar bodies in the English regions. The associations had their own officers, executive committee and publications, and showed interest to a varying degree in both national and local concerns. Fry had intended that the national body, the Federation, should guide and not control the associations, which in theory were autonomous and free to cultivate their own ideas and local area as long as they promoted the work of Liberalism.[33] In the early years, most put the emphasis on electioneering and on the political education of their members. As Krista Cowman has pointed out, the main topics that the WLAs in Liverpool discussed confirmed their status as party organisations: they included housing and municipal affairs, and key foreign policy matters such as home rule and the crisis in the Transvaal; a concerted focus on women's issues did not surface until after the split in the Federation in 1892.[34]

However, as association members throughout the country gained political confidence, they began to take an interest in the debate over suffrage and to heed the arguments of those who wished to see it become an official object of the Federation. Most members, as they came to the issue, were broadly in favour of the vote, but many, like Marylebone WLA, feared its divisiveness and followed Fry's guidance as to their primary purpose.[35] Quite quickly, however, the tide began to turn in the direction of the suffragists, especially in areas such as south Wales where Eva McLaren and Nora Philipps were active in building the organisation and promoting suffrage in newly formed WLAs.[36] Here and elsewhere, many associations followed the lead of Southport and Bristol in making suffrage a formal objective and offered their support to the progressive faction at national meetings. Eva McLaren estimated that of some 204 new associations that were formed after 1889, most moved into the progressive camp. They backed their resolutions and amendments and voted progressives such as the radical Countess of Carlisle, Rosalind Howard, on to the executive committee of the Federation.[37] There was considerable jockeying for position as the moderates attempted to block their advance, but by 1891 the divisions that Sophia Fry so feared if suffrage were to be allowed to dominate proceedings were hardening and the Federation had been carved into two groups.

The progressives, who included Laura and Eva McLaren, Rosalind Howard, Leonora Wynford Phillips, Margaret Sandhurst, Emma Cons and Jane Cobden, were feminist in outlook, with a keen concern for women's rights, for issues of equality and with a desire to link the untapped political power of women to a broad agenda of social and moral reform. Sandhurst and Cobden had stood as the first women candidates in the county council elections of 1888, while the McLarens and Wynford Philipps were opposed to any form of protective legislation that interfered in the free labour of women. They played an active part in a range of organisations, from the British Women's Temperance Association (of which Rosalind Howard became president in 1903) to the Women's Emancipation Union, and all were committed suffragists.[38] They wished to draw attention to women as a class, not just as party workers, and were deeply suspicious of those politicians such as Gladstone who made use of their services but wished to silence their demand for representation. They criticised the moderates with their connections through marriage and family ties to the inner circle of the party for failing to understand that women were insignificant as a political group and that without the vote they would remain so.[39] However, the progressives were also well-connected, albeit in a different way. When Jacob Bright MP refused to pay his dues to the Manchester Liberal Union in 1898, he cited the reluctance of the Liberal Party to put forward a woman's suffrage bill – 'a cowardly and ungenerous attitude' – as the reason. He noted his family's long advocacy of the issue: his wife, sister and nieces all worked for the Cause; his wife Ursula was a leading member of the Union of Practical Suffragists within the Federation.[40] Walter McLaren, Eva's husband, was joint secretary of the cross-party parliamentary committee of supporters and had long championed women's suffrage at national Liberal Party conferences; he and his brother, Sir Charles McLaren, were spokesmen for the suffrage movement at Westminster, along with Corrie Grant, James Stuart and many others.[41]

For their part the moderates, who included Sophia Fry, Eliza Orme, Sophie Bryant, Lady Hayter and Countess Tolstoy, held fast to the view that as women's suffrage was a non-party issue it could not be given prominence in the programme of a party organisation. There were already suffrage societies with energy and influence, they argued, and by adopting the demand officially, they would become one more.[42] The moderates could also point to the divisions within the suffrage movement and warn of the dangers of bringing their feuding into the Federation. As many Liberal women were members of both suffrage societies and associations, this was a distinct possibility. The women's press of these years was filled with dissension over what measure to support and whether married women should be excluded from franchise bills for tactical reasons. By 1892 there were three national suffrage societies lobbying Parliament, each with a different platform. As Sophia Fry had asked the delegates at the Darlington conference in 1889: what kind of franchise would the Federation support? Fry's paper was in many respects the moderates' manifesto: the suffrage question had always been a non-party issue and must remain so.[43]

The moderates were also Gladstonians, and the formal opposition of the leader of the Liberal Party to women's suffrage was an acutely awkward and public fact. Moreover, he had recently reiterated his views in an exchange with Samuel Smith MP who was preparing a franchise bill for its second reading in the spring of 1892. Gladstone's arguments were persuasive. He disapproved of the spinsters' bill, which Smith had drafted because it omitted their married sisters who were 'not less reflective, intelligent and virtuous'. As a matter of legal consistency, he accepted that the vote would and should carry the right of women to sit in Parliament. However, he truly believed that opinion in the country was not ready to sanction such a shift in political behaviour. He worried about any intrusion into the 'precinct of the family' and the 'relations of domestic life' which would be consequent upon a move from the household vote, whereby the husband voted on behalf of his family, to the enfranchisement of the individual. He feared even more the irreparable changes that such a measure might bring to the womanly nature of women, which was the source of their true power, and while a minority of exceptional women had shown themselves capable of public work, he believed, most were not suited for the 'whirlpool of politics'.[44] His appeal to the concept of separate spheres had resonance, allied as it was to an understanding of the restraints that it imposed on those women who did seek to play a public role. This was something that Liberal women and those in the wider women's movement had to acknowledge, either because they genuinely believed that women brought different qualities and abilities to their public work, or because they thought it politic to do so. With their links to the higher echelons of the party, the moderates were perhaps more sensitive to the new role which Liberal women sought to play and cautious about how far they should go. They stopped short of anything that might destabilise gender relations and their own fledgling relationship with the Liberal Party and its organisation. It would be wrong, however, to see Gladstone as implacably opposed to the principle of women's suffrage. He accepted the justice of the claim, but feared its consequences. He also believed that it did not yet command sufficient support in the country, and until it was more than a sectional interest, they should not pursue it as a party.[45] This underscored the widespread view in parliamentary politics that suffrage was a cross-party issue: there were many in the Liberal Party who did not wish to change the consensus.

The splintering of the Federation happened against the backdrop of the general election of 1892. It sharpened the arguments on both sides: the one keen to see suffrage take a prominent place in the election, with local associations holding their constituencies and prospective MPs to account; the other fearful of the disruption the issue might cause. Moreover, it was a problem specific to England and Wales, as the Scottish Federation had included suffrage in its inaugural programme. The annual council meeting in May 1891 became the setting for heated debate and much grandstanding as the moderates attempted to keep their opponents off the executive committee. An important point of contention was the autonomy of the associations and their relationship to the Federation. Did they want a corporate voice on the issue, asked Rosalind Howard, as without an official sanction it became something they could not raise in elections as a legitimate issue.[46] She chivvied those who used Gladstone's hesitation as a deterrent, and suggested they were treating him too reverentially; unless they showed him their firmness on the issue, he was not likely to take it up. The moderates, on the other hand, voiced Sophia Fry's concern at any attempt to lead or even bully the associations into accepting an issue which all might not be agreed upon. Sophie Byles reiterated it in a letter to the *Women's Gazette and Weekly News* in which she expressed fears that if suffrage became a party issue and thus a test of membership, 'many good Liberals, both rich and poor, would leave it'.[47] Another factor was the recent and shrewd decision of Lord Salisbury to pronounce in somewhat guarded fashion in favour of a women's franchise, which may have been an attempt to boost the Conservative vote amongst supporters of the idea, but more likely was a manoeuvre to unsettle the Liberals. It was certainly seen by one Midlands activist as hardening the anti-suffrage contingent in the Liberal Party by making it a party issue.[48] It appeared to confirm the wisdom of the moderates' stand.

At the annual council in May 1892, the progressives finally achieved their goal. Lady Carlisle proposed and Eva McLaren seconded a successful amendment calling on the executive committee to promote the enfranchisement of women. Aware that they no longer commanded the support of the majority of the associations, the moderates on the executive committee decided to stand down and not seek re-election, a move that opened the gates to the progressives and their supporters. A year later, object two of the constitution was reworded to call on the Federation to 'promote just legislation for women (including the local and parliamentary franchise for all women, married, single or widowed, who possess any of the legal qualifications which entitle men to vote) and the removal of all their legal disabilities as citizens.'[49] This signalled to all Liberal politicians the determination of suffragists within the Federation to fight for the legislative interests of their sex.[50] In its explicit call for the removal of marital disability, it mirrored the aims of the Women's Franchise League formed in 1889 on a platform of civic and political equality within and without marriage. Given the number of married women who were active in the Federation and associations by this time, support for a limited widows and spinsters' bill would not have been credible. Rosalind Howard's swift summary of this issue as now 'dead and buried' was a trifle premature, but the position adopted by the Federation swept aside the tactical thinking of both the Central Committee and the Central National Society for Women's Suffrage.[51] It should be noted that there was much radical thought elsewhere in the party on the question of the kind of franchise to be sought. James Stuart MP had intervened in the debate sparked by Gladstone's letter to Samuel Smith by stating that universal suffrage was inevitable and the household vote doomed. Women should be enfranchised, he wrote, as 'intelligent, rational beings'.[52]

As their position was now untenable, Sophia Fry and her allies left the Federation to form the Women's National Liberal Association in which they tried to reclaim the founding principles of the Federation. There was to be absolute local autonomy on questions where there was a difference of opinion in the party, and the maintenance of a common centre of action where there was none. They had no formal programme except for the furtherance of Liberal thought and practice. In effect, they distanced themselves from the friction caused by suffrage. Many in their ranks were suffragists, but akin to Fry's position of disengagement; suffrage was occasionally discussed at annual meetings along with other issues, but in a restrained way. The exception was the debate in 1897 about Faithful

Begg's suffrage bill that disqualified married women, non-resident female property owners, women lodgers and female servants. Mrs Byles roundly condemned this for failing to equalise the position of men and women.[53] The emphasis, however, was on electoral work, and during the general election of 1895, they gave active support to candidates as speakers, canvassers and clerks, thus reinforcing the reputation that Liberal women had gained as essential to local organisation. By 1898, the 'scattered band of women workers' had a countrywide network of 103 affiliated associations.[54] It would be wrong, however, to dismiss them as selfless backroom constituency workers. They were Liberals, with a keen interest in social thought and action, which the annual conference programme reflected in the range of speakers and issues discussed. Along with standard party fare such as taxation of land values, local government, and foreign policy, they examined education, temperance, labour conditions and the Poor Law. This was not surprising given the wider interests of the membership who included Lady Battersea (from the philanthropic National Union of Women Workers), Louisa Hubbard, Susan Lawrence (active in later years in the Fabian Women's Group and the Labour Party), May Tennant (formerly May Abraham, one of the first women factory inspectors to be appointed in 1892), and Mrs Sydney Buxton (from the Women's Industrial Council).[55]

Issues relating to labour and employment were among the few areas outside suffrage where the WNLA was at odds with key members of the Federation such as Leonora Wynford Philipps and the McLaren family. The 1890s witnessed an increasingly polarised debate in the wider women's movement about the use of protective legislation to safeguard the health and well-being of women in industry. It made an appearance at the Federation annual conference in 1891. Laura McLaren led those who believed in a free market for women's labour, an opening up of employment opportunities for working women and a reduction in government inspection and trade union 'interference'. On the opposing side were Lady Dilke, now at the helm of the Women's Trade Union League and vice-president of the Strand WLA, and May Abraham who rallied to the defence of male trade unions and called for more, not less, inspection. Dilke and Abraham prevailed, and the conference rejected Laura McLaren's resolution in favour of one calling for the appointment of women factory inspectors.[56] In subsequent years the Federation continued to look with sympathy on legislation protecting workers in the dangerous trades, but showed reluctance to intervene in other sectors where inequalities might result. However, the schism that left the progressives in command of the Federation also put the free market advocates in a prominent position.

This is perhaps one of the reasons why the WNLA became a sympathetic home where a cadre of labour reformers and trade unionists – Maud Reeves, Margaret Bondfield, Gertrude Tuckwell and Lady Dilke – could give papers on the progress of the women's trade union movement and on the need for protective legislation in shop work and other trades.[57]

Before examining the progress of the suffrage issue in a Federation unfettered by the turmoil prior to 1892, we need to consider the feminist tenor of an organisation whose members were willing to put gender before party. A major vehicle for the developing power of Liberal women was the annual council meeting and conference which provided a forum for the airing of official party policy and those women's issues which the members wished to bring to the forefront of the political stage. The Federation pioneered the concept of party meetings whose main purpose was to inject the women's point of view into politics. Although the Federation in its early years accepted affiliation from both women-only and mixed associations, by 1891 it had asserted a policy of allowing only women delegates to annual meetings; this reinforced its image and purpose as an organisation that was managed and controlled by women. The Victorian suffrage campaign and indeed the wider women's movement had traditionally brought together the skills and hard work of both sexes in mixed organisations, and in a society in which women were barred from the political chambers at both the local and national level this was practicable and wise. The gradual exclusion of men from Federation and association proceedings was therefore a bold statement of independence of thought and action, although as women were not allowed membership of local Liberal unions and constituency bodies, there was also some logic to such a policy. The conferences covered a wide range of subjects. In addition to the generic political topics of the day, they looked at those issues which occupied an increasingly diverse women's movement: employment and factory acts, working conditions and sweated labour; matters of public morality and social purity, including repeal of the contagious diseases acts in India; peace and arbitration in international relations; the advancement of women in local government, education and the work of Guardians; the rights of children; the appointment of police matrons; while abolition of the House of Lords was discussed because of its lamentable record in passing social reform bills.[58] The papers presented were detailed and knowledgeable, as Liberal women brought much expertise to the Federation. The conferences bestowed not only a good general political and economic education on members but became the fulcrum for campaigns and pressure groups, lobbying MPs and giving evidence to government committees. Such activity became an increasingly viable means of obtaining reform, and in their pursuit of social issues and political rights, the Federation became an integral part of the late Victorian women's movement.[59]

In delineating the feminist identity of the Federation and its affiliated associations, attention should be drawn to the centrality of moral reform and the related issues of temperance and social purity. Liberal women were at the forefront of campaigns to cleanse society of its more decadent traits of which alcohol and prostitution were singled out for particular condemnation. Executive members of the Federation such as Rosalind Howard, Florence Balgarnie and Eva McLaren also held office in the British Women's Temperance Association, as in earlier years did Margaret Bright Lucas, who was president of the Bloomsbury WLA and an advocate of the female franchise.[60] They and the BWTA were part of the move from the 1880s onwards to politicise temperance reform and to assert the influence of women.[61] The interlocking of suffrage and temperance which was evident in the formative period of the Federation was even more powerful once Lady Carlisle became president of the WLF in 1894 and subsequently established a suffrage wing in the BWTA following her ascendance to its presidency in 1903. Liberal women, especially those affiliated to the Federation, were characterised by a 'moral arrogance'; they hoped to use the vote, once won, to effect social change and moral progress of which they saw the 'women of England' as the arbiters.[62] The more narrow-minded and puritanical side of this moral fervour was shown in the hounding of Lady Dilke from the annual conference once the sexual scandal involving her husband became public and in Laura Ormiston Chant's attempt to close London's Empire Theatre which was a meeting place for prostitutes and customers.[63] The desire for social purity in public life also pervaded the associations, where members were active in pushing forward the moral reform agenda in their concomitant activities in local government, in temperance and vigilance associations, and in their electoral work for the party.

Nowhere was the autonomy and assertiveness of Liberal women more apparent than in the implementation of the strategy of the 'test question'. From the first WLAs in the early 1880s, there had been those who queried whether they should work for suffrage opponents. Once the Federation was formed and as the debate over suffrage became more prominent, voices from Bristol to Durham and Dundee asked why they should render service to candidates who would not pledge their support for a franchise bill.[64] With pressure from suffrage leaders such as Millicent Garrett Fawcett, the desire to harness women's political associations to the suffrage campaign gained pace and credibility. Particularly controversial was Fawcett's suggestion that they should not only refuse to work for candidates opposed to suffrage, but also desist from working against anyone who had rendered conspicuous service to the cause – a suggestion that would have thrown the electoral landscape into considerable confusion.[65] The Liberals' head office had been aware of the potential damage at an early stage, for during the general election of 1892 it issued a circular warning candidates not to allow Liberal women on to their platforms lest they take the opportunity to advocate women's suffrage.[66] It was undeniable, however, that women in political associations were in a position to exercise power. Liberal women had quickly mastered the skills of electioneering and had devised improved systems at getting out the Liberal vote. By the general elections of 1892 and 1895, they had gained recognition for their efforts, and like the Dames in Primrose League Habitations, had become an essential part of the electoral process.[67] In 1896, a small pressure group called the Union of Practical Suffragists (UPS) was formed within the Federation with the aim of persuading council to adopt a policy whereby candidates would only receive support if their views on suffrage were deemed suitable.[68] It stemmed in part from the practice that some associations had already adopted of interviewing candidates before offering their electoral services – a mark of their desire to be more than political helpmates.[69] However, in its assertion of women's rights over party loyalty, it was a highly contentious strategy, and even Lady Carlisle balked at the idea. It also caused dissension at the local level, as it threatened the cherished autonomy of the associations to manage their own affairs. As Cowman has shown, this led to problems in Liverpool for Nessie Stewart-Brown, a staunch suffragist who sat on the executive committee of the Federation, but who was influenced by the more reticent and divided views of local members; she recognised that such a policy could be counter-productive, as experience in Liverpool had shown that men could be converted to suffrage by their electioneering.[70] UPS members, who included Ursula Bright, Hester Leeds, Anna Priestman and Eva McLaren, were warned that their policy would jeopardise the party's Newcastle programme with its promise of home rule, Welsh disestablishment and temperance reform.[71] This was a persuasive argument that along with members' doubts about party disloyalty held the UPS at bay until 1902 when Rosalind Howard was finally converted. The Federation resolved that in its corporate capacity it could no longer support those candidates who opposed women's suffrage, and that a Federation organiser would only be sent to those constituencies where the candidate pledged to support suffrage in the Commons. Crucially, the associations were allowed the freedom to make their own decisions as to whom they helped.[72]

The question as to how confident Liberal women felt in 1900 about the prospect of a government sponsored suffrage bill materialising in the not too distant future when the Liberals regained power is difficult to gauge. The single-minded focus of the UPS can serve to obscure the doubts and hesitation that lay elsewhere, and there needs to be more research on local Liberal associations before an informed picture can emerge. When the Federation sent a memorial in 1899 to Henry Campbell-Bannerman, the prospective new leader of the Liberals, calling on him to further the cause and to find a place for women's suffrage on the soon-to-be revised party programme, it was signed by only 137 out of a possible 460 associations – a rather tepid response.[73] The associations, as Cowman, Masson and Hollis have shown, were frequently preoccupied with local issues and local politics, and the work of women on school boards, Boards of Guardians and local councils offered an immediate way to influence their communities and to implement those policies and social matters which were dear to their hearts.[74] The Local Government Act of 1894 was a landmark in the right of women to vote and to serve on parish and district councils, bolstered by Walter McLaren's amendment which enabled wives to be qualified for the electoral register in respect of their own property or a residency of twelve months. In the following year, 202 association members were elected to Boards of Guardians and 38 to rural, urban and parish councils.[75] Municipal housekeeping had its satisfactions, and it is perhaps not incorrect to speak of the partial feminisation of local government in this period, which went some way to assuage the lack of the parliamentary vote.[76]

In 1899, the Federation had signalled its radical nature by calling for 'registered adult suffrage': one person, one vote, with a three-month residential qualification.[77] This was a bold move, although the Independent Labour Party and Social Democratic Federation led the way in calling for adult suffrage. There was a concern that the associations had lost their working-class members to the ILP, and although this was linked by some to the Federation's continued insistence on opposing protective legislation, the propertied franchise helped to sharpen the sense of a class divide.[78] In practice, the Federation supported any measure of women's suffrage that was likely to reach the statute books, and this remained its policy throughout the Edwardian years. When Margaret Ashton represented Liberal women on a deputation in 1908 she stressed that they were not asking for a particular form of enfranchisement, as some of their members favoured adult suffrage and others a more limited one.[79] The immediate post-1900 period did generate a sense of guarded optimism. The National Liberal Federation had accepted the principle of the enfranchisement of duly qualified women, and when Campbell-Bannerman met a delegation of Liberal women in 1904, he conceded their good opinion on many social questions and their right to vote.[80] The Liberal cabinet of 1906 contained firm advocates such as Lord Grey and Lloyd George, and there was hope that the implementation of the 'test question' at all by-elections and general elections would change the minds of recalcitrant MPs. Moreover, a resurgent women's suffrage movement in which a well-organised and Liberal dominated NUWSS played a major part was set to generate an increase in popular and political support.

A Liberal landslide in 1906 for a party in which a majority of MPs were committed to women's suffrage should have set the stage for a government-sponsored bill. However, Campbell-Bannerman evaded the issue, in spite of his sympathy with it, and his successor was an unmitigated disaster for the suffrage campaign. As David Morgan has argued, the opposition of Asquith, an anti-suffragist, was quite decisive. He was warned by Elibank, the Chief Whip, on the eve of the general election of 1910 that he could not afford 'to drive the whole Woman's Movement into the most bitter opposition, nor to weaken and in many cases alienate the support of the most active Liberal women workers'.[81] Other complications were the rise of suffrage militancy and its effect on public opinion and MPs, and the vexatious question of what kind of measure should be introduced. Lloyd George defended his vote against the Conciliation Bill in 1910 on the grounds that it would leave out the 'vast mass of working women' with whom he felt in sympathy, and enfranchise those of wealth and property whose 'interests were not in concert with his own'.[82]

In the Edwardian years, Liberal women were pulled in different directions. On the one hand, they continued with their traditional methods of working in concert with sympathetic MPs to try to forward the issue in Parliament. In 1907, the Scottish and English Women's Liberal Federations lined up allies willing to introduce a private member's bill, and rallied their supporters in the Commons to vote for Dickinson's Women's Enfranchisement Bill.[83] In the constituencies, although still controversial and subject to the wishes of associations, the 'test question' which by now included an assessment of the candidates' views on home rule and Welsh disestablishment as well as on opposition to the state regulation of prostitution and for suffrage was beginning to have an effect. Only after the responses were deemed suitable by the Federation area organiser and the association's committee would local members and the organiser then set to work. Between May 1904 and November 1905, this had resulted in the withdrawal of support for seven candidates in twenty by-elections.[84] In 1907, a small ginger group called the Forward Suffrage Union (FSU) was formed within the Federation to lobby for the adoption of a new strategy of withdrawing all help for Liberal candidates until the government introduced a sponsored measure.[85] In its direct challenge to party loyalty, this alarmed suffrage stalwarts such as Lady Carlisle, and gained a hearing but little support in the associations. The WSPU toured the country in an unsuccessful attempt to persuade WLAs to adopt this policy, although as Leneman and Cowman note, the Militants had their admirers.[86]

The repeated failure of the government to fulfil its promises left many suffragist Liberals like Eva McLaren in despair. At both local and national level, the sense of disappointment gave way to frustration and a feeling of betrayal. In such a context it is easier to understand how in 1910, in the absence of a Liberal candidate having been adopted, the Labour candidate, A. G. Cameron, secured the services of the WLAs in West Toxteth, East Toxteth and West Derby – with the approval of the WLF executive committee.[87] The same year in south Wales, in the absence of the government making time for the Conciliation Bill, the Welsh Union decided to work only for Liberal candidates who pledged their support – a policy that the Cardiff WLA put into practice during the general election in December by withdrawing assistance from an anti-suffragist Liberal.[88] In scenes reminiscent of the early 1890s, the annual meeting became once more the setting for fierce debates about suffrage policy, which resulted in loss of members and associations.[89] Resolutions from Tunbridge Wells in 1912 and 1913 calling on all WLAs to withhold assistance from anti-suffrage candidates were defeated, but a similar motion in the Home Counties Union, where suffrage activism was entrenched, was carried by 276 to 24.[90] Such votes were taken against the backdrop of manoeuvring by ministers at Westminster, anxious not to lose a cadre of party workers but unwilling to placate an increasingly militant suffragette campaign, and subject to the complex arithmetic that came with a much-reduced majority. The formation of one more pressure group, the Liberal Women's Suffrage Union, which was organised as an external suffrage society in 1913, was a further sign of an organisation that had exhausted its options.[91]

Claire Hirshfield has suggested that the defeats over suffrage ushered in a 'weariness of spirit' that contributed to the Federation's 'ineluctable decline'.[92] Martin Pugh has argued that the demoralisation of local organisations in these years, especially the women's, was a major factor in the party's protracted decline in the postwar period.[93] Between 1912 and 1914, there was a loss of 68 associations and some 18 000 members from the English Federation, out of a total of 837 associations and 133 215 members in 1912.[94] How many joined the Labour Party following its alliance with the NUWSS over the establishment of an election fighting fund in

1912, or withdrew from party politics in order to campaign directly for the vote is not clear. Nor do we know how many would have returned to the Federation if the onset of war, the granting of women's suffrage in 1918, and the reuniting of all Liberal women in an amalgamated union in 1919 had not made this question impossible to answer. Suffragists like Eva McLaren stayed the course, while others who joined Labour, like Margaret Ashton, did not. The Labour Party was shadowed by an increasingly powerful women's Labour movement and the platform they espoused had considerable resonance with the sort of social reforms which Liberal women had debated over the years. It was inevitable that in the shifting landscape of British politics in the first two decades of the twentieth century some Liberal women might find a new home.

In assessing the strength of feeling about suffrage and its impact on the membership in the later Edwardian period, however, we need to exercise caution. The history of the issue within Liberal women's organisations is one of deep ambivalence and divided loyalties such that there can be no clear distinction between a suffragist majority who were prepared to put gender before party and those who were not. Over the course of 28 years, it was apparent that the overwhelming majority of Liberal women were suffragists, but differed in their degree of commitment and their opinion on its priority in Liberal affairs. The debate was about tactics, not principle. The struggle between moderates and progressives in the early 1890s can serve to obscure the genuine difficulties which many rank and file members had in reconciling a marked sense of their worth as women, and the contribution they felt compelled to make to public life, with their new role as party activists who gained much respect for their electioneering activities. The latter fostered a sense of loyalty to their MP and to local constituencies; through the former, they developed a feminist identity that linked them to the wider women's movement of which they were a part. Such concerns survived the rise of suffrage militancy within and without the Federation. The chequered progress of the UPS and FSU over the introduction of the test question suggests that caution often prevailed. However, the associations could be very bullish in pursuit of a commitment to suffrage from their resident MP, and local members often marched ahead of official sanctions and policy. By 1906, the test question had obviously made inroads into the roster of Liberal MPs, and it could be argued that as the Edwardian years rolled by both Federations and associations were equally willing to flex their political muscle. However, doubts about party disloyalty and the priority given to suffrage also remained to the very end. When Helen Waddell devoted most of her address to the subject of suffrage at the annual council meeting of the Scottish Federation in 1913, she was subsequently criticised by the Dundee delegate who argued that press reports were misleading: the 'suffrage-before-party group in the S.W.L.F' had never yet been a majority of the delegates, and numbered only 37 out of 350 on this occasion.[95]

It is tempting to see the success or failure of the Federations and associations through the prism of suffrage as some historians have done. Suffrage was the natural corollary of a process of politicisation that saw the franchise as a legitimate expectation and not just an aspiration. The period 1880–1914 witnessed a crisis of political identity with new forces emerging. It also marked a new stage in the gendering of politics as women challenged a political status quo that was intrinsically male. As the old century gave way to the new, so the masculine sphere of party politics began a transformation. The demands of Liberal women over suffrage played a part in this process, as did their essential spadework at elections. They developed a political programme which reflected the convergence of membership and ideas with the broader women's movement, and which helped to shape the direction of Radical thought in the 1890s and the policies of New Liberalism after 1900. An ability to influence the political agenda and to decide priorities stemmed in part from a growing self-awareness and self-esteem. The failures over suffrage before 1914 should not obscure this wider achievement.

Notes

1. For a discussion of these networks see P. Levine, *Feminist Lives in Victorian England* (Oxford: Blackwell, 1988); S. S. Holton, 'From Anti-suffrage Slavery to Suffrage Militancy: the Bright Circle, Elizabeth Cady Stanton and the British Women's Movement', in C. Daley and M. Nolan (eds), *Suffrage and Beyond: International Feminist Perspectives* (Auckland: Auckland University Press, 1994).
2. Ibid. and S. S. Holton, 'Reflecting on Suffrage History', in C. Eustance, J. Ryan and L. Ugolini (eds), *A Suffrage Reader: Charting Directions in British Suffrage History* (London: Leicester University Press, 2000), p. 27; R. Billington, 'Women, Politics and Local Liberalism: from "Female Suffrage" to "Votes for Women" ', *The Journal of Regional and Local Studies*, 5, 1 (Spring 1985).
3. For information about Becker's life and work see A. Kelly, *Lydia Becker and the Cause* (Lancaster: Centre for North-West Regional Studies, University of Lancaster, 1992); L. Walker, 'Lydia Becker', *Oxford Dictionary of National Biography* (Oxford: Oxford University Press, 2004).
4. L. Walker, 'Party Political Women: a Comparative Study of Liberal Women and the Primrose League, 1890–1914', in J. Rendall (ed.), *Equal or Different: Women's Politics, 1800–1914* (Oxford: Blackwell, 1987).
5. H. Blackburn, 'Great Britain', in E. Cady Stanton, *History of Woman Suffrage*, vol. 4 (1902), p. 1013.

6. S. S. Holton, *Suffrage Days: Stories from the Women's Suffrage Movement* (London: Routledge, 1996), pp. 56–8.
7. L. Walker, 'Helen Blackburn', *Oxford Dictionary of National Biography*.
8. Billington, 'Women, Politics and Local Liberalism', pp. 5–7.
9. Holton, *Suffrage Days*, pp. 57–8.
10. U. Masson (ed.), *Women's Rights and 'Womanly Duties': the Aberdare Women's Liberal Association, 1891–1910* (Cardiff: South Wales Record Society, 2005), pp. 15–16.
11. See O. Banks, *Faces of Feminism* (Oxford: Martin Robertson, 1981); B. Caine, *Victorian Feminists* (Oxford: Oxford University Press, 1992).
12. E. Orme, *Lady Fry of Darlington* (London: Hodder and Stoughton, 1898).
13. E. A. Pratt, *Catherine Gladstone* (London, 1898), pp. 211–12; see also L. Walker, 'Sophia Fry', *Oxford Dictionary of National Biography*.
14. Walker, 'Party Political Women', p. 167.
15. Women's Liberal Association pamphlet, 8 November 1886.
16. Walker, 'Party Political Women', p. 168; Orme, *Lady Fry of Darlington*, pp. 112–24.
17. Lady Fry addressing the 1892 annual conference, cited in Orme, *Lady Fry of Darlington*, pp. 118–19.
18. Orme, *Lady Fry of Darlington*, p. 131.
19. Women's Liberal Federation (WLF), *Annual Report for 1892*.
20. 'Irish Home Rule and Women in Politics', *Women's Gazette and Weekly News*, 30 March 1889.
21. Walker, 'Party Political Women', pp. 174–5.
22. Mrs Wynford Philipps, *An Appeal to Women*, WLF Leaflet, c.1890.
23. Rev. W. Tuckwell, *Combine! Combine! Combine! An Appeal to Women*, WLF Leaflet, c.1890.
24. WLF, *The Protection of Child Life*, October 1890, London School of Economics, WLF Collection.
25. Walker, 'Party Political Women', pp. 186–7.
26. 'Report of the Birmingham Conference', *Women's Gazette and Weekly News*, 12 January 1889.
27. 'Work in County Constituencies, Report of Conference', *Women's Gazette and Weekly News*, 17 November 1888.
28. *Women's Herald*, 30 May 1891, p. 501.
29. 'Leonora Wynford Philipps Speaking at the WLF Council Meeting', *Women's Gazette and Weekly News*, 15 June 1891.
30. Bristol WLA, *To the Members of the Women's Liberal Federation*, 21 May 1891.
31. Bristol WLA, *Women and the Liberal Party*, c.1891; see also Holton, *Suffrage Days*, p. 57.
32. E. McLaren, *The History of the Women's Suffrage Movement in the Women's Liberal Federation* (London, 1903), pp. 3–4.
33. Orme, *Lady Fry of Darlington*, pp. 126–7; Walker, 'Party Political Women', pp. 169–70.
34. K. Cowman, *'Mrs Brown is a Man and a Brother!' Women in Merseyside's Political Organisations, 1890–1920* (Liverpool: Liverpool University Press, 2004), p. 46.
35. 'Marylebone WLA', *Women's Gazette and Weekly News*, 20 April 1891.
36. Masson, *Women's Rights*, pp. 17–18. Leonora Wynford Philipps was known as Nora Philipps in Wales.

37. McLaren, *The History of the Women's Suffrage Movement*, pp. 4–5.
38. P. Hollis, *Ladies Elect: Women in English Local Government, 1865–1914* (Oxford: Clarendon Press, 1987), pp. 309–17; L. Walker, 'Leonora Wynford Philipps', *Oxford Dictionary of National Biography*.
39. Walker, 'Party Political Women', pp. 187–8.
40. *Women's Suffrage, A letter from the Rt. Hon. Jacob Bright, 30 May 1898*, a pamphlet, Women's Suffrage Collection, Women's Library, London.
41. L. Walker, 'Eva and Walter McLaren', *Oxford Dictionary of National Biography*.
42. E. Orme, 'A Clear Issue', *Women's Gazette and Weekly News*, 15 August 1891.
43. Paper read by Mrs Theodore Fry at the Darlington Conference, 'Relation of the Women's Liberal Federation to the Suffrage Question', *Women's Gazette and Weekly News*, 30 November 1889.
44. *Female Suffrage, A letter from the Rt. Hon. W.E. Gladstone, MP to Samuel Smith, MP, 11 April 1892* (London: 1892), Women's Suffrage Collection, Manchester Central Library.
45. Ibid.
46. 'Report of the Annual Council Meeting', *Women's Gazette and Weekly News*, 15 June 1891.
47. Letter from S. A. Byles, *Women's Gazette and Weekly News*, 7 November 1891.
48. 'Lord Salisbury and Women's Suffrage', *Women's Gazette and Weekly News*, 15 September 1891.
49. McLaren, *A History of the Women's Suffrage Movement*, p. 101.
50. Walker, 'Party Political Women', p. 188.
51. 'Report of the Annual Council Meeting', *Women's Gazette and Weekly News*, 15 June 1891. Both the Central Committee and the National Society supported a spinsters' and widows' franchise on the strategic grounds that such a measure would be more acceptable than the married women's franchise to those MPs who were lukewarm on the subject.
52. *Women's Suffrage, A Letter from James Stuart to the Rt. Hon. W.E. Gladstone, MP* (Edinburgh and Glasgow, 1892), Women's Suffrage Collection, Manchester Central Library.
53. Women's National Liberal Association, *Quarterly Leaflet*, June 1897.
54. Walker, 'Party Political Women', p. 188; Pratt, *Catherine Gladstone*, p. 253; WNLA, *Quarterly Leaflet*, December 1895.
55. WNLA, *Quarterly Leaflet*, December 1895–1899.
56. 'Report of Annual Conference', *Women's Gazette and Weekly News*, 15 June 1891.
57. WNLA, *Quarterly Leaflet*, 1895–99.
58. WLF, *Annual Reports*, 1893–99.
59. Walker, 'Party Political Women', pp. 185–6.
60. M. Barrow, 'Teetotal Feminists: Temperance Leadership and the Campaign for Women's Suffrage', in Eustance et al., *A Suffrage Reader*, p. 71.
61. 'British Women's Temperance Association', *Women's Penny Paper*, 1 March 1890.
62. Walker, 'Party Political Women', pp. 176, 190.
63. *Women's Penny Paper*, 25 May 1889.
64. Bristol WLA, *Women and the Liberal Party*, c.1892; F. Pumphrey (North-West Durham WLA), *A Few Questions for Liberal Women*, n.d.; *Women's Suffrage: Should it be Made a Test Question?*, Address by Mrs Farquharson to the Dundee and District WLA, 28 December 1899.
65. M. G. Fawcett, *Private and Confidential*, printed pamphlet, c.1892, Women's Library.

66. Handwritten memo, June 1892, Manchester Central Library, Women's Suffrage Collection, M50/2/36/42.
67. Walker, 'Party Political Women', pp. 182–3.
68. Anna Priestman, 'Union of Practical Suffragists', *Shafts*, January 1897; Mrs Jacob Bright, *Shall We Work for Candidates who are against Women's Suffrage?*, UPS Leaflet no.1, c.1896.
69. A.W., 'Municipal Work in York', *Women's Gazette and Weekly News*, 23 November 1889.
70. Cowman, *'Mrs Brown is a Man and a Brother!'*, pp. 46–52.
71. M. Taylor, *To the Delegates of the Women's Liberal Federation*, 1896.
72. McLaren, *The History of the Women's Suffrage Movement*, p. 22.
73. WLF, *Annual Report for 1899*, p. 14
74. Cowman, *'Mrs Brown is a Man and a Brother!'*, pp. 122–4; Masson, *Women's Rights*, pp. 36–44; Hollis, *Ladies Elect*, pp. 57–65.
75. WLF, *Annual Report for 1895*.
76. L. Walker, 'The Women's Movement in England in the Late Nineteenth and Early Twentieth Centuries', University of Manchester, PhD, 1984, Chapter 5, 'Women in Local Government'.
77. McLaren, *The History of the Women's Suffrage Movement*, p. 22.
78. C. S. Bremner, 'The Great Woman Question', *Woman's Signal*, 13 June 1895.
79. NUWSS pamphlet, *Women's Suffrage Deputation*, 1908.
80. WLF, *Annual Report for 1904*, p. 16.
81. Quoted in D. Morgan, *Suffragists and Liberals* (Oxford: Blackwell, 1975), p. 70.
82. 'Deputation to Lloyd George', *Common Cause*, 6 October 1910.
83. Leah Leneman, *A Guid Cause: the Women's Suffrage Movement in Scotland* (Aberdeen: Aberdeen University Press, 1991), pp. 43–4.
84. C. Hirshfield, 'Fractured Faith: Liberal Party Women and the Suffrage Issue in Britain, 1892–1914', *Gender and History*, 2, 2 (Summer 1990), pp. 179–80.
85. 'Forward Suffrage Union', *Common Cause*, 15 April 1909.
86. Leneman, *A Guid Cause*, pp. 44–5; Cowman, *'Mrs Brown is a Man and a Brother!'*, pp. 124–7.
87. WNLF executive committee minutes, July and October 1910, Bristol University Library.
88. Masson, *Women's Rights*, p. 74.
89. For a full account of these debates, see Hirshfield, *'Fractured Faith'*, pp. 185–7.
90. WLF, *Annual Reports*, 1912, 1913, 1914.
91. WLF, *Annual Reports*, 1912, 1913.
92. Hirshfield, 'Fractured Faith', p. 187.
93. M. Pugh, *The March of the Women: a Revisionist Analysis of the Campaign for Women's Suffrage, 1855–1914* (Oxford: Oxford University Press, 2000), p. 142.
94. WLF, *Annual Reports*, 1912, 1914
95. Leneman, *A Guid Cause*, p. 137.

Part II
In the Hub of Things: Local Activism and Sexual Politics

5
The National Union of Women Workers and Women's Suffrage

Julia Bush

Unity based upon tolerance of diversity was an article of faith for the National Union of Women Workers. Described by Beatrice Webb as 'almost flagrantly non-political',[1] the Union sought from the early 1890s onwards to create a supportive national network of individual women and affiliated associations committed to philanthropy, education and other forms of public service. Hundreds of middle- and upper-class women gathered at its annual conferences, held in a different city each year, to publicise their own work, to learn from each other, and to celebrate the collective achievements of British womanhood.[2] The Union was pledged 'to promote sympathy of thought and purpose among the Women of Great Britain and Ireland'; 'to promote the social, civil, moral and religious welfare of Women'; to share information 'likely to be of service to Women Workers'; and to encourage the federation of women's organisations at local as well as national level.[3] Importantly, its formal constitution was prefaced from 1900 onwards by the statement that 'This Union is organised in the interests of no one policy, and has no power over the Organisations which constitute it.'[4] The founders of the Union fully recognised that the success of an 'umbrella' organisation depended upon mutual respect among women of varying beliefs and varied social, political and religious background. The desired ethos of gender solidarity in support of gendered social service was carefully perpetuated into the early twentieth century. However, it proved impossible for the Union to distance itself entirely from the concurrent women's suffrage campaign. On the one hand, boundaries between social and political action were becoming increasingly blurred by advances in local government responsibilities, and the gradual extension of women's participation as local voters and elected members of local authorities. On the other hand, Parliament itself was steadily increasing its interventions in the arena of social policy. 'Women Workers' might continue to define their role in terms of gender difference and gender specialisation, but the connections between their work and national government became undeniable. The gathering momentum of the parliamentary suffrage campaign inevitably made itself felt within the self-consciously inclusive National Union of Women Workers. By 1910, affiliated organisations included both suffrage and anti-suffrage societies. Vice-presidents of the Union included both Millicent Fawcett, leader of the largest organisation of moderate suffragists, and Mary Ward, leader of the Women's National Anti-Suffrage League. As these opponents vied for influence within 'the Parliament of Women',[5] the stage seemed set for a showdown that threatened to destroy cherished illusions of unity and even to undermine the Union itself.

The divisive suffrage debates, which rocked the National Union of Women Workers between 1910 and 1913, coincided with the climax of the extra-parliamentary suffrage campaign. However it would be a mistake to interpret the Union's travails as merely a pale imitation of political developments elsewhere. Though there was some instrumental behaviour by leading activists, and external events undoubtedly helped to heighten the temperature of controversy, the National Union responded to the suffrage debate in ways which reflected its own development over the previous two decades. By 1913, Mary Ward had suffered successive defeats in her attempts to prevent the Union from making an active commitment to the suffrage cause. She made a dramatic exit from the organisation, forecasting a disastrous future for what was becoming merely 'another suffrage society'.[6] Yet, there is evidence to suggest that, even at this crisis point, polarisation among the Union's supporters was less extreme than these events suggest. The National Union's engagement with the suffrage question had been varied and continuous since the 1890s, despite its apolitical constitution. It was also very fully recorded, not only through the published reports of annual conferences, resolutions and committee meetings, but also through the diaries, correspondence and later autobiographies of individual participants. A dynamic picture emerges of evolving ideas and policies, and of shifting priorities, rather than of confrontational opposition between suffragists and anti-suffragists. Even at leadership level within the National Union, most women chose to accept the predominance of other, less divisive issues during their annual gatherings. The scarcer evidence of activities in the Union's regional branches suggests that this was still more the case at local level. Unity in diversity appears to have been genuinely prized, by suffragists and anti-suffragists alike, as well as by the many women who made it publicly apparent that their priorities lay with 'womanly' social action rather than with the suffrage campaign in any shape. The National Union provides an interesting site for examining the suffrage debate both as a potential threat to an organisation constructed primarily around other priorities, and as an integral element within such an organisation. Throughout most of the Union's prewar history, suffragism was simultaneously warded off as a dangerously divisive element, and gradually assimilated within various policy agendas. Even at the height of suffrage controversy, when enthusiasts from both camps seemed ready to jeopardise organisational unity, significant numbers of Union members preferred compromise to confrontation. Their confidence in the shared middle ground between suffragist and anti-suffragist supporters of the National Union's core purposes proved eventually to be well-founded. The Union survived its encounter with the suffrage debate, and emerged into postwar Britain as the National Council of Women: a broadly based body of mainly middle-class, socially conservative reformers reunited around an agenda for advancing female citizenship, rather than the narrower concerns of parliamentary politics.

The National Union of Women Workers (National Council of Women) has produced several in-house organisational histories.[7] Rather surprisingly, in view of the size and scope of the Union and the extent of available primary evidence, there is so far no full-length historical analysis of its place within the wider history of British women and their organisations. Serena Kelly's short summary of the Union's records and early development presents an interesting commentary upon its archive that emphasises the 'radical and pioneering' nature of the Union's very existence, despite the fact that it was also 'conservative by temperament'.[8] The complexity of its structure and the professionalism of its record-keeping were symbolic of an organisation which sought to raise women's status as well as their confidence in their work. Frank Prochaska and Patricia Hollis have produced the fullest accounts so far of the Union's role within the web of voluntary social action, philanthropy, public administration and government legislation which together constituted social welfare provision at the turn of the nineteenth century.[9] Their work opens up issues in the Union's general history which deserve more extended discussion than is appropriate here.

In the present chapter, the evolution of the Union's aims, composition and activities provides the context for a selective study of the role of suffragism within an organisation which, despite the dramas of 1910–13, usually chose to focus its main energies in other directions. The origins of the Union will first be explored, from the perspective of participants as well as from the evidence of official records. What did the founders seek to provide for women, and what did they themselves gain from their experience of the Union during its early years? To what extent was the suffrage issue integral to, or alien from, the Union's central concerns in the 1890s? The emergence of the suffrage debate to unavoidable prominence within the Union will be considered in connection with developments in local government and with the separate issue of the Union's rather reluctant affiliation to the suffrage-oriented International Council of Women. The following section explores the ways in which the Union's growing suffragism was manifested (and contested) at different levels within the organisation in the first decade of the new century. Finally, the chapter returns to the successive suffrage confrontations within the Union in the prewar years, and their aftermath for the organisation as a whole. The impact of suffragism upon the National Union of Women Workers was significant, but by no means definitive. The abundant records of suffrage discourse within the Union provide useful insights into lesser-known aspects of the wider national debate on this question. However, the Union also persisted throughout the suffrage campaign in the pursuit of its own deliberately apolitical ideals, centred upon the gendered social duties and capabilities of women rather than upon their constitutional rights or their prospective direct contribution to parliamentary rule.

The National Union of Women Workers was formally constituted in 1895, but its emergence had been a gradual process during the preceding years. From 1876 onwards, Ellice Hopkins and her fellow-crusaders for social purity founded Ladies' Associations for the Care of Friendless Girls in many large British towns. During the 1880s, these philanthropic female reformers discovered the benefits of regular mutual support. A major conference of women workers organised by Lady Aberdeen in 1888 helped to pave the way for a succession of large-scale regional conferences, and for the formation in 1891 of a Central Conference Council that provided organisational assistance on a national scale. The networking skills of Louisa Hubbard and the administrative efficiency of Emily Janes lay behind the success of the early conferences. As editor of *The Englishwoman's Year Book* and the monthly magazine *Work and Leisure*, Louisa Hubbard was exceptionally well-equipped to bring together socially concerned women active in different parts of the country and in different causes. Emily Janes, who became the lynchpin of the Union's central office from 1891 until 1917, was equally effective. From her initial work as Ellice Hopkins's private secretary, she launched out into a ceaseless round of travel, lectures, meetings and correspondence, which paved the way for more formal collaboration among women workers. By the early 1890s *The Official Report of the Central Conference of Women Workers* was already an impressive annual publication, which spread its message to far larger numbers of women than those who managed to attend the conferences. It bore the hallmarks of later National Union publications, which consistently aimed to inform a large, loosely knit membership, both of its own extent and potential influence, and about the content of women's detailed discussions at conferences and committees.

The 1893 *Official Report*, for example, opened with a full account of the organisational arrangements for the most recent conference, managed jointly by the Central Conference Council and the Leeds Ladies' Union of Workers Among Women and Children. Members of the Central Council were listed, headed by the Duchess of Bedford and other titled philanthropists, and already including a number of the women who would become leading figures within the National Union over the next two decades. Presidents of fifteen local Unions of Workers were ex officio Council members, representing cities as far distant as Aberdeen, Glasgow, Belfast, Nottingham, Manchester, Sheffield, Leeds and Birmingham, as well as smaller towns such as Scarborough, Croydon and Cheltenham. It was clear that, unlike so many other national organisations of the period, the emerging Union would not develop simply a centralised, metropolitan perspective upon the matters which concerned it. The listing of earlier conferences and the inclusion of their presidents upon the Council conveyed a due sense of importance and permanence. Details of the organisations represented at the Leeds conference followed next, led by fifteen societies devoted to the Care of Friendless Girls and thirteen branches of the Anglican Girls' Friendly Society (each represented by a genteel Associate rather than a working-class member). A small number of political associations were represented, including the Women's Suffrage Society (Helen Blackburn and Esther Roper) and the Society for the Return of Women to Local Government Bodies (Annie Browne) as well as the Women's Liberal Association and a group of ten women Poor Law Guardians. But these representatives were swamped by women from multiple educational, religious and voluntary social reform groups, extending from women's settlements and Lady Margaret Hall, Oxford, to the Manchester Retreat for Inebriates, the Huddersfield Invalids' Kitchen and the Zenana Bible and Medical Mission.[10]

From the earliest days, women who attended annual conferences seem to have experienced tremendous enjoyment of each other's varied company, sometimes linked to a slightly guilty awareness that such events might be regarded as a self-indulgent talking shop. 'It did seem so splendid to have such a camp of good, earnest, gifted people and to know that they were only representing thousands of others', wrote Mary Clifford after the 1890 conference in Birmingham. As a committed Bristol Poor Law Guardian, she learned 'some valuable things in the Poor Law line', but her overriding impressions were of 'a peaceful and pure and heavenly air prevailing' and of a commendable 'absence of self-assertion'.[11] The distinguished suffragist writer Frances Power Cobbe delivered the valedictory address, upon a religious rather than a political theme. The absence of controversy strongly commended itself to Mary, who was also a suffrage supporter, and she commented upon 'the real and beautiful tenderness for each other' among the women present: 'The love of God seemed so to be underlying everywhere . . . that there was not, throughout the whole, a single jar.' Amongst those experiencing their first conference in 1890 was Louise Creighton, like Mary herself a future president of the Union, and described by her as 'Miss Hopkins thinks her the best woman speaker in England . . . she has a really splendid clear look in her face and a strength and a quick penetrating sword-cut about her.'[12] This slightly formidable future leader was already active in the Girls' Friendly Society and the Mothers' Union, and had helped Mary Ward to pen an influential Appeal Against Women's Suffrage published in the *Nineteenth Century Journal* the previous year. Louise's favourable impressions of the conference were recorded many years later in her autobiography: 'I was much interested by those I met. It was a great joy and surprise to find amongst this collection of rather ordinary looking middle-aged women so much intelligence, capacity and zeal. My eyes were opened to discovering all the work that was going on.'[13] Her suffragist friend Kathleen Lyttelton, also a bishop's wife and another future president, had accompanied her to the conference. Louise's anti-suffragism proved no barrier to their intimate friendship, or to their joint work for the Union and a gradual development of shared views on most other aspects of *Women and Their Work* (as Kathleen titled her didactic text of 1901).[14]

Another conservative suffragist who soon became prominent in the Union was Lady Laura Ridding, again a clerical wife as well as a committed worker against prostitution. As convenor of her local Union of Women Workers, Laura played an important role in organising the 1895 Nottingham conference at which the National Union was formally launched. Her memoir recalls not only her warm appreciation of 'the adventure of encountering new friends or strengthening the love of old ones', but also some of the rather dismissive press coverage which this conference received: 'A leading paper remarked: "How vastly the number of talkers exceeds that of real workers! We should extremely like to know the kind of work the women workers, who are now discussing social questions so freely in Nottingham, really do."'[15] The problem of definition was tackled by Louise Creighton in her first presidential speech in 1895, when she described women workers as 'women who are engaged in some real work whether it be paid or voluntary and who do that work, not for the sake of their own satisfaction, not for the sake of pay, though some may need some pay, but because they look upon their work as a vocation'.[16] Altruistic womanly motivation was all-important within the Union. Equally desirable were the achievement of higher standards and the opening of new avenues for effective public service. The Union constitution of 1895 established the executive committee and, during the following year, the specialist sectional committees which were essential to a better-informed and more powerful organisation in the future.

The transition from a friendly discussion forum to a purposeful, interventionist Union did not occur overnight, and was not universally welcomed by those involved. It presaged a gradual shift in the balance of conference discourse away from abstract questions of morality and social behaviour towards more concrete aspects of social progress, including the need to achieve reforms through collective action rather than merely individual self-improvement. It is no coincidence that 1895 was also the year of the first conference debate upon the parliamentary vote for women. The recent achievement of female representation on the new parish and district councils, and hopes of further responsibilities for women in other branches of local administration, helped to foster enthusiasm for a stronger Union, and at the same time seemed to many members to lend new impetus to the women's suffrage campaign. The terms of the 1895 suffrage discussion were carefully defined, apparently at Louise Creighton's personal insistence. No voting took place, and the session was given a non-confrontational title, which reflected the Union's agreed priorities: 'The Probable Effect on the Position of Women of granting them the Parliamentary Suffrage'. Millicent Fawcett, already prominent within the Union as a campaigner for social purity, stepped forward to defend the suffrage cause. In a speech closely tailored to her audience, she praised 'the social work represented by these Congresses' as 'giving expression to what I believe to be the central principle of distinctive womanhood', namely 'the maternal instinct'. Votes for women would merely strengthen existing work: 'I maintain, therefore, that the change I advocate is strictly in consonance with the womanly character and with the performance of womanly duties.'[17] Anti-suffrage respondents were apparently in short supply. Several women had turned down the organisers' invitation to make a public defence of their views, but this should probably be interpreted as a logical extension of their reluctance to engage in divisive political controversy rather than as lack of personal conviction or anticipation of being outnumbered within the conference. Mrs Henry Sandford, who eventually took up the challenge, delivered a dignified rebuttal of attempts by 'the small, but determined, band who have set their hearts on gaining the franchise . . . to put in a claim to be the representatives of the entire sex'. In her view, 'the vote would be not a benefit but a burden'. It would tend to undermine the partnership and mutual respect of men and women, which provided 'the foundations of domestic peace', and would subject women to 'the bondage of party ties'. Wider consequences would follow, for 'in our loss there would inevitably be involved a loss to the nation'.[18] Though Mrs Sandford's speech drew forth only two other speeches of wholehearted support, the suffragist responses that followed were somewhat muted. Mrs Bright was 'sorry to have to agree to some extent with Mrs Sandford's assertion, that there are large numbers of women throughout the country who do not desire the vote'.[19] Louisa Stevenson reminded the conference of its consensus behind the view that 'women are entitled to opinions . . . having opinions, we are bound to do everything in our power to give expression to them'.[20] Mrs Alfred Booth announced herself 'subdued' but not entirely convinced by Mrs Sandford's speech, despite her own acceptance that 'the noisy political woman among us . . . is not particularly attractive'.[21] As in so many later discussions of women's suffrage, speakers from all sides were anxious to demonstrate their respect for the Union's established traditions of tolerance, and their strong preference for progress through friendly agreement.

Despite a perceptible shift of emphasis, and a corresponding strengthening of organisation, the National Union of Women Workers remained a predominantly conservative organisation. Compromise was a necessary condition for a broad-based existence, and did not relate only to disagreements over the suffrage issue. Supporters and opponents of protective legislation for women in the workplace sometimes found themselves at loggerheads at conferences, but managed to achieve peaceful coexistence. Religious affiliation was a still more potentially divisive issue. As early as 1890, Mary Clifford had noted the 'rather Churchy' tone of the conference, and commented, 'I think it's very sweet of the Non. Cons. to endure with entire meekness the unconscious attitude of superiority that Church people take.'[22] When Beatrice Webb decided to resign from the executive committee of the Union in 1896, it was primarily upon the basis of her dislike of its assumptions of Christian (mainly Anglican) orthodoxy. She found some sympathisers among fellow-members, but was told that prayers before meetings were necessary as 'the Union would lose membership if it were not understood to be deliberately Christian'.[23] This stance was not enough to prevent Jewish women's organisations from affiliating to the Union, and indeed, by 1901, Lady Battersea (Constance Rothschild) had been elected president. Beatrice herself valued other aspects of the Union sufficiently to remain a member of its Industrial Sectional Committee for several years. In her case, membership was influenced by her awareness of the Union's tactical importance to an aspiring Fabian and social researcher. Despite her characteristically superior attitude towards an organisation 'thoroughly typical of provincial English middle class', she respected its potential influence upon 'the silent good and narrow women who do so much to form the undercurrents of public opinion',[24] and shared at least some of the Union's consensual views on the characteristics of womanhood and the centrality of motherhood to society. At the Nottingham conference of 1895, she was one of the many silent anti-suffragists.

Ten years later both Beatrice Webb and Louise Creighton had changed their minds on the issue of votes for women. Beatrice had moved on into more radical political circles, but her published recantation in 1906 revealed traces of the social conservatism that had led her to reject suffragism for so many years. Women still possessed 'their peculiar social obligations', but now required the parliamentary vote in order to fulfil those functions more responsibly and effectively.[25] Louise Creighton's recantation took place at the National Union conference in the same year, as well as in the columns of *The Times*.[26] In these statements, and especially in her later memoirs, she placed as much emphasis upon the continuities in her fundamental views as upon her pragmatic adjustment to changing circumstances. Remembering an early suffrage meeting at which she and her husband had actually been persuaded by Lydia Becker to sign a suffrage petition, she wrote: 'I was very keen to promote the work and efficiency of women in every way, and whilst I was a great believer in their real equality with men, I was clear too that on the whole their work and the nature of their influence were different.'[27] In relation to the Union, she recalled that 'the number of advocates probably increased, though we were not at all as a body active in the matter, and my opinion did not change, that women would be more useful if they kept outside actual political life and free from party politics'.[28] In accordance with this view, she refused to join a suffrage organisation even after 1906, despite her speeches and writings in favour of moderate suffragism. Perhaps more than any other individual leader, she embodied the Union's widely shared desire to transcend political divisions in order to assert higher priorities. Women's contribution to social progress depended upon personal development, family duty, religious faith and participation in a wide range of womanly social action rather than purely upon obtaining the parliamentary vote. Consensus among conservative suffragists and reformist anti-suffragists upon this broad platform of beliefs held the National Union together in 1895, and continued to help assuage the more demanding suffrage conflicts of the prewar years.

The 1895 Union conference had let the suffrage genie out of the bottle, and established suffragism as a legitimate subject for debate in this consciously apolitical setting. However, votes for women by no means dominated the agenda of conferences over the next few years, and barely registered in the work of the branches and of most specialist Union committees. When the subject resurfaced, it often did so indirectly. The Manchester conference of 1896 contained a session on 'The Duties of Citizenship' which dwelt mainly on women's responsibility for making effective use of the powers they already possessed in local government and well-organised philanthropy. In an oblique reference to suffragism, Louise Creighton reminded members that they 'need not be always expressing opinions; it is by what we are and what we do that we must try to show how women can best serve the cause of humanity'.[29] Her presidential address in 1897 warned members of the 'loss of sense of proportion' associated with single-minded campaigning around such issues as 'the Parliamentary Suffrage, and Oxford and Cambridge Degrees', and urged them to consider other reform priorities, for example in relation to women's employment.[30] Despite its desire to avoid polarising debate, the Union had decided in 1896 to introduce an important innovation. Delegates at General Meetings of the Union were to be permitted to vote on policy resolutions. The intention was clearly to exert firmer influence upon government policy, and at the same time silence critics of the conference as mere ineffectual talk. Early resolutions were passed unanimously, in support of such uncontroversial matters as the condemnation of atrocities against Armenian Christians and recommendations for the improved training for midwives. Yet, here was a tempting new opportunity for the Union's more determined suffragists to make their mark.

As the century drew to a close, resolutions began to multiply in connection with women's roles in local government. Members of the Women's Local Government Society (WLGS) took a leading part in pressing these initiatives within the Union. The WLGS was a long-standing Union affiliate and a stronghold of suffragism, despite its official neutrality on the subject. Its support was steadily strengthened by government policies that simultaneously opened some doors to women representatives whilst closing others. Women were first admitted, and then excluded, from the London County Council. Next, the abolition of London vestries and the introduction of London boroughs excluded them from areas where they had long been active. Meanwhile their general exclusion from county and borough councils was a long-standing grievance, especially when the Education Bill of 1902 threatened to abolish the School Boards that had contained women members for thirty years. In 1901, WLGS leaders prompted the

Union to resolve that 'for the work of County Councils and of County Borough Councils the co-operation of women with men is essential'; there was also a specific Union demand for women's admission to London councils.[31] Connections to the suffrage cause remained indirect, for many anti-suffragists viewed local administration as an acceptably 'domestic' extension of womanly social reform. However, the way was being prepared for a far more critical Union decision the following year. On the back of a long and indignant discussion of women's exclusion from education authorities, two short, straightforward conference speeches made the case for a resolution 'That without the firm foundation of the Parliamentary franchise for women, there is no permanence for any advance gained by them'.[32] This first direct suffrage resolution, carried without any further discussion, was to become pivotal to the Union's prewar conflicts.

Louise Creighton obviously recognised the danger, for she tried and failed soon afterwards to persuade the Union to rescind its general policy on resolutions. In a tense debate at the 1903 conference, she reminded members that 'all should be represented, and all should have the opportunity of meeting, to learn to understand one another, and discover the points on which we agree: that we should be a Union, not a body expressing a policy'.[33] Henrietta Barnett, the suffragist co-founder of the Toynbee Hall settlement, seconded her proposal to discontinue resolutions, invoking the Union's established traditions of inclusiveness and its strengths as a focus for 'subtle spiritual forces'.[34] Not for the last time, a debate ostensibly concerned with the constitutional rulebook extended into a deeply serious consideration of the Union's true purpose.

Supporters and opponents of votes for women found themselves in agreement over the desirability not merely of a tolerant, broadly representative Union of Women Workers, but also of distinctive ways of working together towards shared objectives. Rejection of the adversarial methods of party politics, in relation to women's central social concerns, was widely shared by conservative suffragists who hoped that their enfranchisement would prepare the way for improved methods of parliamentary government. Speakers on both sides of the debate, and from various points across the spectrum of suffrage opinion, drew parallels with the proceedings of the annual Anglican Church Congress, which seemed to some to offer a more attractive and appropriate role model. Yet, as some women reminded others, the Congress was supplemented by an Anglican Convocation which had the constitutional power to reach collective decisions and thus to act decisively as the ruling body of the Church. The Union's reputation and ability to influence events seemed bound up in its ability to pass resolutions on the matters which its members felt to be most important.

Despite universal respect for Louise Creighton, there was a new note of insistence and urgency in some speeches, which reflected the evolution of political events and of the Union itself since the suffrage debate of 1895. 'Already it has been our privilege to exert influence in the passing of certain legislative Acts affecting the future of women', claimed the highly conservative Ellen Joyce: 'To cease to put our views into shape would be a retrograde step.'[35] The suffragist Mrs Randall Vickers felt 'quite sure that delegates [would] not take the trouble to leave their homes if the Conference [was] to serve no other purpose than that of talk'.[36] The hunt for an acceptable compromise was on. From a distance, Laura Ridding proposed a qualifying amendment that permitted passage of resolutions within limiting terms, including the requirement for a two-thirds majority. 'Everything depends upon the spirit in which things are done', observed Miss Leppington, who advocated trust in 'the wisdom and gentleness of our Executive to carry these things without friction'.[37] In the same conciliatory spirit, a vote on Louise Creighton's recommendation was avoided. The issue was referred back for further consideration and by the following year a compromise had been reached. Voting on resolutions continued, under restrictive conditions intended to minimise conflict within the Union and to protect the feelings of minorities.

The 1903 debate had sounded a warning to Union members. The parliamentary suffrage resolution was allowed to stand quietly for a number of years without further controversy, whilst there was general support for women's continuing progress in local government. However, the issue of the parliamentary franchise was not likely to remain dormant for long. The affiliation of the Union to the International Council of Women in 1897 had added to suffragist members' confidence in advancing their cause through its channels. Anticipation of this outcome probably reinforced the reluctance of some leading British women to make a commitment towards internationalism in the first place. It was well known that Lady Aberdeen (the ICW president) was an enthusiastic suffragist, while the international body as a whole had its origins within the American suffrage movement. The 1899 international congress in London roused mixed emotions among the leaders of the National Union of Women Workers. According to Beatrice Webb, 'the more experienced English women, whilst organising it admirably, mocked at it in private'.[38] The American veteran Susan B. Anthony roused 'thunders of applause' when she took to the stage alongside other suffragist speakers at one of the largest gatherings of the week, chaired by Millicent Fawcett.[39] But neither Beatrice nor Louise Creighton was impressed. In 1904, a radical International Woman Suffrage Alliance was established, alongside a Standing Committee on Suffrage and Rights of Citizenship within the ICW itself. Such developments continued to seem distant from the conservative environment of Union conferences. The Union's rather half-hearted engagement with internationalism was a less reliable indicator of developing currents of opinion than the evidence of members' activities within its branches and sectional committees. Such activities were extensively reported in annual reports during the first decade of the twentieth century and this source, together with surviving manuscript records of Union work below national leadership level, provides a valuable perspective upon the membership's limited role in their Union's evolving suffrage commitment.

The origins of the National Union of Women Workers lay in a huge variety of local organisations. Despite the strengthening of its central administration and leadership from 1895 onwards, respect for diversity of opinion at national conferences reflected the realities on the ground. Not even Emily Janes could provide a completely accurate picture of where the Union began and ended. *The Annual Handbook* listed organisations affiliated nationally to the Union and the membership figures for local Unions, but in 1911, she admitted the impossibility of an accurate headcount since each separate branch contained both individual members and representatives of locally affiliated societies.[40] Local records immediately reveal that the Union took different forms in different places, and that suffragism might feature prominently, marginally or not at all. The Peterborough branch, founded in 1896, contained around 150 members by 1906, and held three well-attended meetings each year, beginning with prayers and concluding with tea. Its executive council included representatives of various Anglican groups, including the Mothers' Union, the Girls' Friendly Society, the Church Missionary Society and the Church of England Temperance Society, alongside Baptist and Wesleyan Missionary Societies, the Society for the Propagation of the Gospel, the Bible Society, two more temperance organisations, various groups protecting the interests of young women, individual Poor Law Guardians and a scattering of teaching and nursing associations. The Women's Co-operative Guild provided the only evidence of direct involvement by working-class women, and suffragist societies were noticeably absent.[41] The Torquay branch seems to have been still more emphatically middle-class, and strongly averse to militant suffragism. Its president, Minna Gray, penned an outraged letter to Emily Janes in October 1906 threatening resignation in protest at the Union's apparent sympathy with Militants whose methods had 'done irreparable damage to the cause of women'. The following month her protest statement against Millicent Fawcett's public support for imprisoned Militants received backing from 17 out of 22 Torquay committee members, of whom only two 'distinctly approve[d]'.[42] The Bournemouth branch, on the other hand, was founded in 1909 by leaders who carefully followed advice from headquarters to 'invite, without distinction, the leading women workers in the neighbourhood'. Affiliated societies soon included both the National Anti-Suffrage League and the National Union of Women's Suffrage Societies, as well as a fine array of organised mothers, girls, educators, temperance workers, church workers and Poor Law Guardians. In accordance with central policy, the branch considered setting up its own sectional committees in specialist areas. However, the suffrage issue itself was ruled out-of-bounds at local level. In 1912, Bournemouth 'decided against putting this question to its members', as it had been invited to do by Head Office: 'The Bournemouth Branch was known to be sharply divided on this question and the Council judged it wiser to confine its energies to those matters upon which its members were practically united.'[43]

The evidence from individual branches in the Union's annual reports shows that their activities varied widely, reflecting the enthusiasms of the most active local members rather than necessarily the priorities established by the Union's central executive and annual conference. Suffrage campaigning was not a priority even where local suffrage groups were affiliated, and even during the period from 1910–13 when this issue took up a considerable amount of the central leadership's time and energy. Some branches feared internal conflict, some probably felt that the suffrage was being adequately campaigned for elsewhere, and many seem to have been genuinely more enthusiastic about other causes. There is an interesting discrepancy between the heated leadership debates and large national conference majorities for suffragist resolutions in the prewar years, and the published local branch reports dwelling almost entirely on different matters. When the Bromley branch held its first annual meeting in October 1908, members 'received with applause' an announcement that the local executive had decided 'to do nothing either to advance or resist the movement in favour of Parliamentary votes for women', since 'many of those present were anxious to join the Branch if it did not involve them in the Franchise Controversy'.[44] Considerable attention was devoted by this branch, and most others, to women's role in local government, on the other hand. Women were urged to use their local franchise, and to put themselves forward for public office (often by Women's Local Government Society speakers). Other popular issues for branch meetings were rescue work, maternal and child welfare, employment conditions, the recent Poor Law Report, and housing improvements. The Manchester branch, one of the largest in the country and one which certainly included many suffragists, celebrated Margaret Ashton's election as the first female city councillor, but included no direct reference to the parliamentary vote in its report. Instead members attended lectures on 'Factory Law as it affects women and children', heard speakers on 'Citizenship' and 'Women and India', and organised a Special Conference to oppose the circulation of objectionable literature.[45] In Dundee Louise Creighton spoke to 'a large audience' on 'The Meaning of the Demand for Women's Suffrage'; other meetings during the year turned to Domestic Economy classes, the work of the Mothers' Union, and 'Educational Ideals'.[46] Hull members were meanwhile perpetuating old-fashioned philanthropy by organising their own crèche for working mothers.[47] By 1912, Emily Janes had begun to publish her own edited digest of the multiplying local reports. Many of the same issues continued to predominate, supplemented by current debates over the new National Insurance Act and the prospective Criminal Law Amendment Act (intended to suppress the white slave trade). Her report made a particularly strong appeal for more women in local government and illustrated the role of Union branches in recommending suitable candidates. She also emphasised the minor successes of some branches in attracting working-class women, rather than merely working on their behalf, but without concealing the fact that this was more often an aspiration than a reality.[48]

There was always a strong temptation for Emily Janes and other national leaders of the Union to attempt to expand their influence over the branches, for all the Union's pride in its diversity. Administrative efficiency, and the Union's financial solvency, depended upon a degree of centralisation, quite apart from the collective impact made by marshalling the branches' support behind important causes. Specialist sectional committees at national level were intended to help bridge the gap between central office and the regions, as well as to sustain discussion between conferences and increase Union expertise. By 1914 the Union had nineteen committees, dealing with such subjects as education, rescue and preventive work, housing, industrial reform, public health and public service. Most committees invited branch representatives to attend their national meetings, and communicated with members on a more or less regular basis through reports of their work or requests for local information. Branch records show that the response to such invitations was very variable. Despite attempts to spread Union democracy, the most active committee members tended to be national experts (like Beatrice Webb) or members of the Union's national leadership; constitutional limits were placed upon the power of committees to make or express policy for the Union as a whole, suggesting some fears that committees might be hijacked by unrepresentative groups of enthusiasts. Unlike the ICW, the National Union of

Women Workers firmly rejected proposals to form a suffrage sectional committee.[49] But this did not prevent its legislation sectional committee from regularly addressing the subject as it pursued its remit of surveying and attempting to influence prospective parliamentary Bills concerning the welfare of women and children. Opportunities existed for this committee to exert internal influence in the suffrage cause, through both its branch contacts and its leverage within the Union's executive committee. Fortunately, its minute book for the period 1906–13 has survived, and provides interesting evidence of the committee at work.[50]

For most of this period, the suffragists Laura Ridding and Margaret MacDonald led the legislation committee. Its business ranged widely, including debates over legislation concerning education, health, housing and employment, as well as direct lobbying of government departments on behalf of the appointment of 'Police Matrons' and to draw attention to 'Road Traffic Dangers'. Positioned between the Union's branches and its executive committee, the committee made the most of its influence. Some subjects, such as the proposed medical inspection of school children, lent themselves ideally to the uncontroversial involvement of branch members in gathering and submitting detailed evidence. Others prompted the committee to lean upon its executive. The suffrage issue was almost constantly on the parliamentary agenda during these years, so it is not surprising to find it regularly present on the committee's agenda too. Few attempts were made to appease anti-suffragism within this particular forum. In May 1906, the committee decided to add its own representative to a suffrage deputation to the prime minister, alongside the Union executive's nominee. In February 1907, Margaret MacDonald wrote on behalf of the committee to all Union branches, reminding them of the Union's parliamentary suffrage resolution and urging them to support not only the promised legislation to admit women as local councillors, but also the forthcoming women's franchise proposal: 'Your branch may be glad to write and ask its local members of Parliament to be in their places and support Mr Dickinson's bill.'[51] The Manchester branch reported back by 19 April that it had lobbied its MP as requested, but 'Tunbridge Wells did not think it wise owing to divided opinion to take action on the Suffrage Bill, but would watch for the Local Authorities Bill and try to convince local members to support it'. Winchester also 'had differences of opinion among the members on the Suffrage Question', and proposed holding a local debate.[52] These lukewarm responses did not deter the committee from passing a resolution pressing all branches to 'call meetings for the study of the subject, understanding that by so doing they do not necessarily pledge themselves to one side or the other'.[53] In 1908, another formal request was made to the branches for suffrage support, and in June, the committee was enthusiastically behind the Union executive's decision to rally support for a large London suffrage demonstration. In 1910, 1911 and 1912 further committee resolutions were passed pressing the Union executive (as well as the government) for stronger action to advance votes for women.

The Union executive's letter of instructions to those planning to participate in the June 1908 'Suffrage Procession' provides vivid evidence of the organisation's willingness, by this stage, to lend highly visible public support to the cause, despite the reservations of some members. Women were urged to walk rather than drive in the procession, to gather behind the Union's banner, and to 'persuade their friends to accompany them'. Those who chose to drive had the option of 'a special N.U.W.W. brake'; alternatively, they were 'asked to allow their coachmen to tie the enclosed ribbon with the national colours to their whips, in order to show that they belong to the N.U.W.W. group . . . those walking might also wear a small piece of the same ribbon'.[54] Perhaps an anti-suffragist backlash was inevitable. In July 1908, the Women's National Anti-Suffrage League was launched, and soon after accepted as an affiliate of the National Union of Women Workers. Mary Ward, its chief inspiration, had been associated with the Union since the 1890s in connection with her settlement work and play schemes for London children, and prominent supporters included Lucy Soulsby (a member of the Union's executive) and a small number of other, mainly elderly, Union stalwarts. The new League adopted objectives that committed it to advancing women's work in local government, as well as to opposing their parliamentary enfranchisement; within a year, Mary had decided to call a halt to the Union's growing suffrage activism. As a long-time member and honorary vice-president, she was no doubt aware of the divisions of opinion at grassroots level, and hoped to capitalise upon latent resentment for the benefit of her own organisation. Her first move was to condemn the Union's participation in a Trafalgar Square suffrage demonstration through the *Anti-Suffrage Review*, followed by an attempt to persuade the Union executive to review the whole issue of official representation at public meetings and demonstrations on controversial issues.[55] Mary proposed to introduce a resolution on this subject at the 1910 conference, and threatened to make a prior personal appearance at the executive committee to press her case. The Union's official reports on the arguments which followed can be supplemented from the private correspondence between Mary Ward and Louise Creighton, who found herself awkwardly placed between her old friend and former anti-suffragist colleague and her current associates on the executive, some of whom were far more ruthless suffragists than she was herself. Louise begged Mary to refrain from an intervention that would be certain to provoke an even stronger suffragist commitment from 'the small body of the violent'.[56] She hoped to carry a compromise resolution which, without referring directly to the suffrage question, would commit the executive to a policy review after the conference. This tactic eventually succeeded in averting an ugly confrontation, at least temporarily, but not before the Union had felt obliged to seek legal advice on whether its suffrage resolutions contravened its constitutional pledge to organise 'in the interests of no one policy'.

Manuscript notes on an anxious executive meeting reveal that Louise was not alone in trying to conciliate the Union's anti-suffragist members. Laura Ridding made a long speech extolling the Union's special qualities of harmony and respect for differing views, before recommending that the Union should abstain entirely from suffrage discussion if this was what was needed to maintain its unity.[57] At the 1910 conference, she was as good as her word, for she used her authority as Union president to ban the display of both suffrage and anti-suffrage literature. An unprecedented vote of no confidence was angrily proposed by some suffragists and defeated by others, including Louisa Knightley, who then went on to chair a post-conference suffrage meeting.[58] Though there were suffragist as well as anti-suffragist peacemakers on the Union executive, there were also members who had entirely abandoned their earlier dislike of internal controversy. Millicent Fawcett published a triumphant review of suffrage progress during 1910 in the Union's *Occasional Paper*, openly ridiculing organised anti-suffragism.[59] Mary Ward, who had suffered an embarrassing defeat in a public debate with Mrs Fawcett the previous year, was equally prepared to take up cudgels again. During 1912, she initiated a campaign to prevent the Union from endorsing a stronger resolution in favour of the parliamentary franchise. Encouraged by the progress of her own organisation, which by this date had amalgamated with well-funded men to form the National League for Opposing Women's Suffrage (NLOWS), she was confident of her support from anti-suffrage women below leadership level and had high hopes of rescuing the Union from a suffragist takeover. In November 1912, an Extraordinary Meeting of the National Council of Women (the governing body of the Union) was called at the request of 58 members 'to consider the Franchise and Registration Bill now before Parliament as it affects women'.[60] Despite her efforts among the branches, and the support of Gladys Pott, secretary of the NLOWS, Mary found herself heavily out-gunned. The suffragists came still better prepared, having persuaded Louise Creighton herself to propose their resolution.

Millicent Fawcett seconded it, and they won the day by 199 votes to 59, with 13 abstentions. A final effort to defeat suffragism within the Union was made a year later, when Mary Ward participated in an ill-tempered debate over constitutional reforms intended to help the organisation to retain its dissenting minority. Both appeasing suffragists and indignant anti-suffragists were roundly defeated, on this occasion by an even larger margin.

The outcome of the Union's suffrage debates in 1912 and 1913 was never seriously in doubt, given the critical stage of the suffrage campaign in Parliament and the country, and given the fact that Union representatives at national conferences had been consistently voting for suffrage resolutions since 1902. However, the speeches on these occasions deserve careful attention. They reveal the underlying continuities within a socially conservative organisation, and the shared viewpoints of many suffragists and anti-suffragists, as well as the nuances of different types of suffrage support and opposition. Mrs Allan Bright, the Union president, had the unenviable task of chairing the 1912 meeting. Nearly 300 women from across Britain came together one November morning in Central Hall Westminster, rather than the debate being cushioned by the lengthier discussions and social events of an annual conference. The resolution before them reiterated the decision of 1902, with the rider that Members of Parliament were urged 'to vote so as to ensure that no Bill shall be passed which does not include some measure of Parliamentary Suffrage for Women'.[61] Mrs Bright used her introductory speech to pour oil on troubled waters, reminding members of the Union's 'primary object, which [was] to promote the religious, moral and social well-being of women', and of the fact that the Union had been 'founded on the spirit of prayer'. The Union had been uniquely successful in drawing together 'women representing such different religious and political faiths, but who are all one in their great desire to promote the well-being of their sex, and the safe-guarding and protection of the children who are dearer to many women than their own lives'. She next made a point of commending the womanly qualities of each of the leading speakers in turn: Mrs Creighton, 'practically the mother of this very large and flourishing Union'; Mrs Fawcett, 'a model in fulfilling those practical obligations of a wife and mother which are the dearest of all ties'; Mrs Ward, 'who . . . has done so much for children'.[62]

No one present could be left in doubt about the centrality of the Union's gendered social values to the debate, and especially to the spirit in which it should be conducted. Most of the speeches that followed attempted to uphold these good intentions. Louise Creighton's speech was so conciliatory that she was able to deny that it was 'a suffrage speech' at all. Instead, she dwelt on the familiarity of the resolution, the importance of combining 'enthusiasm, devotion, zeal, with fairness and toleration', and her respect for the Union's anti-suffrage minority.[63] Millicent Fawcett also spoke with magnanimity, but with a more forceful emphasis upon the need for the Union to be seen to take 'practical action' on the suffrage issue: she sometimes wished its executive committee 'were not quite so mild', and urged the necessity of taking risks, even including the risk of losing members.[64] Mary Ward's speech was the most inflammatory of the morning. Whilst claiming to speak in defence of the Union's political neutrality and its traditions of tolerance, and underlining her support for its local government work, she ridiculed the view that women's progress depended upon the franchise and asserted that the suffrage resolution would 'split the Union in two', leaving 'permanent bitterness and separation behind'. The strengthened suffrage commitment was unconstitutional, since it broke the Union's pledge to refrain from divisive political action. 'I should like to know what question could be more political than the question of Woman Suffrage', she proclaimed, before condemning the abandonment of 'the very ideals which led to the founding of the Society', alleging a dishonourable retreat from constitutional agreements made in 1910, and predicting that 'if you pass this Resolution you will succeed in breaking up a Society which had in it a touch of something universal and divine'.[65] Seventeen other women expressed their views before the vote was taken, eight defending and nine rejecting the resolution. Among the opponents were several who declared themselves as suffragists who had decided to prioritise the future of the Union and its work above the current conflict, despite the critical stage of the parliamentary debate. It cannot have been easy for Mrs Alfred Booth, who had spoken up for suffragism in 1895, to take this position, and perhaps still less so for the aged Mary Clifford. They found themselves argued down by implacable younger suffragists. Miss D. S. Potter pointed out that nowadays 'nearly all the questions dealt with by the Union were political questions'.[66] Ada Nield Chew, representing the National Union of Women's Suffrage Societies, injected a note of class hostility into the proceedings with her comment that 'they had already heard a good deal of the need of work amongst the poor, who needed the help of people better off. What they really needed was the opportunity to help themselves – the vote, in order that they might use it to do away with the conditions of life that dragged them down.'[67] Here was an uncompromising voice of twentieth-century suffragism, pressing an argument that had already been heeded by Louise Creighton and Beatrice Webb, as well as by Millicent Fawcett.

The debate of 1913 was a still more uncomfortable affair for the anti-suffragists and their suffragist sympathisers. Laura Ridding (an experienced peacemaker) had chaired a subcommittee which considered possible constitutional means of softening the suffragist blow to organisational unity. She brought the group's emollient recommendations for conference approval, but failed to obtain it. Fired up by their November success and by the escalating suffrage conflict outside the conference, members refused to accept proposed restrictions on the annual number of resolutions, linked to new safeguards for minorities through a requirement for three-quarters, rather than two-thirds, voting majorities. In an effort to turn back the clock, as well as to help the anti-suffrage cause, a 'No Resolutions' pamphlet had been circulated within the Union during the year. Other women wanted to propose a veto solely on 'Resolutions on controversial subjects'.[68] Louise Creighton had despairingly dreamt up an elaborate new scheme of 'alternative resolutions' that even her greatest admirers found hard to understand.[69] In vain did the opening speakers appeal for calm and impartial consideration of the many alternatives, as the more intransigent women leapt into the fray with long speeches and multiple amendments which stoked up a heated debate. 'Are we going to become an exciting battleground of contending factions, or are we going to bring the Union back to its splendid attitude of wise neutrality?' demanded Mrs Mackeson, on behalf of the mainly anti-suffragist Shropshire branch.[70] Lady Dorothy Wood feared that changes which gave the executive increased power to manage resolutions, and thus control policy, would drive away 'the ordinary woman who, many would agree, constituted the main part of the Union'.[71] Mrs Grogan claimed to speak as 'a plain, ordinary woman', and on behalf of her whole branch, she advocated the 'St Andrews' attitude of strict neutrality towards subjects of acute controversial character': 'if these wedges are allowed, and if members fall away, and we just exist in a crippled condition, the fault will be with those who drive in these wedges between our members and the bond of union'.[72] Other speakers went so far as to name the suffrage issue that lurked in every corner of the debate. Debate veered from details of the internal rulebook to the role and impact of the Union upon national affairs, and ultimately to the overall impact of the suffrage campaign upon the Union itself. Both suffragists and anti-suffragists stood disunited and dismayed at the prospect of still greater disunity in the future. But their dismay was not enough to prevent a decisive defeat for Mary Ward and her supporters as each vote was taken.

The aftermath of the Union's climactic prewar suffrage debates proved much less catastrophic than some had feared (and perhaps some had secretly hoped). Despite Mary Ward's alarmist predictions in *The Times* and in private letters to Louise Creighton,[73] only one local branch and one major organisation (the NLOWS) seceded from the Union, together with 46 individual resignations over the following months. The Union's annual report for 1913–14 was able to claim 'increased activity in all departments of its work', signified by six new local branches, six new affiliations and the growth of overall branch membership from 6507 to 7057.[74] Many anti-suffragists evidently followed Lucy Soulsby's advice, in a letter read out after the vote at the 1912 Extraordinary Meeting, to stay within the Union. Meanwhile Mary carried out her threat to launch a rival organisation. By the spring of 1914, she had succeeded in persuading some prominent suffragists as well as anti-suffragists to join her in a Joint Advisory Committee, designed to bring women workers' influence to bear on legislation through sympathetic Members of Parliament. Its objectives included an ostentatious commitment to refrain from any discussion of parliamentary suffrage.[75] Louise Creighton rejected Mary's pressing invitations to become involved in this new venture, but their friendship survived intact.[76] Both women privately lamented the toll exacted by public controversy, and both remained aware of the extent of their shared attitudes towards many aspects of women's work. Their friendship was safeguarded by ongoing beliefs, which continued to uphold the Union into the war years and into a postwar world where women's suffrage was no longer controversial. Parliamentary politics apart, the Union was able to assert the continuities of its faith in women's progress through collective social action; women's importance to the nation as wives and mothers, as well as civic improvers; and women's ability to work alongside men, complementing masculine efforts towards social improvement as well as making their own distinctive contribution.

The suffrage campaign and the National Union of Women Workers were mutually influential throughout the early history of this organisation, rather than simply during the conspicuous dramas of 1910–13. Periodic discussions of suffragism brought the question directly into contact with Union business, but the suffrage views of members were also indirectly linked to their opinions on other subjects within its remit. Debates over the Union's purpose, and the related subject of its constitution, connected with parallel discussions amongst suffragists and anti-suffragists over the most suitable means of influencing national government. With or without the parliamentary vote, Union members believed that women were citizens whose gendered influence upon government and society was necessary to fulfil Britain's potential and to safeguard the national and imperial future. This belief was strengthened by evidence of the British government's growing acceptance of a measure of social welfare responsibility. Both suffragists and anti-suffragists invoked the power of public opinion, and attributed due importance to women's share in shaping it. They also converged to celebrate women's own contribution towards their achievement of improved education and legal status. From this perspective, differences over the suffrage issue were differences over the means to an agreed end. Whilst women on both sides of the suffrage argument invoked high principles, and in the heat of battle sometimes claimed a yawning gulf between their outlook and that of their opponents, it is important to recognise that they were often arguing from very similar premises. This was particularly true within an organisation like the National Union of Women Workers, which attracted large numbers of rather conservative suffragists as well as many rather progressive anti-suffragists. In this context, there was a genuine basis not only for shared social action, but also for a genuine dialogue over the prospects for greater female influence upon local and national affairs. The Union's direct and indirect engagement with suffragism helped to stimulate women's thinking about the methods as well as the policies of government, providing a platform for many gradations of suffrage and anti-suffrage opinion. Some women changed their minds over the female franchise as a result of their Union experiences. Others found a certain amount of common ground, without actually reaching agreement on the vote. This extended debate over the best means of female influence, in a context of broadly agreed social ends, prepared the way to a rapid healing of suffrage rifts after 1918.

Union members attempted to define appropriate womanly contributions towards gendered social reform upon the basis of their understanding of women's innate qualities. A largely positive view of gender differences, and especially of female moral and social attributes, was central to Union discourse in the 1890s and remained highly important into the postwar period. It helped to underpin the female case against votes for women, yet at the same time formed an almost equally vital component of conservative suffragism. Believers in essential womanhood faced various complicating factors, as they attempted to translate their convictions into practice. Inescapable issues of social class division hovered over many Union debates, especially after the turn of the century. Suffragists wrestled with the dilemma of the married women voter, alongside the threat of adult suffrage, while anti-suffrage women raised the spectre of a mass 'ignorance vote', potentially susceptible to subversive socialism. These were difficult issues for middle- and upper-class Union members on both sides of the suffrage divide. Were some women perhaps more womanly, and therefore more trustworthy, than others? Would additional responsibilities in public life bring out the best in women, or would some kinds of political involvement dilute their special qualities and give rein to their weaknesses?

By the early twentieth century the democratic challenge posed by the prospective involvement of 'ordinary' (and even working-class) women in decision-making was becoming prominent within the Union's own constitutional discussions, as well as within the suffrage debate. Argument over the nature of the 'political', and the extent to which this category might benefit from feminine reform, could also be found in both locations. Was politics merely a neutral term to describe the business of government and public administration, or did it necessarily encompass the 'rough and tumble' of party politics? Many supporters of the female vote shared the anti-suffragists' distaste for public propaganda and mass electioneering, and more specifically for the compromising of individual moral judgement, which party loyalty was believed to represent. Once again, the issue was not one that could be reduced to a simple choice between suffrage and anti-suffrage. It related to more profound questions about the nature of womanhood and the rightful contributions of women to British society and government.

The Union's records illustrate the complexity of women's views across a broad spectrum of issues which related both directly and indirectly to the suffrage debate. Agonised and sometimes confused disputes within the National Union of Women Workers during 1912–13 threatened a destructive polarisation of opinion on this subject. For a brief period the external pressures imposed by the militant campaign, and the government intransigence which fuelled it, seemed likely to overwhelm the Union's deep-rooted tolerance and its well-established faith in womanly priorities which superseded mere 'masculine' politics. Yet, even at the climax of the suffrage conflict most Union members remained anxious to restore peace through an acceptable internal compromise. This was the case within Union branches up and down the country, as well as at the suffrage-related National Council meetings of the prewar years. From a longer-term perspective, the peacemakers' persistence seems as significant as the strength of feeling among warring suffragists and anti-suffragists. It represented more than a mere sentimental desire for friendly harmony. The Union's success in eventually weathering the suffrage storm reflects the reality of women's public service across the suffrage divide, based upon a bedrock of shared beliefs and some shared uncertainties about distinctively feminine roles and responsibilities. The postwar success of this most broadly representative of women's organisations provides a warning against overstating the defining impact of suffragism upon the ideology of the mainstream British women's movement. Union members brought other priorities to their branch meetings and to their National Council, both before and after the war. Collective commitment to the implementation of votes for women could generally be accommodated alongside existing gender conservatism, rather than needing to supplant it.

Notes

1. B. Webb, *The Diary of Beatrice Webb*, edited by N. and J. MacKenzie, vol. 2 (London: Virago Press, 1986), p. 84.
2. Between 1890 and 1914, annual conference attendance seems to have been in the range 400–600. For membership numbers, see note 40 below. The Union's governing body consisted of the majority, but not all, of those present at conferences. Branches and affiliated organisations were represented on a formal basis at the governing General Council. This became known as the National Council of Women, after the NUWW affiliation to the International Council of Women in 1897. The NUWW as a whole adopted the title of the National Council of Women (NCW) in 1918.
3. *Report of the Annual Meeting of the NCW, 1901* (London: NUWW, 1901), p. 24.
4. Ibid.
5. This term was coined by the national press and widely adopted by Union members from the late 1890s onwards.
6. *NUWW Handbook and Report 1912–13* (London: NUWW, 1913), p. 213.
7. See P. Adams, *NCW Golden Jubilee Book* (London: NCW, 1945); I. Grant, *The National Council of Women: the First Sixty Years* (London: Odhams Press, 1955); D. Glick, *The National Council of Women of Great Britain: the First One Hundred Years* (London: NCW, 1995).
8. S. Kelly, 'A Sisterhood of Service: the Records and Early History of the National Union of Women Workers', *Journal of the Society of Archivists*, 14, 2 (1993), p. 173.
9. See F. Prochaska, *Women and Philanthropy in Nineteenth Century England* (Oxford: Clarendon Press, 1980); P. Hollis, *Ladies Elect: Women in English Local Government 1865–1914* (Oxford: Clarendon Press, 1987).
10. *Official Report of the Central Conference of Women Workers, 1893* (Leeds: Fred Spark and Son, 1893).
11. Letter included in G. Williams, *Mary Clifford* (Bristol: J. W. Arrowsmith, 1920), pp. 181–3.
12. Ibid.
13. L. Creighton, *Memoir of a Victorian Woman*, edited by J. Covert (Bloomington: Indiana University Press), p. 90.
14. K. Lyttelton, *Women and Their Work* (London: Methuen, 1901).
15. L. Ridding, 'The Early Days of the National Union of Women Workers', p. 7, MS account in Ridding Papers, Hampshire Record Office, 9M6873/35.
16. Quoted in Glick, *National Council*, p. 7.
17. *Women Workers. Official Report of the Conference, 1895* (Nottingham: James Bell, 1895), pp. 78–9.
18. Ibid., pp. 81, 82, 87.
19. Ibid., p. 88.
20. Ibid., p. 91.
21. Ibid., p. 105.
22. Williams, *Mary Clifford*, p. 182.
23. Webb, *Diary*, vol. 2, p. 102.
24. Ibid., p. 84.
25. B. Webb, *The Times*, 5 November 1906.
26. Speech reported in *The Times*, 27 October 1906.

27. Creighton, *Memoir*, p. 145.
28. Ibid., p. 116.
29. *Women Workers. Official Report of the Conference, 1896* (Manchester: J. E. Cornish, 1896), p. 6.
30. *Women Workers. Official Report of the Conference, 1897* (Croydon: Roffey and Clark, 1897), p. 5.
31. *Report of the Annual Meeting of the NCW, 1901* (London: NUWW, 1901), p. 27.
32. *Report of the Annual Meeting of the NCW, 1902* (London: NUWW, 1902), p. 66.
33. *Handbook and Report of the NUWW, 1903* (London: NUWW, 1903), p. 118.
34. Ibid., p. 119.
35. Ibid., p. 122.
36. Ibid., p. 121.
37. Ibid., p. 123.
38. Webb, *Diary*, vol. 2, p. 162.
39. Ridding, 'Early Days', p. 11.
40. *Handbook and Report of the NUWW, 1911–12* (London: NUWW, 1911), p. 97. An attempt to tabulate local membership by including members of locally affiliated organisations as well as individual members led to the impressive total of 1 620 902, but this did not take account of women's multiple organisational memberships. An even larger total, reflecting even more double-counting, would have resulted from inclusion of the recorded memberships of national affiliates. Instead, the NUWW published an annual list of national affiliates (without membership numbers), and from 1906 onwards a list of local branch membership numbers based upon individuals and representatives of locally affiliated organisations (not differentiated). Membership on this understated basis rose from 4373 in 1906 to 7057 in 1914.
41. Peterborough NUWW minute book, 1896–1906, London Metropolitan Archives, NUWW/NCW archive ACC/3613/08/025.
42. Minna Gray to Emily Janes, 30 October and 13 November 1906, NUWW/NCW archive ACC/3613/3/1/B.
43. Bournemouth NUWW minutes, 1909–22, NUWW/NCW archive ACC/3613/08/069.
44. *Handbook and Report of the NUWW, 1909–10* (London: NUWW, 1909), p. 83.
45. Ibid., pp. 104–5.
46. Ibid., p. 89.
47. Ibid., p. 95.
48. *Handbook and Report of the NUWW, 1912–13* (London: NUWW, 1912), pp. 107–17.
49. A suffrage committee was proposed then rejected by the NUWW executive committee in 1909.
50. Legislation Sectional Committee Minute Book, 1906–13, NUWW/NCW archive ACC/3613/01/070.
51. Ibid., 22 February 1907.
52. Ibid., 19 April 1907.
53. Ibid., 3 May 1907.
54. Correspondence re Women's Suffrage, letter from Norah Green dated 5 June 1908, NUWW/NCW archive ACC/3613/3/1/B.
55. See manuscript draft of rough notes on Mrs HW's Resolution at EC meeting (undated, 1910), NUWW/NCW archive ACC/3613/3/1/B.

56. Louise Creighton to Mary Ward, 26 October 1910, Pusey House, Oxford, Ward papers 6/3. See also letters from Louise Creighton on 21 September and 17 November, and from Mary Ward on 22 September, Ward papers 3/3/1.
57. Draft of rough notes (undated, 1910) includes a full record of Laura Ridding's speech.
58. See Louisa Knightley's journal, 10, 11 and 14 October 1910, Northamptonshire Record Office K2922.
59. *Occasional Paper*, September 1910, pp. 12–15.
60. *NUWW Handbook and Report, 1912–13* (London: NUWW, 1912), p. 199.
61. Ibid., p. 203.
62. Ibid., pp. 200–2.
63. Ibid., pp. 203, 206.
64. Ibid., p. 208.
65. Ibid., pp. 211–13.
66. Ibid., p. 215.
67. Ibid., p. 215.
68. *NUWW Handbook and Report, 1913–14* (London: NUWW, 1913), p. 167.
69. Ibid., p. 168.
70. Ibid., p. 174.
71. Ibid., p. 176.
72. Ibid.
73. *The Times*, 22 November 1913; Mary Ward to Louise Creighton, 6 and 22 December 1913, Ward papers 3/3/1.
74. *NUWW Handbook and Report, 1914–15* (London: NUWW, 1914), p. 67.
75. See J. Bush, 'British Women's Anti-Suffragism and the Forward Policy, 1908–14', *Women's History Review*, 11, 3 (2002), pp. 431–54, pp. 447–8. A 'private and confidential' list of women and Members of Parliament 'who have joined the Committee' reached the NUWW executive in March 1914, NUWW/NCW archive ACC/3613/3/1/B.
76. See correspondence between Mary Ward and Louise Creighton, December 1913–April 1914, Ward papers, 3/3/1 and 6/3.

6
The Women's Co-operative Guild and Suffrage

Gillian Scott

Founded in 1883 as part of the English consumers' Co-operative Movement, the Women's Co-operative Guild (WCG)[1] campaigned actively for women's rights. Rather than constituting a 'dual affiliation', the distinctive position it occupied at the cusp of the working-class and the women's movement constituted the basis of a new organisational identity, primarily defined by a feminist analysis of the circumstances of its members – predominantly working-class housewives who shopped at the Co-op stores. The WCG generally characterised this group as 'married working women', signifying that although not typically in paid employment they worked hard in their homes. Operating as a self-styled 'trade union of married women', in the years before World War One, the WCG took up various 'Citizenship' campaigns to improve their situation. With tens of thousands of members, highly democratic procedures and a formal position of party-political neutrality, the WCG succeeded in bringing this previously unrepresented constituency into public life, broadcasting their needs and views on a range of social and political questions that included but was by no means limited to the suffrage.

To explore the fine grain of these developments, we begin by tracing the early growth of the WCG from socially conservative origins to a broad alignment with the aims of the women's movement. We then turn to the Guild's pioneering work for divorce law reform and maternity care in which its disclosures of the wrongs of working-class wives generated an expansive conception of the reforms needed to improve their situation and underscored the urgent need for their direct political representation. Finally, we consider the WCG's involvement with the suffrage agitation, and its efforts to hold in equilibrium the claims of class and of sex in relation to political reform.

The first priority for the early WCG was to reassert the rights accorded to women within the Co-operative tradition. Since the 1840s, consumers'

Co-operation had evolved as a democratically controlled and collectively owned trading scheme to supply working people with decent and affordable food, paying back a share of profits to members as a dividend or 'divi'. By 1900, with 1 780 000 members and a share capital of £23 256 000,[2] it consisted of hundreds of self-governing societies (retail stores or 'Co-ops'), federated into the Co-operative Wholesale Society (CWS) for supplies, and the Co-operative Union (CU) for education and propaganda purposes. This leading institution of working-class self-help offered women exceptional opportunities that reflected both a utopian socialist past[3] and a material reality: the Co-ops' survival and growth depended upon women's trading loyalty. Never constitutionally excluded from the movement, women enjoyed, in principle at least, equal membership rights – to vote, to own shares, to earn dividend, and to have access to educational provision.

Yet, the practice often fell short of the theory. Many Co-operators believed that women's proper place was the home and that they lacked the capacity to deal with facts, figures and policy-making. They did most of the shopping, and even collected the 'divi', but few attended Co-operative meetings, and still fewer spoke at them. 'What are men always urged to do', asked Alice Acland, wife of a prominent Co-operator,[4] 'when there is a meeting held at any place to encourage or start Co-operative institutions? Come! Help! Vote! Criticise! Act! What are women urged to do? Come and Buy!' They could be independent members so why not also have 'our meetings, our readings, our discussions?'[5] The Women's League for the Spread of Co-operation (soon renamed the WCG) was thus launched at the 1883 Co-operative Congress with 50 members, a regular women's column in *Co-operative News*, and in 1886 a £10 grant from the Co-operative Union (CU).

At the outset, however, there were few signs of the WCG's later radicalism. More apparent was an orthodox domestic ideology. Early Guild leaders cared deeply about propriety. Alice Acland disavowed the 'vex'd question of women's rights',[6] maintaining that women could do much 'without departing from our own sphere, and without trying to undertake work which can be better done by men'.[7] 'Quiet influence,' she explained, 'in the home, and from home to home, cannot fail to have an effect.'[8] By 1885, there were 376 members and ten branches, and needlework and dressmaking classes were popular branch activities. When a guildswoman departed from these norms, there were protests. Mrs Ben Jones boldly proposed that when at Co-operative meetings with their husbands, women might, if invited to do so, speak from the platform.[9] Subsequent correspondence in the women's pages made it plain that some members disapproved of women speaking in public on behalf of the Guild.[10] For the respectable working-class, as for their middle-class superiors,[11] it was unfeminine and immodest for a woman to draw attention to herself at a mixed public gathering.

The infant WCG also faced prejudice from male Co-operators who objected to the very concept of a women's organisation. In 1885, Miss Webb (vice-president) reported that 'some of the most unjust criticism comes from co-operators, or so-called co-operators. We are told by some that "we should do more good staying at home and educating our children".'[12] Another obstacle to organisational growth was the belief of many potential recruits that they could not leave their homes. Some, like Mrs Layton, saw only practical difficulties: 'I was far too busy. I thought a meeting in the middle of the week quite impossible. I still had to wash and iron for my living.'[13] Others could not even imagine going to a meeting. A Norwich branch secretary found that when 'asking mothers to come out for an hour or two to enjoy themselves, they nearly all make one answer – "Oh, Thank you! But I never go out, my daughter will come, or my husband and children will come".'[14]

With the whole social and economic structure, legal system, customs and beliefs buttressing women's subordinate position, it is not surprising that in the 1880s the WCG, uncertain about its purpose and its claims on the wider movement, remained fragile. Dynamic growth only began with the emergence of a leadership that had the courage and the confidence to work against the grain of dominant values about a woman's place, and to envision the WCG as a project to mobilise Co-operative women for active citizenship, making full use of Co-operative resources in the process.

This radical approach came from two sources: middle-class feminists with socialist leanings looking to connect with working-class women, and working-class women activists from suffrage and trade union backgrounds. The single most important figure in the Guild's history was Margaret Llewelyn Davies, General Secretary from 1889 to 1921, an upper-middle-class woman from a privileged yet enlightened background. Her father, John Llewelyn Davies, was a Christian socialist; her aunt, Emily Davies, a mid-nineteenth-century equal rights feminist, founded Girton College, Cambridge; her mother, Mary Crompton, was from a progressive Unitarian family.[15] For Margaret, all this meant a good education and the opportunity to find personal fulfilment not in marriage but in constructive social work. This led her to Co-operation and the WCG which became, as she later wrote, 'the pivot of my work'.[16]

Davies's determination that the Guild should mobilise the energies and capacities of working-class women was strengthened by the family's move, in 1889, from London to the parish of Kirkby Lonsdale in Westmorland.[17] This brought the Guild national office close to the mill towns of Lancashire and Cheshire, heartland of the industrial revolution, and the birthplace of Co-operation with well-established societies in almost every town. Here, the large-scale employment of women in the textile industry had fostered a strong tradition of female trade unionism and working-class suffragism. This was fertile soil for Guild growth and a source of valuable allies for Davies.[18]

Emblematic of this new alliance was the relationship between Davies and Sarah Reddish, employed from 1893–5 as the WCG's first full-time paid organiser. From a working-class Co-operative background (her father was secretary and honorary librarian for the Bolton Society), Reddish began work in the textile industry aged 11. A trade unionist who later worked for the Women's Trade Union League, she was also prominent in northern suffragism. Her political values and experience made her an inspirational co-worker for Davies who, years later, paid tribute to Sarah Reddish 'whose life was devoted to the causes of women and labour'.[19]

Davies and Reddish's first step was to anchor the WCG firmly within the Co-operative movement. In the 1890s, a new constitution was devised which, modelled on the CU, established the WCG as a federation to which branches affiliated on condition that members belonged to a Co-operative Society and subscribed to a Guild Central Fund. Branches were clustered into districts and sections, to maximise contact, meetings and educational work, resourced by the centre. In 1892, a national WCG festival was held, and from 1893 an annual delegate Congress to agree policy for the coming year, carried out by an elected Central Committee and a national office.

Careful attention to organisational nuts and bolts soon yielded results. Between 1890 and 1894, membership jumped from 1640 to 7511, and branches from 54 to 170. Yet, growth was not without cost. In the same period, expenditure leapt from £19 to £245,[20] underlining the difficulty of organising mainly unwaged housewives. As the *Annual Report* noted, 'the addition to our income from new branches can never equal the increasing outlay necessary upon the growth of the whole work of the guild'.[21]

To make up this shortfall, strong arguments and effective lobbying techniques were devised to unlock funds from the wider movement. The Guild was working to the 'aims and policies of the Co-operative Union', it pointed out, and was convinced that there were 'unutilised forces' which could be put at the Union's disposal 'but for lack of funds'.[22] In May 1894, when the CU Central Board received a Guild deputation on this matter, Davies explained that 'they did not want to make an undue claim upon the Union, but last year the Board was good enough to vote the sum of £50. This year she hoped the Board might see its way to double that amount. [Laughter].'[23] The grant was duly increased to £100 and through subsequent increments took account of membership growth, more than doubling the income from subscriptions and making possible initiatives that would otherwise have been impossible. By 1899, with 12 537 members in 262 branches, the Guild was becoming a standard feature of Co-operative culture wherever the movement was active.[24]

The point of building the WCG, however, was not in any simple sense to serve the actually existing Co-operative movement. Davies and the women that she drew around her conceived of the WCG as far more than a mechanism for increasing sales. Politically astute, they understood its considerable potential for the organisation of working-class women and began to foster initiatives to make the Guild a progressive force in the movement and in national life. As Davies wrote in 1892:

> Self governed, free from outside patronage, with money at its back, it ought to become a very powerful instrument for bringing all kinds of help to women in their different capacities ... There is a good deal yet in the lives of women that is not exactly rose coloured, and changes are not very likely to occur without determined action on the part of women themselves.[25]

As part of the process of promoting rank and file democracy, the WCG introduced a new and emancipatory discourse about working-class wives' great but previously untapped capacities for public service. As Sarah Reddish pointed out, the 'influence and power of women in the home are everywhere acknowledged to be great. Why should they be so much undervalued in society?'[26] Such words were aimed in part at Co-operative officials, to win support for the Guild, but also at new members whose lack of experience and formal education meant that they lacked self-confidence. The WCG stressed that guildswomen were capable and resourceful; their daily work of running the home had equipped them with skills and aptitudes which only required the right organisational setting to be channelled into public work. In the Guild, they found unique opportunities to acquire new skills. 'Great progress', it was reported in 1897, 'has been made in bringing out new speakers.'[27] For many, organisational life was transforming and empowering. Mrs Bury, a housewife in her forties and a former mill-worker, experienced the 1893 Guild conference as 'a revelation':

> Here was the very opportunity that I had been seeking but never put into words. I had longings, aspirations, and a vague sense of power within myself which had never had an opportunity for realisation. At

> the close of the meetings I felt as I imagined a war-horse must feel when he hears the beat of the drums.[28]

The development of the WCG through the 1890s made it far more than the sum total of its parts. What evolved was highly innovative: a new model of active female citizenship, grounded in the experience and the capacities of ordinary members, and generative of a distinctively working-class feminism. As Sarah Reddish wrote in 1894:

> We are told by some that women are wives and mothers, and that the duties therein involved are enough for them. We reply that men are husbands and fathers, and that they, as such, have duties not to be neglected, but we join in the general opinion that men should also be interested in the science of government, taking a share in the larger family of the store, the municipality and the State. The WCG has done much toward impressing the fact that women as citizens should take their share in this work also.[29]

Steadily, the WCG's expanding conception of women's sphere, combined with a burgeoning sense of guildswomen's agency, began to be channelled into constructive projects of social and political reform. The suffrage campaign was to be one major commitment but, as Davies later wrote, guildswomen did not 'wait for the vote to tackle some of the most urgent problems' of their lives.[30] In particular, the citizenship campaigns orchestrated by the WCG in response to two reform initiatives of the Liberal government – to promote radical divorce law reform and to win maternity benefit as part of the new National Insurance scheme – demonstrated its determination to ensure that even disenfranchised working-class wives should have their views represented in legislative proceedings that would affect their lives and underscored the absurdity of a legislature that excluded the female sex from its proceedings.

The process of building the WCG revealed much about the grim circumstances of many women's lives. Davies herself was personally shocked by what she witnessed in members' homes during her speaking tours: the 'hard battles being waged against heavy odds, or the marks which such fights have left behind them ... struggles with want, concealed under thick coverings of pride; daily work done under the weight of constant ill health; unselfish devotion rewarded by lack of consideration.'[31] Traditionally, she pointed out,

> When women married, they retired behind a dark curtain on which was embroidered all sorts of beautiful sentiments about the beauty of

> motherhood and the sanctity of the home; but now the curtain was being withdrawn, and from the discussion that had taken place they had learned much of the sufferings of married women, the pain and misery that were going on behind the curtain.[32]

This problem was analysed by Mrs Nash in a Guild paper, *The Position of Married Women* (1907). In 1869, she pointed out, Mill had described the wife as the 'bond-servant of her husband'. Since then the idea had gained ground that married women were entitled to more than a life of drudgery. 'We might say', Mrs Nash commented acidly, that they have 'been promoted from slaves to servants', with the important qualification that while a servant could ask for better wages and conditions, a wife could not bargain with her husband over her home and her children.[33] Without some intervention from the women themselves, progress would be slow and they faced the problem of their isolation. It was 'difficult for each woman separately to assert herself against the unjust claims of home',[34] and injustices were often hidden from view by the convention that 'the privacy of the home is sacred'.[35] But here, surely, was an opportunity for collective action: 'the Guild can be a kind of trade union, through which we can spread better ideas'.[36]

Mrs Nash thus proposed an identity for the WCG that was to serve for decades to come. It linked the Guild with the labour movement, made explicit its role in representing a particular constituency, and left open the field of practical endeavour. While Mrs Nash endorsed the need for the Guild to work for the vote, in a far-sighted way, she indicated other desirable goals for campaigning work: to entitle married women to a share of the family income, to make decisions concerning her children, and even to challenge the 'repulsive'[37] divorce laws that bound her to a cruel husband. There was also a case to be made for the provision of 'an allowance from the State' so that the welfare of the mother and her children would not rest entirely upon the 'good fortune and character of her husband'.[38]

While many of these reforms were decades away, a more immediate opportunity for collective action arose in 1910 when, in recognition of its status as an organisation of about 25 000 Co-operative women, the WCG was invited to give evidence to the Royal Commission on Divorce and Matrimonial Causes. Under the terms of existing legislation, divorce proceedings were available only to the rich – poorer people were limited to legal separation without the possibility of remarriage – and for those who could afford divorce, the law enshrined a sexual double standard whereby a husband could divorce his wife for an act of adultery while a wife had to prove a cause in addition to adultery.

It is hard to overstate how sensitive and taboo a subject divorce was in 1910. Mindful of the stigma attached to the very idea of a failed marriage, the Guild leadership moved cautiously. At the 1910 congress, with over 500 delegates present, expecting conflicting opinions, a senior guildswoman moved a resolution condemning the sexual inequality of the existing divorce laws and calling for cheaper proceedings.[39] She made, it was reported, 'a weighty and restrained speech, with a grave sense of the difficulty and responsibility of her task'. She was seconded by a midwife who 'spoke from intimate personal knowledge of the lives of women. The audience listened with great attention and a discussion was fully anticipated.' But 'not a single delegate rose to speak. They were prepared to vote instantly,' and 'a forest of hands showed itself immediately and silently. There were only five raised against it.'[40] Here was emphatic evidence that working women, often supposed to be the group most in need of the protection of unbreakable marriage vows, wanted, in the words of one journalist, 'cheap and easy divorce'.[41]

The Guild office then set about collecting evidence, written statements from members giving explicit and intimate details of marriage and childbirth, for submission to the Commission. The contents of these 131 manuscript letters explain why divorce elicited greater 'strength and earnestness of feeling' than any other subject in the Guild's history. Nearly every woman had first or second-hand knowledge of the 'hidden suffering' endured within failed marriages. The most shocking cases described violence, marital rape, forced miscarriage and abortion: evidence that the women bore the 'great mass' of the suffering. 'No woman', Davies observed, 'could inflict on a man the amount of degradation that a man may force on a woman.'[42]

'My cousin', wrote one member, 'married a man who has behaved most brutally towards her, has broken her teeth, blacked her eyes, and bruised her body.' Another described women who always tried to induce an abortion on discovering that they were pregnant because 'the husband will grumble and make things unpleasant, because there will be another mouth to fill and he may have to deprive himself of something'. In another case, the husband 'always thrashes his wife and has put her life in danger in his anger on discovering her condition'. There were instances of syphilitic men infecting their wives and children. 'Husband physically rotten', one member tersely reported, 'through bad life previous to marriage. Compelled wife to cohabit – result three children with sore eyes and ears, and mentally deficient.'[43] Married women clearly recognised the concept of rape within marriage, even if the law did not, and the experience of being 'compelled' was a recurring theme. 'I had not the same privilege as the beasts of the field. No one can possibly imagine what it is unless you actually go through it, to feel you are simply a *convenience* to a man.'[44]

This material made a great impression on the empirically minded liberal members of the Commission, not least because of the Guild's credentials as a democratic working-class organisation. The sweeping recommendations of the Majority Report, published in December 1912, sought to abolish the ways in which divorce law discriminated between rich and poor, and between men and women, and to establish divorce as the legal closure of a relationship already dead. These embraced many of the measures supported by the WCG but did not extend to mutual consent and serious incompatibility as grounds for divorce, or to the institution of female court officials, which it also advocated.[45] Nevertheless, religious and conservative opposition held up legislation and reform was further delayed by the war. It is indicative of the advanced nature of the recommendations of both the WCG and the Majority Report that it took several decades for them to be enacted: the sexual double standard was abolished in 1923 but mutual consent was not introduced until 1969 while marital rape was not legally recognised until 1991.[46]

The advanced position of the WCG on the question of divorce law reform reflected the fact that its conception of the problem and its resolution was not limited to a legislative framework. As Davies pointed out to the Commissioners, even if 'unjust laws and public opinion were changed, the greater physical weakness, the conditions of maternity, the difficulty of monetary independence, would still put power in the hands of men and give opportunities for its abuse'.[47] At the same time, the Guild's base in the working-class movement, its support for trade unionism, and its participation in the Co-operative project of social and economic transformation, meant that it viewed legal reform as only one of a number of different strategies available to improve the position of the constituency it represented. This gave it the confidence to argue that alternative social and economic arrangements could and should be made so that a married woman had alternatives to an unhappy marriage rather than being bolted in by her dependence on a male wage-earner.

Yet, the divorce law reform agitation stretched to breaking point the WCG's relationship with the Co-operative movement. Co-operative officials, encouraged by pressure from Catholic co-operators, demanded that the Guild drop divorce law reform as a condition of the award of its annual grant (£400 by 1914). The subject of divorce was thus linked to the vital question of women's autonomy. For the Guild leadership, democratic control over policy-making procedures was an essential element of its work and reputation. As the Central Committee explained in a statement to the membership: 'Our freedom has in the past allowed us to fight for our co-operative ideals, and for a higher status for married women, and to create an effective demand for justice and equal fellowship.'[48]

At the 1914 Congress, which took the decision to reject the annual grant rather than lose control over its own policy, delegates, representing 32 182 members in 600 branches, queued to speak to the emergency resolution. 'Guildswomen', said one, 'wanted to work with the men side by side, not as subordinates with restrictions, for they possessed the powers and abilities of adult women (Hear, hear, and applause).' 'This matter of divorce', she went on, 'they had been considering for the past four years; but for how many years had women been suffering?' The vote was passed with no dissentients and prolonged cheering.[49] The determination with which guildswomen defended their autonomy surprised even Margaret Llewelyn Davies. As she wrote to Leonard Woolf, 'I had no idea the strength and unity of feeling wd. [sic] be so great.' And that it should be connected with divorce 'was all the more remarkable ... Someone said the Guild had found its soul, it has certainly found it feet.'[50]

The WCG's work for divorce law reform highlighted the complexity of the project of female emancipation and the impossibility of reducing it to a single reform, even one as emblematic as the vote. The interlinking of economic, cultural and political aspects of women's oppression was similarly apparent in the Guild's campaign for maternity rights. In 1910, when preparation of a state scheme of National Insurance was announced, the Guild applied to the Chancellor of the Exchequer for information about provision for women, and was invited to send a private and informal deputation. To ensure that the deputation would be armed with some facts, the Guild undertook a survey among the membership. The findings showed that 'the great mass of wage earners are unable to provide adequately, and that the provision is usually at the cost of the woman'.[51] At their meeting in March 1911 with Sir Rufus Isaacs (standing in for the Chancellor, Lloyd George), Guild officials argued for national care of maternity, detached from insurance schemes since these did not reach those most in need. In a direct exchange with Isaacs illustrative of the Guild's success in securing a hearing for ordinary women, Mrs Layton, a former midwife, explained that even when the husband gave everything he could from his wages, the only way the wife could cover the cost of the confinement was 'by going short herself'. The husband 'had to be kept going for the work's sake, and it would break her heart to starve the children'. When Sir Rufus asked how much was needed, she answered 'nothing less than £5'; he said that this was 'impossible', and suggested 30 shillings instead.[52]

The Guild was galvanised into action by news that a Bill would be introduced during the forthcoming parliamentary session. The spring Sectional Conferences were reorganised to consider married women's needs in relation to state insurance and to make their own proposals. As Davies explained to delegates in Manchester, 'little public thought' had been given to 'married women's conditions and needs, and the urgency of providing for maternity had not been realised'. The additional cost of maternity, an estimated £3–£5, far exceeded average earnings, and as the contributory scheme excluded those most in need, the great need was for centrally funded municipal schemes of maternal care. In the short term, however, the Sectional Conferences called for National Insurance to include provision for married women's sickness, invalidity and maternity needs.[53]

When the National Insurance Bill was published, the Guild gave a qualified welcome to its recognition of 'the common responsibility of the whole nation for some of the worst results of our social and industrial conditions'. In particular, its inclusion of maternity benefit for wives of insured men, and married women insured in their own right, though 'small in amount' represented 'a beginning which may be developed into more complete provision'. But the Guild strongly objected to Lloyd George's exclusion of 'non-working' women from health cover. This was 'a most serious blot', and a massive undervaluation of the vital importance of their endless hard work caring for the home and bringing up the family.[54]

The General Secretary returned to this failing at Congress, later that year. Mr Lloyd George, she said, 'needed a little reminder of the fact that they were workers (hear, hear). They had to make a great stir and show the Chancellor of the Exchequer that women who remained at home were workers, and their work was as arduous as any other kind of work and just as valuable (hear, hear).' Delegates unanimously resolved that married women should be eligible for state contributions. Among other proposed modifications of the proposed scheme was the important demand that the 30-shilling cash payment should be the property of the mother.[55]

The Guild office promptly began to make a 'great stir'. During the various stages of the Bill's passage, it collaborated with the Women's Labour League (WLL), the National Federation of Women Workers (NFWW), and other women's groups, organising deputations to Lloyd George, the lobbying of MPs and the Co-operative Parliamentary Committee, national and local public meetings, and letters to the press. The 'sense of injustice', wrote Davies and Harris in a letter to the

Westminster Gazette, 'rests on the fact that the claims of married women are unrecognised as regards medical, sick sanatorium, or disablement benefits unless they happen to be wage earners. Non wage-earning women form an army of six to seven million of workers in the home, from whom life extracts more than any other class.' These women should be fully entitled to the state contribution since 'provision for the needs of the whole family is the joint work of both parents, the man's wages and the woman's domestic labour (which has its direct money value) being equally indispensable'.[56]

As a result of these representations, sections of the Bill were redrafted to give married women the option of paying into the scheme, although qualifying for only half the state contribution in the absence of an employer's share. However, mindful of the potentially 'disastrous' impact of married women's health problems on the funds of insurance societies, the Chancellor could not countenance their eligibility for full sick pay. In addition, the 30-shillings maternity benefit was to be the property of the husband unless the wife had separate insurance, with a safeguard (clause 19) that men who spent the money for some other purpose would be liable for prosecution.[57]

This question of the ownership of maternity benefit became the subject of a major Guild campaign in 1913 during the passage of an amending Bill to the 1911 National Insurance Act. The recently created WCG Citizenship Sub-Committee arranged for a Guild deputation to meet with the Commissioners drafting the Bill, at which there was 'prolonged and animated discussion'. The Guild's main contention was that prosecution under clause 19 would not serve its purpose, and that by right the cash benefit should belong to the wife. What women needed at such a time, Davies insisted, was the maternity benefit and their husband's wages – not his imprisonment.[58]

Yet this measure was still not included in the published Bill making it necessary for the Guild to lobby hard at the next, Committee, stage. Guildswomen sent resolutions and letters to MPs; examples of cases where the husband had misspent the benefit were collected and sent to MPs on all sides;[59] support was obtained from the Co-operative Parliamentary Committee and communications despatched to the press.[60] Guild officials attended the relevant sessions of the Parliamentary Standing Committee,[61] and, witnessing the overwhelmingly masculine character of the proceedings, agreed on the need 'not only for women to be present to watch Bills in which they were interested' but also to sit on the committees.[62]

The five Labour MPs on the Committee spearheaded the opposition to the Guild's position with 'a definite line against the view that it should be her property'.[63] Despite the fact that a Labour/suffrage alliance had been agreed the previous year, there was a marked unwillingness to support women's rights. To the contrary, George Roberts spoke of his 'abhorrence against the unnecessary intervention of the State between a man and his wife'.[64] The Committee did recommend that the benefit should be the wife's legal property but when the Bill reached the Report stage, Labour members were again obstructive, moving that either husband or wife should be authorised to receive the benefit.[65]

The WCG now rose to the challenge of explaining its position to the whole House in preparation for the vote. Branches were urged to write to MPs of all parties,[66] a fresh memorandum was prepared, and in less than a week, a petition was drawn up, signed by 700 women with 'practical knowledge of administration and public work . . . members of town councils, boards of guardians, insurance committees, nursing and midwives' associations, women sanitary inspectors and health visitors',[67] and sent with a covering letter to all MPs and to the press.

In the Commons, the issue was taken as a free vote and debated for over two hours. Once again, Labour members led the opposition with the assistance of Lloyd George, among others. Contributions in support of the Guild position included Mr Snowden's comment that Mr Roberts 'heartily approves of the last part of the tenth commandment. He would place the man's wife in the same category as the man's ox and the man's ass.'[68] The Labour amendment won by 9 votes but Lord Robert Cecil, 'who had previously received a small Guild deputation', successfully moved a further amendment requiring that the husband could only receive the benefit if authorised by the wife.[69]

In the words of the *Manchester Guardian*: 'If the House of Commons had gone about women's suffrage, it could not have done anything better than its debate on the maternity benefit.'[70] For the Guild, this was 'the first public recognition of the mother's place in the home, and the first step towards some economic independence for wives'. Two important principles had been admitted: that 'the wife, by her work (though unpaid) in the home, contributes to the support of the family'; and that 'just as an employed woman's earnings are her own, so money due to a woman as mother shall be legally hers'. Another point had thus been added 'to the Wives' Charter, of which the first was the Married Women's Property Act'.[71]

While the WCG was not a suffrage organisation, the suffrage demand was central to its identity as a democratic women's organisation and related to the whole thrust of its citizenship work. As Margaret Llewelyn Davies wrote in 1897, the demand for the vote was 'part of the great movement for the freedom of women, which will give them their true status in society and lead to a trustful and respectful comradeship between men and women'.[72] Despite what might appear as a natural alliance, it took more than two decades for the Guild to adopt a formal position of support for female enfranchisement, at the 1904 Congress. This time lag reflects the complexity of the organisational work that it took to achieve such a consensus. The Guild's base in the broad church of the Co-operative movement meant that the women it recruited came from enormously diverse educational and political backgrounds. For many, the demand for the vote and inclusion in the masculine sphere of politics could appear as improper or irrelevant. As the General Secretary noted in 1908, there remained 'a section of our members who have not seen the connection between the vote and their home and store, while some branches have refused to take part in our campaign'.[73]

The majority support for the suffrage demand in 1904 did, however, register a growing level of awareness, even a process of conversion, among guildswomen concerning their democratic rights, and a deepening appreciation that different aspects of their lives converged in the claim to citizenship, defined by Davies as being 'above sex, party, class and sect . . . A citizen is a human being, belonging to a community, with rights and duties arising out of a common life.'[74] Three strands of Guild activity drove this process forward. Firstly, the ideas of educated, often middle-class, feminists, who saw the WCG as a means of transmitting to working-class women 'the message of the movement for the emancipation of women',[75] and whose ideas were expressed in the women's pages of *Co-operative News*, and in Guild educational papers; secondly, the Guild's organic relationship with working-class suffragism in the north-west of England; thirdly, its expanding involvement with municipal politics.

The use of feminist arguments increased steadily during the 1890s. In 1897, following the second reading of a woman suffrage Bill, Guild Sectional Conferences discussed 'Why Working Women Need the Vote'.[76] In Bristol, Mrs Martin criticised the standard anti-suffrage claim that 'women's "sphere" is the home' where their interests were looked after by 'fathers, husbands, and brothers'. While the 'happy home life' of some women might make them content with men's laws, she argued, also echoing J. S. Mill, we do not 'legislate for justice-loving men and women any more than we build prisons for honest men and women'. The vote was needed 'for the *protection* of the home', so that married women could gain entitlement to child-custody, a share of their husband's income, and, for women in paid employment, to their own earnings.[77]

The Guild was also closely associated with working-class suffragism in the north-west of England where the number of Guild branches expanded rapidly from 7 to 262 between 1889 and 1899.[78] Many of these were integral to the suffrage networks, involved in passing resolutions, lobbying trades councils and MPs, and organising reform meetings.[79] The large Darwen and Bolton branches were heavily involved in collecting signatures of 'cotton operatives to a petition for the enfranchisement of women'.[80] Sarah Reddish, a leading member of the North of England Women's Suffrage Society led the 1901 deputation to the House of Commons in 1901 to present a petition of almost 30 000 Lancashire female textile workers' signatures.[81]

While feminist ideas and the groundswell of working-class suffragism increased rank and file support for the suffrage demand in the WCG, the decisive factor for the 1904 resolution was its involvement in municipal politics. Although explicitly excluded from parliamentary politics by the 1832 Reform Act, women had been gradually admitted, as voters and as candidates for office, to those branches of local government deemed closest to their feminine responsibilities beginning with School Boards and Poor Law Boards in the 1870s.[82] From the early 1890s, the Guild supported female candidates standing as Poor Law Guardians and for School Boards.[83] In 1894, 22 guildswomen were elected as Poor Law Guardians, increasing to 36 in 1898;[84] in 1900, Sarah Reddish was among those successful in gaining a School Board seat.[85]

It was municipal activism that finally confronted the Guild with the top-down parliamentary pressure on local democracy and brought the suffrage question before the whole organisation. When the 1899 Local Government Act abolished parish vestries, on which women were entitled to sit, and replaced them with Borough Councils, from which they were excluded, the WCG Central Committee asked all branches to write to MPs protesting against the change, but to little effect.[86] In a similar vein, the 1902 Education Act replaced School Boards with local education authorities, providing only for the co-option of women members, not their direct election. This move, condemned by the 1903 WCG Congress as 'undemocratic and reactionary',[87] convinced the Central Committee that it would be appropriate to bring the matter of parliamentary representation before Congress in the following year. As Davies commented, 'this treatment of women is not taking place without effect. Women have been roused and they realise the weakness of their position without a vote.'[88] At the 1904 Congress, Sarah Reddish made a forceful case for women's enfranchisement on equal terms with men,[89] urging the 'great need for all women to join together to work for the removal of the sex disability. This was a sex question and no matter what their position in life, they ought to join together in order to remove all disability.' She was not, she continued, going to 'shirk the word political'. If they

> eschewed politics – as they were not going to do – it would mean that they would take no part in government, and people who took no part in government left themselves to be absolutely governed by others, and the fault of that was they would govern them from their (the governors') own standpoint.

The resolution was passed with only twelve opposing votes.[90]

This explicit affiliation to the suffrage cause was a significant moment for the WCG, and, given its 18 556 members in 359 branches,[91] for the suffrage movement. As the 'women's suffrage revival' got underway from 1905,[92] the WCG established a dedicated Suffrage Fund and collaborated with the suffrage societies in lobbying MPs for their support of private members' bills, leafleting, petitioning, passing resolutions, and participating in deputations to the House of Commons, demonstrations and processions.[93] During the 1906 election campaign, the Guild sent to all Cabinet members copies of a 'united manifesto' calling for the parliamentary franchise for women, with signatures from labour, political and temperance organisations, including the North of England Weavers' Association and the Independent Labour Party.[94]

The Guild's suffrage work had two distinct foci. As a Co-operative organisation, it set out to win the equal-rights suffrage position in the mainstream of the movement. As a working-class women's organisation, it sought to channel guildswomen's energies into national and local suffrage campaigns while seeking to enlarge the voting qualifications to benefit married working-class women.

In regard to the Co-operative movement, the immediate prospects were not auspicious. In 1906, the CU executive ruled out a woman's suffrage resolution because it was 'political'. The Guild deplored this 'unsympathetic attitude' because it ignored both women's rights and the potential benefits to the movement of the enfranchisement of large numbers of female Co-operators.[95] Undeterred, the Guild office began a two-year propaganda campaign. Leaflets were sent to all societies explaining why women needed the vote while a postal ballot of guildswomen's husbands showed overwhelming support for the Guild's position.[96] At the 1908 Co-operative Congress, Mr Tweddell, Chairman of the Co-operative Parliamentary Committee, moved the resolution calling for a government Bill to enfranchise women. It was passed almost unanimously, 'only one voice being heard in opposition'.[97] Yet, as Davies pointed out, the effort it had taken to get the motion on the order paper demonstrated that even in their own movement it was only through 'extreme watchfulness and distasteful self-assertion' that women's needs were considered.[98]

Winning the support of the Co-operative movement for women's enfranchisement was in line with the Guild's priority of strengthening links between the working-class movement and the women's movement. Yet, the WCG's attempt to hold together working-class and feminist interests in the suffrage movement was under increasing strain. A strong body of opinion in trade union and Labour Party circles, including some guildswomen, opposed the extension of the suffrage to women on the same terms as men on the grounds that this would disproportionately enfranchise propertied women and strengthen the anti-Labour vote. Many middle-class suffrage activists, on the other hand, viewed any move towards universal suffrage as a liability that would discourage Liberal and Conservative support for their cause. The complex debate about the relationship between sex, class and electoral reform intensified as suffrage reform stalled under Asquith's Liberal government. At Guild Congress in 1904, the 'sex-equality' position had triumphed despite strongly held opposing views. Mrs Gasson, of the WCG, observed that if women were enfranchised on equal terms with men, many of them gathered in the hall 'would not qualify as they were neither householders, owners, occupiers or lodgers'. Gertrude Tuckwell, representing the Women's Trade Union League (WTUL), regretted being in the 'horrible position of differing from Miss Reddish' but explained that the WTUL priority was 'the working women'. They wanted to 'put the power into the hands of the people who were suffering' and not the 'property-owning class who had had it too long already'.[99] Countering such points, Reddish stressed that the key difference between the 'adult suffrage' and 'sex-equality' positions was tactical. They all wanted adult suffrage, the question was: 'how were they going to get it? They had no political power.'[100] For the adult suffrage women, however, the answer was to oppose any suffrage reform short of universal enfranchisement as 'class and property' legislation.[101]

The debate between different sections of the working-class women's movement went on in the women's pages of *Co-operative News*. Ada Nield Chew, a WTUL organiser, accused the suffrage societies of duping their working-class members: 'women who would not benefit at all are to work for and support a measure which would only benefit rich women, on the understanding that their turn will come some day'.[102] Davies countered that as men had not 'abolished a property qualification for themselves, it is a mistake to cut ourselves off from being able to support any measure which we considered satisfactory as a step towards adult suffrage'.[103] The need was to secure women's right to the vote so that future reform would bring adult rather than manhood suffrage (for which there was support on the Labour side). The WCG 'Manifesto on the Enfranchisement of Women' supported in principle any bill that did not disqualify married women and was likely to enfranchise a large proportion of working women.[104] In contrast, in 1905 the Labour Representation Committee determined not to support any measure short of adult suffrage. In the same year, the Adult Suffrage Society was formed, claiming a commitment to universal suffrage but in practice, mainly active in opposing the limited female suffrage bills that came before the Liberal government.[105]

The WCG patiently sought to extend the scope of private members' bills. In 1906, the General Secretary wrote to the press proposing that home-occupiers' wives should also qualify for the vote, eliciting a favourable response from the Liberal MP, W. H. Dickinson, who was introducing a Women's Enfranchisement Bill. A Guild memorandum then went to all MPs but for 'tactical reasons' (the conviction of many suffragists that any adult suffrage tendencies would weaken its chances), the measure was not included and the Bill fell for want of time at its second reading in March 1907.[106] Dickinson's second attempt, later in 1907, did include voters' wives[107] but made even less progress. In 1908, the Stranger Bill was confined to the removal of sex disability from the existing franchise. It aroused little enthusiasm from the Guild and in any case got no further than its second reading.[108]

More promisingly, the 1909 Howard Bill, proposing residential suffrage for men and women, also passed a second reading before being turned back. For the Guild this was an improvement on Stranger's Bill[109] but Mrs Fawcett, of the National Union of Women's Suffrage Societies (NUWSS), regarded it as 'practically universal suffrage', and claimed that it 'alienated all Conservative and much moderate Liberal support, and was taken in the face of the strongly expressed protests of all the suffrage societies'.[110] This attitude created hostility among working-class women in the suffrage movement, including some guildswomen, who were being asked to support limited bills from which they would not immediately benefit.[111] At the same time, the growth of direct action, and the increasingly undemocratic practices of the Women's Social and Political Union (WSPU) were splitting the suffrage movement and alienating many working-class women from broad sexual solidarity.[112]

The debate at the 1908 Co-operative Congress reflected tensions about militancy and about the property qualification upheld by Stranger and his ilk. Seconding the suffrage resolution, Mrs Hodgett emphasised that 'she was not a militant suffragette' but represented 25 000 Co-operative women who believed that they should have the same rights of citizenship in the state as they enjoyed in the 'Co-operative State within a State'.[113] Mr Redfearn asked what, precisely, it would mean to give the vote to women. He insisted that the 'militant suffragettes were satisfied with the terms of the recent limited franchise bill of Mr Stranger'.[114] Davies responded by stressing that outweighing the property qualification was the need for the vote to tackle the 'grave injustices, hardships, and miseries' in women's lives,[115] while Mr Tweddell reminded delegates that they wanted only to pledge Congress to the principle of women's suffrage rather than to any particular piece of legislation.[116]

At the 1909 Guild Congress, irritation at the NUWSS's attitude to the Howard Bill and growing unease about Militancy found expression in a resolution stating that only adult suffrage would be 'consistent' with the Guild's aims of establishing equality between 'men and women, married and single, rich and poor'.[117] As the voting numbers (238 to 232) make plain, the question was closely fought. Nevertheless, formal refusal of any reform short of adult suffrage implied an indefinite deferral of women's political rights. Neither the Liberals nor the Conservatives had any reason to introduce adult suffrage, and Labour – the only party which did – had ignored the matter until roused by the women's agitation, still seemed more intent on orchestrating opposition to a limited female suffrage than on pressing for adult suffrage, and was, in any case, the minority party.

To keep alive the claims of women while honouring Guild support for adult suffrage, Davies played a prominent role in the People's Suffrage Federation (PSF). Formed to obtain 'the parliamentary vote for every adult man and woman', with only a short residential qualification,[118] the PSF transferred to the suffrage platform the Guild aim of 'Equal Fellowship of men and women'.[119] While Davies refused to criticise the WSPU, maintaining that their agitation was ensuring that women's interests would not be ignored, she was highly sensitive to the social inequalities that ran through the whole suffrage question. 'The Limited Bill is so obnoxious to us', she explained in an interview to *The Woman Worker*. 'We feel that a personal, and not a property basis, is the only democratic one. Any property or tenancy qualification would place the working-class women at a disadvantage.'[120]

The PSF became the organisational means by which guildswomen continued to be active in the movement, with many branches affiliating to it directly.[121] It gained support from other working-class women's organisations, including the WLL, the WTUL and the NFWW. Also involved were leading labour and socialist women (Mary Macarthur, Margaret Macmillan), left-wing politicians and academics (Arthur Henderson, George Lansbury, Bertrand Russell, the Webbs) and a number of progressive Liberals.[122] It was thus well placed to put pressure on Liberal and Labour MPs to take the women's cause more seriously, and to outflank anti-feminists in the Labour Party. More than two years of patient effort by the PSF was a key factor in securing a majority vote at the 1912 Labour Party conference for a resolution stipulating that 'no Bill can be acceptable to the Labour and Socialist Movement which does not include women'.[123]

The 1912 vote opened a period of close collaboration between the NUWSS and the Labour Party[124] which drew the Guild back into mainstream suffrage agitation, its efforts now co-ordinated by its Citizenship Sub-Committee, formed that year.[125] Guild branches were encouraged to press MPs to vote for amendments to the 1912–13 Reform Bill to 'enfranchise married women'.[126] Early in 1913, the WCG Central Committee joined with other suffrage organisations and the WLL in condemning the Speaker's ruling against the women's suffrage amendment, and demanding a government-sponsored adult suffrage bill as the only measure capable of restoring 'the lost confidence of the women'.[127] And guildswomen joined the NUWSS-organised Women's Suffrage Pilgrimage to London in July 1913.[128]

Although mass suffrage agitation lapsed with the outbreak of war, when franchise reform again appeared on the political agenda in 1917, the WCG was among those organisations bringing forward the women's case, and then sustaining pressure for the abolition of residual forms of sex discrimination from 1918 to 1928.[129] Despite its limitations, the 1918 Reform Act delivered the municipal and the parliamentary vote to virtually all Co-operative women, and was hailed by the Guild not as the end of the struggle but the beginning of its next phase. This is, proclaimed a Guild leaflet, *The Vote at Last*, 'a tremendous new fact, and Guildswomen must seize hold of it and consider what it means'.[130]

In its campaigning work prior to World War One, the WCG created an original unity from its dual commitments to working-class advancement and to women's rights. In the Co-operative movement and in its citizenship work it demonstrated that even disenfranchised working-class wives could, if properly organised, intervene effectively in public life. In late nineteenth-century British society, the working-class housewife occupied a marginal space: 'Without money of her own, with no right even to housekeeping savings, without adequate protection against a husband's possible cruelty, with no legal position as a mother, with the conditions of maternity totally neglected, married women in the home had existed apart voiceless, and unseen.'[131] It was, Davies conceded,

> perhaps inevitable that the mother should have been publicly overlooked, for the isolation of women in married life has, up to now, prevented any common expression of their needs. They have been hidden behind the curtain which falls after marriage, the curtain which women are now themselves raising.[132]

Guild organisation carried feminist ideas to such women and fed back their experience – of married life and of maternity – in ways that significantly extended the scope of the women's movement, demanding not only women's entry into the public sphere but also social intervention to secure justice in the private sphere. The WCG did not single-handedly advocate maternity benefit and other allowances for married women, or highlight issues of domestic violence and sexual abuse, or, indeed, win the vote. However, it certainly played a pioneering role in defining working-class wives as a collective group with shared interests, and in enabling some of their number to express their point of view and take action to improve their situation. In Davies's words, the outstanding fact about the Guild movement was thus, 'the emergence of the married working woman from national obscurity into a position of national importance'.[133]

Notes

1. G. Scott, *Feminism and the Politics of Working Women: the Women's Co-operative Guild, 1880s to the Second World War* (London: UCL Press, 1998).
2. G. D. H. Cole and R. Postgate, *The Common People 1746–1946* (London: Methuen, 1966), p. 437.
3. B. Taylor, *Eve and the New Jerusalem* (London: Virago, 1983).
4. 'Arthur Acland, Liberal MP and Oxford Academic', in Joyce M. Bellamy and John Saville (eds), *Dictionary of Labour Biography*, vol. 1 (London: Macmillan, 1972).
5. Cole and Postgate, *The Common People*, p. 216.
6. Ibid.
7. Ibid.
8. *Co-operative News*, 13 June 1885, p. 580.
9. 'Meeting of the WCG', *Co-operative Congress Report* (*CCR*), 1885, pp. 71–2.
10. *Co-operative News*, 27 June 1885, p. 621.
11. G. Stedman Jones, 'Working-class Culture and Working-class Politics in London 1870–1900: Notes on the Remaking of the Working Class', in *Languages of Class, Studies in English Working-Class History 1832–1982* (Cambridge: Cambridge University Press, 1983).

12. 'Meeting of the WCG', *CCR*, 1885, pp. 71–2.
13. 'Memories of Seventy Years by Mrs Layton', in M. Llewelyn Davies (ed.), *Life as We Have Known It by Co-operative Working Women*, 1931 (London: Virago, 1977), p. 39.
14. M. Llewelyn Davies, *The Women's Co-operative Guild* (Kirkby Lonsdale: Women's Co-operative Guild, 1904), p. 21.
15. 'J. Llewelyn Davies', *Dictionary of National Biography*, 1912–21 (Oxford: Oxford University Press, 1927). B. Stephen, *Emily Davies and Girton College* (London: Constable, 1927).
16. Davies, article for *Norges Kvinder*.
17. A. Birkin, *J. M. Barrie and the Lost Boys* (London: Constable, 1979), p. 46.
18. J. Liddington and J. Norris, *One Hand Tied Behind Us* (London: Virago, 1978).
19. *Co-operative News*, 3 March 1928, p. 13; Davies, *The WCG*, pp. 28–32; Liddington and Norris, *One Hand Tied Behind Us*, pp. 93, 291.
20. 'Report of the Women's Guild', *CCR*, 1894, p. 55.
21. Ibid.
22. Ibid., p. 56.
23. 'WCG deputation to the Central Board', *CCR*, 1894, p. 3.
24. WCG, *Annual Report*, 1898–99, p. 3.
25. 'Report of the Women's Guild', *CCR*, 1892, p. 56.
26. Miss Reddish, *Women's Guilds with Special Reference to their Claims on the Attention and Support of Educational Committees. Co-operative Educational Committees' Association Annual Meeting* (Bolton: Henry Smith, 1890), p. 3.
27. *Co-operative News*, 10 April 1897, p. 387.
28. Davies, *The WCG*, p. 61.
29. 'Report of the Women's Guild', *CCR*, 1893–4, pp. 58–9.
30. 'Peaceful Campaigns by Two Old Campaigners', typed MS, 1933, 'Material . . .', 1, item 41.
31. *Co-operative News*, 4 February 1899, p. 114.
32. *Co-operative News*, 27 May 1911, p. 667.
33. R. Nash, *The Position of Married Women* (Manchester: CWS Printing Works, 1907), pp. 3, 5.
34. Ibid., p. 9.
35. Ibid., p. 12.
36. Ibid., p. 9.
37. Ibid., p. 13.
38. Ibid., p. 11.
39. WCG, Central Committee Minutes, 5–6 May, 28 May, 2 June, 4 June, 8–9 September 1910.
40. 'Miss M. Llewelyn Davies', Minutes of Evidence taken before the Royal Commission on Divorce and Matrimonial Causes, 1912, III (Cd. 6481) PP 1912–13, XX, p. 150.
41. *The Nation*, 23 July 1910, Gertrude Tuckwell Collection.
42. 'Miss Davies', Minutes of Evidence, pp. 150–1.
43. Ibid., p. 156.
44. Ibid., p. 157.
45. *Report of the Royal Commission on Divorce and Matrimonial Causes*, 1912 (Cd. 6478), PP XVIII, p. 113.

46. L. Stone, *Road to Divorce: England 1530–1987* (Oxford: Oxford University Press, 1990), ch. XIII; J. Weeks, *Sex, Politics and Society: the Regulation of Sexuality since 1800* (Harlow: Longman, 1989), ch. 13.
47. 'Miss Davies', Minutes of Evidence, p. 161.
48. *Co-operative News*, 20 June 1914, pp. 807–8.
49. Ibid., 20 June 1914, p. 808; WCG, *Annual Report*, 1914–15, p. 4.
50. MLD to Leonard Woolf, n.d., Monks House Papers, University of Sussex.
51. 'Report of Women's Guild', *CCR*, 1911, p. 198.
52. 'Memories of Seventy Years by Mrs Layton', in Davies (ed.), *Life As We Have Known It*, p. 49.
53. *Co-operative News*, 15 April 1911, pp. 481–2.
54. Ibid., 13 May 1911, p. 600.
55. Ibid., 24 June 1911, p. 809.
56. Ibid., 12 August 1911, p. 1044.
57. Ibid., 14 October 1911, p. 1319.
58. Ibid., 28 June 1913, p. 827.
59. Ibid., 23 August 1913, p. 1083.
60. Ibid., 2 August 1913, p. 975.
61. National Insurance Act (1911) Amendment Bill Standing Committee C., 'A Bill to Amend Parts I and II of the National Insurance Act 1911, 22 July–31 July 1913', Parliamentary Debates, Commons, Official Report Fifth Series, LVI, Seventh volume of Session, 56 H.C. Deb. 5s, London: HMSO, 1913.
62. *Co-operative News*, 23 August 1913, p. 1083.
63. Ibid.
64. National Insurance Amendment Bill, Standing Committee, p. 3102
65. *Co-operative News*, 23 August 1913, p. 1083.
66. Ibid., 19 July 1913, p. 916; 23 August 1913, p. 1083.
67. 'Report of Women's Guild', *CCR*, 1914, p. 254.
68. *Parliamentary Debates, Commons, Official Report Fifth Series*, LVI, Seventh Volume of Session, 56 H.C. Deb. 5s, London, HMSO, 1913, p. 1533.
69. Ibid., pp. 1537–44.
70. *Co-operative News*, 16 August 1913, p. 1039.
71. Ibid., 23 August 1913, p. 1084.
72. M. Llewelyn Davies, Mrs Martin, *Why Working Women Need the Vote* (Manchester: Co-operative Printing Society, 1897), p. 8.
73. 'Report of Women's Guild', *CCR*, 1908, p. 147.
74. *Co-operative News*, 29 October 1904, p. 1338.
75. Cole and Postgate, *The Common People*, p. 217.
76. *Co-operative News*, 10 April 1897, p. 387; 17 April 1897, p. 410.
77. Davies and Martin, *Why Working Women Need the Vote*, p. 12. Faithfull Begg's Bill was 'talked out' at Committee stage in July.
78. WCG, *Annual Report*, 1898–9, p. 3.
79. Liddington and Norris, *One Hand Tied Behind Us*, ch. 9; J. Liddington, *The Life and Times of a Respectable Rebel, Selina Cooper 1864–1946* (London: Virago, 1984).
80. WCG, *Annual Report*, 1899–1900, p. 20. Liddington and Norris, *One Hand Tied Behind Us*, ch. 9.
81. WCG, *Annual Report*, 1901–2, p. 5.
82. P. Hollis, *Ladies Elect Women in Local Government*, 1865–1914 (Oxford: Oxford University Press, 1987).

83. WCG, *Annual Report*, 1892–3, p. 7; 1894–5, p. 7.
84. Davies, *The WCG*, p. 135; WCG, *Annual Report*, 1894–5, p. 24; 1897–8, p. 8.
85. WCG, *Annual Report*, 1899–1900, pp. 18–19.
86. Ibid., p. 14.
87. 'Report of Women's Guild', *CCR*, 1903, p. 166.
88. Davies, *The WCG*, p. 141.
89. 'Guild Congress Supplement', *Co-operative News*, 23 July 1904, p. 917.
90. Ibid.
91. 'Report of Women's Guild', *CCR*, 1904, p. 170.
92. Ibid., 1905, p. 175.
93. Ibid., 1905, p. 176; 1906, p. 161; 1907, p. 154; 1909, p. 167.
94. Ibid., 1906, p. 161.
95. WCG, *Annual Report*, 1906–7, p. 14.
96. 'Report of Women's Guild', *CCR*, 1909, p. 167.
97. 'Discussion on Report: Women's Suffrage', *CCR*, 1908, pp. 353, 358.
98. Ibid., p. 357.
99. 'Guild Congress Supplement', *Co-operative News*, 23 July 1904, p. 917.
100. Ibid.
101. Ibid., 10 December 1904, p. 1507.
102. Ibid.
103. Ibid., 17 December 1904, p. 1559.
104. 'Report of Women's Guild', *CCR*, 1905, p. 176.
105. Liddington, *Selina Cooper*, p. 166.
106. 'Report of Women's Guild', *CCR*, 1907, pp. 154–5.
107. Ibid., 1908, p. 147.
108. Ibid., 1909, p. 168.
109. Ibid.
110. M. G. Fawcett, *Women's Suffrage: a Short History of a Great Movement* (London: T. C. & E. C. Jack, 1912), p. 70.
111. S. S. Holton, *Feminism and Democracy: Women's Suffrage and Reform Politics in Britain, 1900–1918* (Cambridge: Cambridge University Press, 1986), pp. 60–2.
112. H. Mitchell, *The Hard Way Up: the Autobiography of Hannah Mitchel, Suffragette and Rebel*, 1968 (London: Virago, 1977), chs 11–16; Liddington and Norris, *One Hand Tied Behind Us*, ch. 11; Liddington, *Selina Cooper*, ch. 12.
113. 'Discussion on Report: Women's Suffrage', *CCR*, 1908, p. 355.
114. Ibid., p. 356.
115. Ibid., p. 357.
116. Ibid., p. 358.
117. 'Report of WCG Congress', *Oldham Chronicle*, 26 June 1909, Gertrude Tuckwell Collection.
118. WCG, *Annual Report*, 1909–10, p. 11.
119. Ibid.
120. *The Woman Worker*, 10 November 1909, p. 437.
121. *Co-operative News*, 1 July 1911, p. 855.
122. Ibid., 1 December 1909, p. 504; 'Report of Women's Guild', *CCR*, 1910, p. 231; Mary Macarthur and M. Llewelyn Davies to Gladstone, Gladstone Papers, LXXXIII, British Museum Add. MS 46067 f.331 (1909).
123. L. Garner, *Stepping Stones to Women's Liberty* (London: Heinemann, 1984), p. 17.

124. Liddington and Norris, *One Hand Tied Behind Us*, p. 247; Liddington, *Selina Cooper*, ch. 1.
125. WCG, Central Committee Minutes, 22–23 August 1912.
126. 'Report of Women's Guild', *CCR*, 1913, p. 240.
127. *Co-operative News*, 8 February 1913, p. 180.
128. Ibid., 8 August 1913, p. 1003.
129. WCG, Central Committee Minutes, 12 January, 9–10 February, 5 March 1917.
130. M. L. Davies, *The Vote at Last!* (London: Co-operative Union Ltd., 1918).
131. M. Llewelyn Davies, 'Preface', in C. Webb, *The Woman with the Basket: the History of the Women's Co-operative Guild* (Manchester: the Guild, 1927).
132. M. Llewelyn Davies, 'Introduction', *Maternity Letters from Working Women*, 1915 (London: Virago, 1978), pp. 8–9.
133. Davies, 'Preface'.

7

'To make the world a better place': Socialist Women and Women's Suffrage in Bristol, 1910–1920

June Hannam

In 1913, writing in the *Bristol and Clifton Social World*, Councillor Margaret Ashton from Manchester wrote that 'it is the linking up of public administration with the daily life of the people that women councillors can most effectively help the community . . . the joint effort of men and women working together in public as in private that obtains the best result'.[1] These words would have struck a chord with women who were active in the socialist movement in the early twentieth century. Their motivations for engaging in socialist politics were varied, but nearly all emphasised the importance of doing something to improve the lives of working people, in particular women and children – Lucy Cox, for example, who joined the Bristol Independent Labour Party in 1916, claimed in an interview later in life that the hardships endured by her parents to give their children an education, and the loss of young men from her village during World War One, had made her determined to enter politics to 'make the world a better place . . . These were the two things that made me join the Labour Party – poverty and war.'[2] Socialist women joined a mixed-sex party because they hoped to work alongside men to make a better world for both sexes. At the same time, both in their theory and in their practice, they highlighted the specific difficulties faced by women in the workplace and in the home and drew a link between socialism and women's emancipation. In the immediate prewar years the women's suffrage movement, one of the most burning political issues of the day, provided a new context in which socialist women attempted to pursue their different interests.

Historiography

We have long been aware of the extent to which socialist and suffrage politics were inextricably linked. A central feature of socialist ideology was a commitment to the emancipation of both sexes and the 'Woman Question' was debated extensively in socialist organisations from the late 1880s onwards. Nonetheless, women found that, despite the rhetoric of equality employed by socialists, their concerns were marginalised in a movement that emphasised class and the needs of the male worker. Before the turn of the century, many socialist women challenged this marginality and sought to develop a more woman-focused socialism.[3] This became a key issue in the decade before World War One as the women's suffrage campaign brought concerns about sex inequality to the forefront of politics. Women's suffrage highlighted in an acute form the tensions that already existed between sex and class and the subject was fiercely debated within socialist groups and in the socialist press. Many socialist women, and some men, became involved in the suffrage campaign itself as well as using the issue to raise questions about the commitment of socialist groups to working for women's emancipation as a key part of the project of constructing a new society. Indeed, it was members of the Manchester branch of the socialist group, the Independent Labour Party (ILP), who first established the Women's Social and Political Union (WSPU) in 1903 – an organisation that was to become famous throughout the world for its Militant methods.[4] The shifting political tactics at a national level have been charted in detail, in particular the split between the WSPU and the ILP in 1907, and the development of an alliance for electoral purposes between the Labour Party and the constitutionalist group, the National Union of Women's Suffrage Societies (NUWSS), in 1912.[5] The Labour Party pledged not to endorse any measure to extend the franchise unless it included women, while the National Union agreed to support Labour candidates in selected constituencies. An Election Fighting Fund Committee (EFF) was established for this purpose and contained many ILP suffragists.[6]

One focus of histories of suffrage and socialism has been on the tensions between the two movements and on the difficulties faced by socialist women as they attempted to reconcile competing loyalties to their sex, their class and their party. Attention has been drawn to the reluctance of socialist groups, and of the Labour Party,[7] to give wholehearted support to the demand for women's suffrage and to the debates over an adult versus a limited suffrage measure that took place at all levels of the labour movement.[8] The Social Democratic Federation, a Marxist party, took an adult suffrage position while the ILP, a group committed to an evolutionary route to socialism and far less likely to appeal to class antagonism, was the one political party that gave a formal commitment to the demand for women's suffrage on the same terms as men. Nonetheless in both groups women complained that the leadership did not give priority to franchise reform and in the case of the ILP that members of the National Administrative Council lacked commitment to women's suffrage despite the official policy of the organisation.[9]

A second focus of attention has been on the contribution socialist women made to the suffrage campaign and the difficulties that they faced in reconciling their suffragism and their socialism. It has been suggested that socialist women brought a new dimension to suffrage politics by raising the specific concerns of working-class women and by their emphasis on the need for a broad and democratic basis for the franchise. Biographies of leading suffrage campaigners coupled with studies of local activists have made us far more aware of the complex choices that socialist women had to make as they faced the dilemma of where to put their energies.[10] Some, for example, left socialism altogether to give a full-time commitment to women's suffrage, others joined suffrage groups but continued to be active within socialist politics, while yet others gave a much lower priority to the suffrage campaign. Individual women shifted their priorities and allegiances over time, moving between groups and between tactical positions.

The situation at a local level was particularly fluid and it is difficult to discern a distinctive pattern in the choices that were made.[11] Despite splits at a national level the WSPU, with its origins in the ILP and its emphasis on methods of campaigning that were familiar to socialists, continued to attract the support of socialist women, for example in Liverpool, Glasgow and Leeds.[12] In Lancashire, however, textile workers, described by Liddington and Norris as radical suffragists, at first established their own organisations but then continued their work within the decentralised and non-party NUWSS. In the north-east too, the ILP members Lisbeth Simm, Florence Harrison Bell and Ethel Bentham were leaders of the North East Society for Women's Suffrage, a branch of the NUWSS. They ensured that the NESWS gave support to the Labour candidate in Jarrow in the 1906 election despite the non-party stand of the National Union.[13]

Although the literature on suffrage and socialism is extensive, the focus has been on the engagement of socialist women and men and their organisations in the suffrage movement and the influence that they had on the campaign. Attention has also been paid to the importance of suffrage in helping to shape socialist women's political identities. Less has been written about the effects of the suffrage movement on the structure of socialist politics and women's experiences within that politics. Did the suffrage movement make a difference to the theory and practice of socialist groups? What space was there for women to raise their 'own' issues within those groups and did suffrage alter the ways in which socialist groups sought to recruit women members? To what extent did engagement in suffrage politics have long-lasting effects?

It will be suggested in this chapter that the most effective way to explore these questions is through detailed local studies. It was at the level of the branch that most women and men engaged in political activities and developed their political identities. It was here that they formed close friendships, took part in specific campaigns and made links with the community. The importance of looking at the culture of local branches and the relationship between organisational structures, politics and everyday life has increasingly been recognised. Eleanor Gordon's study of women and the labour movement in Scotland before 1914, for example, explores the range of groups and activities in which women were involved and provides important insights into the attitudes of local socialists to women as a political constituency.[14] In a more recent study of Liverpool, Krista Cowman examines the extent to which women's suffrage affected the outlook and practices of local socialist groups before 1914, while a number of studies have been undertaken of Labour Party branches in the interwar years.[15]

This chapter seeks to add to this literature through a study of the relationship between suffrage and socialism in Bristol, drawing on comparisons with other local areas where appropriate. It will focus not only on the prewar period but will also consider the immediate postwar years in order to assess any long-term development in the attitude of local socialists towards women members and 'women's emancipation'. In particular it will seek to test Pat Thane's suggestion that women played an important role in building up labour and socialist politics from a local base and helped to ensure that women's suffrage and women's rights became firmly established on the radical agenda by 1914.[16]

Bristol socialism

In the immediate prewar years, there were two well-established and substantial socialist groups in Bristol, the Bristol Socialist Society (BSS) and the Independent Labour Party. The BSS had been formed in the 1880s and was associated with the Social Democratic Federation (renamed the Social Democratic Party in 1909). It had 600 paying members, 'long experience, fighting traditions, and propaganda strength', as well as links with the trade unions, in particular through Ernest Bevin and Ben Tillett of the Dock Workers' Union.[17] Bristol had one of the largest ILP branches in the country, with approximately 600 members in 1912–13.[18] There was a separate branch in East Bristol, one of the poorest districts in the city, that was affiliated separately with the national party.[19] The local ILP had grown in strength after Walter Ayles, an engineer, moved to Bristol in 1910 to become the full-time general secretary and organiser of the Bristol branch. He improved its organisation, attracted new members and, with the establishment of the Kingsway Hall in 1911, ensured that there would be a recognised space for socialist activity. In 1913, the ILP newspaper, *Labour Leader*, wrote of a 'booming Bristol branch' that had held 300 propaganda meetings in the course of the year and was about to launch a membership drive to increase numbers to 1000.[20] On the other hand this was an uphill struggle. The branch minutes record the apathy of many members and the extent to which lack of funds hampered propaganda activities.

In line with national policy, the ILP was affiliated to the local Labour Representation Committee, established in 1905. The BSS remained outside of the LRC but there was usually co-operation between all three groups during election campaigns and also for propaganda purposes. Both the BSS and the ILP were critical of the Labour Party, however, for its failure to pursue socialist policies and the Bristol ILP threatened to disaffiliate from the LRC in 1912. It eventually drew back from taking this step on the condition that the ILP would be free to co-operate with other groups during election campaigns and would be able to act independently. Despite these tensions, the LRC enjoyed increasing success at municipal elections with the number of Labour councillors rising from one in 1910 to eight in 1914 (including one alderman), the majority of whom were ILP members.

In contrast to many other local areas, socialist women in Bristol do not appear to have taken a prominent role in the suffrage movement until after 1911. This can partly be explained by the nature of the suffrage movement itself. Bristol was one of the first cities to establish a women's suffrage society in 1868. Its leading members were also active in the Bristol Women's Liberal Association and this close relationship with liberalism continued into the twentieth century.[21] A local supporter of the WSPU, Emily Blathwayt from Batheaston, near Bath, claimed that the Bristol NUWSS was too sympathetic to the Liberal Party. She suggested that the members from Clifton, who were drawn from professional and business families, 'seem to be what I call Liberal Primrose Leaguers'.[22] The WSPU also had an active branch in Bristol. The city was seen as a key area in which to develop militant activities because one of its MPs, Augustine Birrell, was a Cabinet minister. Annie Kenney was sent to Bristol as a full-time organiser in 1908 and she drew support from a range of social groups including middle-class women with independent means from Clifton, schoolteachers, nurses and working-class women such as Annie Martin who was a member of the Women's Co-operative Guild. The WSPU held numerous meetings outside of factory gates in 1909 and 1910 and established a shop opposite the Wills tobacco factory in order to attract working-class women.[23]

On the other hand, the Bristol WSPU was not as closely rooted in the local labour and socialist movement as it was in many other cities, in particular in the north of England. This may partly reflect the fact that women workers were not well organised in the city – most of them were employed in the clothing industry or in the new factory trades manufacturing food products, confectionery and tobacco, in all of which trade unionism was weak. Key women propagandists in the late nineteenth-century socialist movement in Bristol, including Enid Stacy, Katherine Conway (later Bruce Glasier), Miriam Daniell and Helena Born, who attempted to bring together socialism and women's emancipation, had all left the city by the mid-1890s and their place had not been taken by others in the intervening years. This can be compared with Glasgow where socialist women played an active part in the WSPU. For example, Isabella Bream Pearce, who in the 1890s was president of the Glasgow Women's Labour Party and wrote a women's column in the *Labour Leader* under the pseudonym 'Lily Bell', became honorary secretary of the Scottish WSPU. Between 1906 and 1908, Isabella again wrote as Lily Bell, this time editing a suffrage column in the influential ILP newspaper *Forward*. Tom Johnston, the editor, was sympathetic to the militant suffragettes, and ensured that *Forward* carried numerous articles on women's suffrage, provided extensive reports on suffrage meetings and welcomed contributions from WSPU members up to the outbreak of war.[24] In Manchester too, socialists took a leading part in all branches of the suffrage campaign.[25]

Women's political space

What spaces did socialist women have in which they could raise the question of women's suffrage? The issue of whether women should be organised separately within socialist groups, including whether the socialist press should have specific women's columns, was always the subject of controversy among feminists. On the one hand it was argued that working-class women were more likely to feel comfortable in a single-sex group, where they could gain confidence, and that such groups raised the possibility that women would achieve greater autonomy and would highlight the inequalities that they faced as a sex. On the other hand it was suggested that women's groups would keep women separate from mainstream socialist organisations and would ensure that they, and their concerns, would remain marginal to the socialist project.[26]

The establishment of the WSPU, which was seen as a rival for the allegiance of working-class women, did encourage socialist organisations to set up their own women's groups. In 1904, the SDF supported the formation of a national women's organisation for the party and encouraged the setting up of Women's Circles in local branches. The ILP did not have a separate women's organisation at national level but many local branches established women's groups and ILP members predominated in the Women's Labour League (WLL), an organisation set up to give support to the Labour Party.[27] Women's columns were also established in the socialist press, including *Justice* and the *Labour Leader*, the official organs of the SDF and the ILP respectively, as well as in many local papers. In Bristol women could join the Women's Circle in the BSS or the Women's Mutual Improvement Class (WMIC) in the ILP and there was also a branch of the WLL in the city.

The extent to which women used any of these spaces as a vehicle for pursuing women's suffrage depended very largely on the specific political context of their local area and on whether there was an active group of suffragists in the local socialist movement. Socialist women who were keen to prioritise women's suffrage argued their case in a variety of different spaces, regardless of the characteristics of any specific women's group. In East Leeds, for example, the same women were active in the WSPU, the ILP and the Women's Labour League, although at a national level the League advocated support for an adult rather than a limited suffrage measure. By contrast, the different women's groups in the Bristol labour and socialist movement did not give much attention to women's suffrage before 1912. Members of the WLL, for example, were involved largely in industrial issues during 1910 and 1911 and in work for the municipal elections. They assisted male trade unionists in their attempts to organise women workers in boot making, box making and tailoring and collected money for Rhondda Valley miners who were on strike.[28] At election time, they took part in canvassing and helped bring women to the polls. The most experienced member, the president Emily Webb, who was also national secretary of the Railway Women's Guild, seconded a resolution at the 1913 WLL national conference that called on the government to place the issue of women's suffrage before the House of Commons in the current session and demanded a government measure that contained clauses on women's enfranchisement. She did not, however, emphasise the suffrage cause in her day-to-day politics in

Bristol. This may have been because, as a long-standing member of the Board of Guardians, she gave priority to social questions and had little time to pursue other issues.[29]

Bristol socialists and suffrage

Bristol socialists became far more involved in the suffrage campaign after 1911 and the subject was more frequently discussed at socialist meetings. This was partly connected with the arrival in Bristol of key individuals who saw women's suffrage as important. It was also linked to the development of the alliance between the Labour Party and the NUWSS in 1912 and then the decision of the EFF to target East Bristol as one of the constituencies in which it would give support to a Labour Party candidate. It has already been noted that Walter Ayles became a key figure in the Bristol ILP in 1910. He was a pacifist and a keen supporter of women's rights, including women's suffrage. His wife Bertha, who shared his views, worked as a part-time organiser for the Women's Labour League in the south-west and also in Lancashire and took an active role in the Bristol branch of the ILP.[30] They ensured that the Bristol ILP passed a resolution calling on the government 'to remove all disabilities based upon the fact of sex' and, at a meeting of Pilgrimage marchers in 1913 Walter Ayles seconded a resolution that women's suffrage should be introduced immediately.[31]

In the same period Annie Townley, a working-class organiser for the EFF and a member of the ILP moved to the area to spearhead the EFF campaign in East Bristol.[32] Once there she encountered difficulties from the Bristol NUWSS. Many members disagreed with the new policy of forming a closer relationship with the Labour Party and this led to resignations from the committee. The cautious attitude of the local NUWSS is revealed by the fact that as late as 1914 it was noted that the *Common Cause* was sold on the street by Miss Jeffreys, 'our pioneer in this unattractive but necessary work'.[33] No EFF group was established in Bristol and therefore Annie Townley had to work directly under the London committee.[34]

As soon as she arrived, she made contact with fourteen different Labour organisations and trade unions, including the WLL, the East Bristol ILP and the local Labour Representation Committee and sought their support for a resolution calling for the government to introduce a measure to enfranchise women. She also organised numerous suffrage meetings in East Bristol where she worked closely with Mabel Tothill, a middle-class socialist who lived and worked in the local University Settlement and who became secretary of the East Bristol Women's Suffrage Society.

The *Common Cause* reported that the campaign was a great success; by May 1913 200 friends of suffrage had been enrolled and several representatives of labour organisations added to the East Bristol Committee.[35] It was noted that this was such a poor district, with women suffering from low pay and inadequate housing, that they had been unable to give time or money up to now. Nonetheless, those already organised in the Women's Co-operative Guild, the WLL and the Railway Women's Guild were now 'rallying with enthusiasm for the fight'.[36] One member of the WLL, for example, probably Bertha Ayles, paid for handbills requesting men to send postcards to their MPs calling for them to vote for the inclusion of women in a franchise bill on the widest possible basis and these were distributed to all male trade unionists.[37] After Annie Townley had moved a resolution of support for women's suffrage at the East Bristol ILP, which was passed, members of the women's section began canvassing every Wednesday and took a copy of the labour newspaper, *Daily Citizen*, to each house.[38]

The success of the campaign was attributed to Annie Townley 'whose tact and ability have won her golden opinions from all sorts of people'.[39] The National Union had long been aware that class hostility made it unlikely that working-class women or male trade unionists would give any sympathy to the suffrage cause unless speakers they could trust approached them. Therefore, the NUWSS employed socialist women from a working-class background as organisers, including the ILP members Selina Cooper and Ada Nield Chew. Annie Townley, the wife of a textile trade unionist and socialist, clearly fitted well with this policy and Walter Ayles claimed that she had 'succeeded in winning the confidence of local trade unionists, which was critical to maintaining Labour Party support for women's suffrage in the area'.[40]

After a special campaign in April 1913 Annie Townley carried out registration work in the district and proclaimed that this had been a great success 'especially among the Committee [of the National Union branch] themselves who never before had heard Labour speeches, or met Labour men'.[41] The campaign became even more intensive after July when the prospective parliamentary candidate for East Bristol, alderman Frank Sheppard, withdrew from the fight and Walter Ayles took his place.[42] Meetings were held every week, addressed by both male and female speakers, and in the autumn, there was a special campaign in which meetings were held throughout the constituency. Speakers included Helena Swanwick, a leading figure nationally in the EFF, Ada Nield Chew and local Labour Party/ILP councillors. The *Common Cause* thanked 'our friends' among the Labour Party for giving their time to help in the campaign although they were preparing for the municipal elections.

Mr Burleigh, the campaign secretary for Walter Ayles, was singled out for particular praise since his 'local knowledge made him invaluable in the post'.[43] There were some tensions, however, between the Bristol and East Bristol branches of the ILP. The former expressed concerns that their paid secretary was now putting so much effort into his election propaganda that he was neglecting his duties to the branch. They were reluctant at first to respond positively to the request from the joint secretaries of the labour and women's suffrage campaign to give support at meetings since it was felt that the Central branch had been ignored despite the fact that some of its wards were in East Bristol. Nonetheless, two months later the Bristol branch agreed to co-operate and to help with registration work.[44]

Ayles himself was crucial in persuading the local labour and socialist movement to take women's suffrage seriously since he was personally committed to women's emancipation. He was a persuasive speaker and held 'excellent' meetings in Bristol where, in dealing with the 'women's question' he 'carried the war into the camp of the "Anti's" in downright style'.[45] As more people became involved in the East Bristol WSS Mabel Tothill became president of the group and was able to give up the role of secretary, which was taken on by Mrs Bottomley. Little is known about the latter's background although both she and her husband addressed local meetings on women's suffrage. The momentum of the campaign, including regular meetings and joint labour and suffrage demonstrations, was kept up until the outbreak of war. After each large meeting, new 'Friends' were enrolled and in February 1914, it was reported that a collection of 13 shillings had been taken which was 'exceptionally good for East Bristol'.[46]

Although the newspapers of the NUWSS and the ILP praised the campaign in East Bristol and held this up as a shining example of joint activity and co-operation between the two groups, this glossed over continuing tensions between the local NUWSS and the ILP and Labour Party. These became particularly acute during World War One when Ayles took a stand against conscription – a position that was embarrassing for the NUWSS. At the same time, the National Union made a decision to suspend EFF activities during the war, including registration work. This was a blow for East Bristol where the EFF had played a pivotal role in the decision of the ILP and LRC to run a candidate in that area. Holton has provided a detailed account of the negotiations that took place between East Bristol and the national leadership, which eventually led to a continuation of support for Ayles in East Bristol. She notes his impassioned argument to the NUWSS executive that if they denied him their support it would strengthen those within the Labour Party who were hostile to the women's suffrage movement and that 'in East Bristol there is now more animosity to the middle classes than there was at the outbreak of war'.[47]

The class differences between the Bristol NUWSS and the East Bristol WSS did little to give women a sense of solidarity with one another. In the north-east Lisbeth Simm expressed a similar suspicion of women from wealthy, non-labour backgrounds when she complained that the local WSPU organisers had 'little idea of the poverty of the region or the hardship their fund raising would produce'.[48] In Bristol, women socialists were more likely to emphasise the close working relationships that they had with other male socialists. For example, the handbills that they distributed to male trade unionists were headlined 'Organised Workers of Bristol! Bristol Working Women appeal to Bristol Working Men'.[49] Most of the leading Bristol campaigners were married to male activists in the labour movement, as was Lisbeth Simm herself, but that does not provide a complete explanation for their attitudes. Many of the members of the East Leeds ILP who belonged to the WSPU had husbands in the socialist movement and yet they were willing to express their autonomy and to continue to support the policies of the WSPU even after 1912, when these were in conflict with the Labour Party and the ILP at a national level. In Bristol, it appears that because the suffrage campaign was rooted in the attempt to get a Labour candidate elected, the Bristol East WSS threatened to become autonomous from the NUWSS rather from the socialist and labour movement.

Women's role in socialist groups

There were many similarities in both of the main socialist organisations in the ways in which women engaged in socialist politics, regardless of whether their particular group was supportive of women's suffrage. On the one hand, there was space for individual women who were confident of their abilities, to take on key roles. Several women were members of the executive committee of the Bristol Socialist Society and they took part in discussions on all questions including finances, unemployment, co-operation with the ILP and election propaganda. Jane Tillett often chaired the meetings, Miss Gregory acted as treasurer and women were selected as representatives on the Right to Work Committee, a group that drew together all the main labour and socialist organisations in the city. Its demand was that 'every citizen of either sex be provided with useful work or healthy maintenance'.[50] Jane Tillett was also elected as a

Poor Law Guardian. Before 1912, women did not play a prominent role within the Bristol ILP. Key figures such as Emily Webb were active instead within the Women's Labour League. In 1912, however, Bertha Ayles was elected as vice chairman and then as chairman of the Bristol branch and, along with Mrs Lean, was a delegate to the LRC.[51] Mrs Still and Miss Carter were also elected as two out of the four branch representatives to the executive committee.

Most women engaged in socialist politics through the women's groups attached to the branches. In both the BSS and the ILP, these had very similar characteristics. They were seen as spaces where women would become educated on socialism or topical issues – for example in 1912 the Bristol ILP women's class had a lecture on the Wages Board Act.[52] They also encouraged a collective response to any problems affecting working women or their families, thus in 1910 the BSS Women's Circle suspended its meeting to assist the female cardboard box makers who were trying to organise themselves into a trade union. Women's groups could be a way to attract women into the socialist and labour movement since political activities were intertwined with social events. The Bristol WLL, for instance, held coffee suppers with music to make themselves 'sociable' and to introduce women to their work and claimed that 'the teas and socials have brought profit and enjoyment'.[53]

We are now far more aware of the importance of the social and cultural life of local socialist groups, including music, dances, rambling and cycling as well as educative politics for attracting men and women into the movement.[54] As part of the Bristol ILP membership drive in 1913, a cycling corps was formed 'for the purpose of doing missionary work in the surrounding villages'.[55] The BSS was very similar and had a cycling section and a rambling committee that recommended members to distribute literature when they were out walking.[56] Social events were also crucial for providing much-needed funds – profits from the Dance Committee, the annual Bazaar and the Garden Fête helped to keep the Bristol ILP afloat in the prewar years, in particular when it proved difficult to collect subscriptions. Men were of course involved in these activities as well as women, but it does appear that there was a gendered division of labour. Men were responsible for doing much of the organising, in particular for key events such as the Bazaar, whereas women, who were usually their wives and daughters, made goods for sale. In the Brislington ward, for example, men guaranteed to raise £5 in two months to purchase materials for the Women's Sewing Class for the Bazaar.[57] The Women's Class was also regularly asked to provide catering for conferences and other events.[58]

Suffrage and branch life

What was the impact, if any, of the women's suffrage campaign on roles of women within the Bristol socialist movement and of attitudes towards them? The BSS gave very little priority to 'women's issues' in this period, including women's suffrage. The official position of the Social Democratic Party was that it supported the demand for an adult suffrage measure but the suffrage question was given a very low priority within the organisation. In Bristol, the question of women's suffrage was rarely raised at meetings despite the fact that this was a period in which considerable publicity was given to the issue in the national and local press. Reverend Ramsay, a city councillor and ILP member, was due to speak on the subject of Votes for Women in 1910 on behalf of the WSPU, and in November of the same year Jane Tillett chaired a meeting of the Women's Co-operative Guild on the subject of adult suffrage, but most attention was paid to industrial unrest.[59]

In contrast, as noted above, ILP members in East Bristol did become extensively involved in the suffrage campaign. As early as January 1912 a demonstration was organised on behalf of women's suffrage at Barton Hill Baths; Bertha and Walter Ayles attended as delegates from the Bristol branch. Activity then intensified when the EFF targeted the constituency. The East Bristol WSS struggled financially, but used socials and concerts both to raise funds and to attract members. Activities included entertainment and competitions such as 'hat trimming (men only), potato races and candle lighting' combined with talks on women's suffrage. Mabel Tothill thought that the existence of the East Bristol WSS was largely tied up with the fortunes of the Labour candidate and the suffrage campaign boosted membership of both sexes in the Bristol East ILP.[60] This had a knock-on effect for the Bristol branch. In reporting on the 'booming' life of the branch, the *Labour Leader* noted in particular 'the growing activity on the women's side of the movement, the members of which have done extremely useful work'.[61]

During this period the presence of women was far more obvious at key labour sites of activity – when the Bristol Branch decided to establish a newspaper, *Bristol Forward*, in 1914, the women's movement had its own space allotted along with Trade Unions, the LRC, the ILP and Anti vaccinators.[62] At the May Day demonstration in 1914, among the speakers on the platform were Mrs Townley, for the NUWSS, Mrs Brodie for the Poor Law Guardians and Mrs Tillett for the Women's Branch of the Dockers' Union.[63] Although speakers at ILP branch meetings were predominantly male, Annie Townley, Ada Nield Chew and Muriel Wallhead all gave talks on women's suffrage.

It is difficult to know how far women's own view of themselves as political activists was changed by their involvement in suffrage campaigning. There are times when we can glimpse an increase in confidence. In 1912, for example, the secretary of the Bristol WLL reported that 'while several of our members can express themselves at an indoor meeting we are terrified at the thought of saying a few words at an outdoor meeting; if we could overcome this and hold outdoor meetings in the summer we should gain many new members'.[64] Two years later the vice president Mrs Higgins, an ILP member, used a different tone when she urged women to become involved in the tramway workers' dispute. She gave a 'stirring speech, driving home the fact that this was the women's fight as much as the men's and that it behoved the women to be up and doing'. This led to the appointment of a committee that aimed to hold a mass women's meeting 'so that an urgent appeal could be made to all women to come along and help in this heroic fight'.[65] In this period too, the Women's Mutual Improvement Class nominated Mrs Higgins as a vice president of the Bristol branch and this was endorsed by the executive committee.[66]

Such activities, however, were still juxtaposed in the Bristol ILP with a view of women as primarily fund-raisers and organisers of social events. In discussing the growing activity on the women's side of the movement the Bristol ILP singled out the members of the dance committee, 'whose efforts have been untiring', while East Bristol ILP praised the 'lady comrades' for activities on behalf of the sale of work and the bazaar.[67] The language used is also instructive, with socialists still being equated with men. In urging members to come along and lend a hand in propaganda work and the making of socialists the Bristol East ILP added 'Put your backs into it, men!' and on another urged that 'every worker should report himself to the secretary'.[68] Women were often put forward to stand as Poor Law Guardians, but were less likely to be encouraged to be candidates for city council elections where the emphasis was placed on returning Labour *men*. Women rarely held official positions within the two local branches or within the wards, while at a meeting of the South Western Counties ILP there was only one female delegate.[69]

There is little evidence that issues of specific interest to women were being pursued by the local ILP. Walter Ayles's programme for change in Bristol emphasised public allotments, the municipalisation of the docks and the trams, and public health questions. Women were mentioned specifically only in relation to municipal lodging houses.[70] Issues brought to the attention of the ILP that related to women, such as an enquiry into the hours of work and employment of girls, were referred to the WMIC.[71] Neither the ILP as a whole, nor women activists within it, tended to raise broader issues about the gender division of labour and the subject was treated with humour by the local ILP. For example, reporting on a garden fête it was noted that the event 'was a success, although there was quite a noticeable scarcity of male members. Possibly they were at home minding the babies!'[72]

These attitudes can partly be explained by the strength of the 'ideology of separate spheres' that permeated both the socialist and the suffrage movements. Eleanor Gordon, for example, argues that in Scotland the ILP and the WLL, dominated largely by ILP women, based their case for women's enfranchisement on the view that women had distinct moral attributes and would bring something different to political life. They saw women's role as bound up with domesticity and motherhood and therefore their public roles would democratise and humanise society. As a corollary of this, however, women were viewed primarily as the wives, mothers and sweethearts of socialists and their roles tended to be seen as separate and auxiliary.[73] Walter Ayles certainly saw women as having a distinctive role to play. He argued that 'we must have economic freedom' and that 'to get this the help of women is imperative. Their experience and advice is invaluable. But to give this fully *they must have political freedom.*' He concluded that winning East Bristol for Labour 'will be the greatest blow yet struck in the cause of women's freedom and the social redemption of England'.[74]

Krista Cowman comes to similar conclusions in Liverpool. Here socialist women had been actively involved for a number of years in the WSPU, but the local ILP continued to discuss women speakers in terms of their attractiveness or their gentle qualities. Cowman argues that 'domestic ideology continued to have direct bearing on the opportunities socialism offered women for public political activity. Topics offered to women speakers tended to be restricted and practical experience limited.'[75] Thus, for most women, political activity took place on the periphery – in non-aligned socialist societies or groups. She also suggests that although socialist involvement in the WSPU simultaneously increased the opportunities for women to play a part in socialist activities, they were still marginalised since they became identified as suffrage speakers and nothing else. Thus, suffrage became added to fundraising, educating and catering as suitable areas of political work for women.

In many respects, suffrage activities could reinforce the view that men and women played different roles and had different strengths. Reporting on EFF work in the constituencies the *Labour Leader* pointed to East Bristol and North Monmouth where 'great activity is being shown by the women, both in the quiet work of organization (in which women suffragists have shown that they excel) which should tell heavily when the General Election comes along'.[76] The way in which the suffrage movement was described in the socialist press is instructive – reference is made to 'woman suffragists and labour' or to the 'joint campaign for suffrage and labour', which implied that the two issues were separate. The circumstances in which suffrage propaganda arose in East Bristol – as part of a campaign to ensure that a Labour candidate was elected – meant that the arguments for women's enfranchisement could be framed in terms that emphasised the benefits to Labour rather than the implications for women themselves and their emancipation. Indeed, the *Labour Leader* argued that local forces were hopeful of the 'added strength which will come to them at election times in the support of the electors' wives – now for the first time awakened to a live interest in politics, and coming to them directly from the labour standpoint'.[77]

Bristol socialism and women's suffrage after 1914

The East Bristol WSS continued its work among the local community during the war. The society took part in the Prince of Wales fund, using the suffrage shop as a headquarters where members attended three times a week to receive applications from local working women who needed assistance. The president, Mabel Tothill, was on the executive of the Lord Mayor's Committee that dealt with female unemployment and aimed to provide training in needlework and cookery. The WSS still held regular meetings with speakers on a variety of topics and continued to carry out registration and other work connected with future elections.[78]

A close connection was still sustained between the East Bristol WSS and the WLL since the same key women were members of both. As noted above, the Bristol WLL was far less active, in particular in relation to women's suffrage, before Bertha Ayles arrived in the city. Bertha, however, suffered from a heart complaint and at the end of 1913, after the birth of her son, decided to reduce her political commitments.[79] By this stage, however, other local women such as Mrs Higgins were prepared to take leadership roles and during World War One Annie Townley became far more involved in the WLL. By 1916, she was president, and the following year secretary, of the Bristol branch. She attended the annual conferences of the League where, in 1917, she seconded a resolution on the importance of women being electors and sought to remove a clause on residential qualifications in the new Franchise Bill.[80]

Annie Townley, Mrs Higgins and Mabel Tothill also became far more active in the Bristol branch of the ILP during the war, representing the party at numerous conferences and acting as delegates to affiliated organisations. In 1915, Annie Townley was elected as vice chairman of the branch, with her husband as the literature secretary, and in 1916, she became chairman. In common with many other ILP members, the three women added work for peace to their interest in work for suffrage. Mabel Tothill was secretary of the local advisory committee set up to help anyone victimised as a conscientious objector. Annie Townley joined the Women's International League and during the annual conference of the WLL, held in Bristol in 1916, she expressed the hope that the League would 'give a lead for men to follow in their conference'. She proposed a resolution on ILP lines that called for a speedy end to the war, a peace by negotiation and a system of mediation by neutral powers. She claimed that she was 'not afraid to join a campaign to stop the war' and wanted the Labour Party to take some definite action.[81]

It could be argued that the women's suffrage campaign was a vehicle for giving a high profile to individual women who then, in the context of war, found further opportunities to take a leading role in the ILP. Annie Townley took over as chairman of the ILP when Frank Berriman was arrested for resisting conscription and she also carried out Walter Ayles's organising work when he too was imprisoned.[82] She generally kept the branch informed about women's activities in wartime, giving a talk on 'Women and War' and reporting on the week's mission organised by 'women comrades' on behalf of the Women's Peace Crusade.[83] Women continued to maintain a higher profile, and to develop their careers, both in the ILP and in the Labour Party after the war. Annie Townley remained as chairman of the Bristol branch of the ILP until 1921. Mabel Tothill was elected to the City Council in 1920 – the branch minutes record pride in the fact that the first woman elected to the Council was from the ILP – and she became vice chairman of the branch in 1921.[84] A younger woman, Lucy Cox, who had worked closely with Walter Ayles during the war, took an active part in the postwar ILP. Her political journey had begun with suffrage but then took a different direction. She later recalled that at sixteen she was 'strongly feminist, at twenty strongly pacifist and at twenty-two joined the ILP – that is my record'.[85] In the 1920s, Lucy spoke at propaganda meetings throughout the region and was a delegate to the ILP Divisional Conference and the Bristol North election committee.[86] It may also have been the influence wielded by these leading women that ensured that the local group supported the candidature of Minnie Pallister who was standing for the NAC of the ILP.

This was a difficult time for the ILP as it had to work out its role in relation to the ILP and it was reported that the Labour Party 'absorbed the efforts of many of our comrades', in particular women such as Annie Townley who became a full-time women's organiser for the Labour Party in the south-west. After the war the Labour Party's new constitution, that allowed for individual membership for the first time, coupled with a different organisational structure in which constituencies were encouraged to set up women's sections, provided a changed context for women's engagement in politics. In Bristol, the long period of sustained campaigning through the East Bristol WSS, the WLL and the ILP before and during the war did lay the groundwork for the formation of strong women's sections in the city, the most successful of which were in East Bristol.[87] In 1918, for instance, it was reported that in Bristol East 50 per cent of voters in the general election of that year were women.[88] Local women do appear to have gained in confidence by this stage. In 1919, for instance, a number of working women signed the petition presented to the City Council for the building of 5000 houses. They pointed out that women, who spent more time in the home than men, 'are peculiarly interested in securing the best arrangements for health, comfort and well being of the inhabitants'. They requested that the plans being considered by the Council should be 'submitted to some experienced women' and suggested that a women's advisory committee should be appointed.[89]

Nonetheless, women in the ILP and in the Labour Party were still largely engaged with fundraising – the bazaar committee to support Ayles's candidature for Parliament were all female and women were often thanked for organising successful suppers and reunions. Only nine women were put forward as candidates for the City Council in the interwar years, seven of whom were successful. Indeed, Marge Evans, a local ILP and Labour Party activist, claimed that 'the Party was dominated by men . . . we've still got a terrific fight about getting women representatives on to committees and for women's rights'.[90] Of even greater significance is the fact that women were seen, and saw themselves, as working to support socialism and the Labour Party. There is little in the minutes of the St George West Ward women's section and the Bristol East Divisional Labour Party or in press reports, to suggest that women were prepared to push for controversial issues that affected their own position as women or that challenged the gendered nature of local politics. This contrasts to some extent with the situation in Manchester where Karen Hunt suggests that the local women's section could be awkward. The long history of suffragism in the city contributed to a determination that women should make effective use of their hard-won citizenship and they did raise controversial questions such as birth control. Nonetheless, even here she found that women were still expected to be responsible for social events and fundraising.[91]

Conclusion

It has been suggested here that a great deal can be understood about the texture of the relationship between suffrage and socialist politics from detailed local studies. When women, and men, became involved in socialism in their localities they sought to do something for the community as well as for just their class or their sex and they worked across a broad front in order to achieve their objectives. At times this involved working with other socialist and labour groups – for instance in the Right to Work Committee or in organising May Day demonstrations – or it might involve working with groups that were outside the labour movement, such as women's suffrage organisations. The particular ways in which such connections worked, and the potential consequences for women's own political development and their role within socialist groups, varied between local areas. In Bristol, the fact that socialist women became involved in suffrage politics in the context of the EFF–Labour electoral alliance meant that there were fewer conflicts with male comrades over loyalties and priorities. This can be compared with the situation in East Leeds where there was conflict in the local Women's Labour League and ILP about whether it was acceptable for those who were also members of the WSPU to heckle Philip Snowden, a Labour MP, when he visited the constituency. The WSPU member Mrs Dightam claimed that it was right to do so since the Labour Party had fallen from its ideals in failing to support women's equality.[92]

Suffrage politics played a key role in influencing the ways in which socialist and labour women constructed a political identity for themselves. Claire Collins argues that after 1912 the WLL, far from drawing closer to the suffrage movement, developed an identity in opposition to that of suffragists and emphasised loyalty to the Labour Party and to class politics.[93] This can certainly be seen in the north-east where Lisbeth Simm and Florence Harrison Bell moved away from suffrage politics after 1909 to give more of their energies to the Women's Labour League. There were personality and class tensions with members of the NUWSS and therefore in the immediate prewar years Simm and Bell took no part in the EFF campaign in the area.[94] In Bristol East women worked in a variety of groups – the WSS, the Women's Co-operative Guild, the WLL, and the Women's Class in the ILP – but their identity as women was closely intertwined with their identity as socialists, and as Labour Party supporters, and thus they were prepared to leave the NUWSS if it went back on its support for Walter Ayles. Thus, women's suffrage may have been placed on the socialist and Labour Party agenda by 1914, and provided a vehicle for individual women to take a higher profile in the movement. Nonetheless, political equality could be defined as the opportunity for women to support the mixed-sex ILP and the Labour Party and did not mean that issues of particular relevance to women, such as birth control, would be given priority or that gender inequalities would be challenged. As Marge Evans reminds us, the broader question of women's rights and women's emancipation was a long way from being realised in the theory and practice of Bristol socialism and labour politics after 1918.

Notes

1. *Bristol and Clifton Social World*, 1913.
2. *The News*, 21 July 1978.
3. J. Hannam and K. Hunt, *Socialist Women: Britain, 1880s to 1920s* (London: Routledge, 2002), chapter 3.
4. For an account of the links between the Pankhurst family and the ILP, see P. Bartley, *Emmeline Pankhurst* (London: Routledge, 2002) and J. Purvis, *Emmeline Pankhurst: a Biography* (London: Routledge, 2003).
5. A. Rosen, *Rise Up Women! The Militant Campaign of the Women's Social and Political Union, 1903–1914* (London: Routledge & Kegan Paul, 1974).
6. The most detailed account of the development of the alliance can be found in S. Holton, *Feminism and Democracy: Women's Suffrage and Reform Politics in Britain, 1900–1918* (Cambridge: Cambridge University Press, 1986); see also J. Vellacott, *From Liberal to Labour with Women's Suffrage: the Story of Catherine Marshall* (Montreal: McGill-Queen's University Press, 1993).
7. The Labour Party was not formally committed to socialism at this stage. It was an alliance of trade unionists and socialists, in particular the ILP.
8. See, for example, Holton, *Feminism and Democracy*; Hannam and Hunt, *Socialist Women*, chapter 5.
9. For a detailed discussion of the views of the SDF and the ILP respectively on the 'Woman Question' and women's suffrage, see K. Hunt, *Equivocal Feminists: the Social Democratic Federation and the Woman Question, 1884–1911* (Cambridge: Cambridge University Press, 1996) and J. Hannam, 'Women and the ILP, 1890–1914', in T. James, T. Jowitt and K. Laybourn (eds), *The Centennial History of the Independent Labour Party* (Halifax: Ryburn, 1992).
10. For example, see J. Hannam, *Isabella Ford, 1855–1924* (Oxford: Blackwell, 1989); S. Fletcher, *Maude Royden: a Life* (Oxford: Blackwell, 1989); J. Liddington, *The Life and Times of a Respectable Rebel: Selina Cooper, 1864–1946* (London: Virago, 1986); D. Nield Chew (ed.), *Ada Nield Chew: the Life and Writings of a Working Woman* (London: Virago, 1982). A key text for understanding working women's involvement in the suffrage movement at a local level remains the pioneering study by J. Liddington and J. Norris, *One Hand Tied Behind Us: the Rise of the Women's Suffrage Movement* (London: Virago, 1978).
11. For an overview of local suffrage activities, see J. Hannam, '"I had not been to London". Women's Suffrage – a View from the Regions', in J. Purvis and S .S. Holton (eds), *Votes for Women* (London: Routledge, 2000); L. Leneman,

'A Truly National Movement: the View from Outside London', in M. Joannou and J. Purvis (eds), *The Women's Suffrage Movement: New Feminist Perspectives* (Manchester: Manchester University Press, 1998).

12. K. Cowman, *'Mrs Brown is a Man and a Brother': Women in Merseyside's Political Organizations, 1890–1920* (Liverpool: Liverpool University Press, 2004).
13. Liddington and Norris, *One Hand Tied Behind Us*; D. Neville, 'The Women's Suffrage Movement in the North East of England, 1900–1914' (unpublished MPhil thesis, Newcastle-upon Tyne Polytechnic, 1991).
14. E. Gordon, *Women and the Labour Movement in Scotland, 1850–1914* (Oxford: Clarendon Press, 1991).
15. Cowman, *'Mrs Brown is a Man and a Brother'*; M. Worley (ed.), *Labour's Grass Roots: Essays on the Activities of Local Labour Parties and Members, 1918–1945* (Aldershot: Ashgate, 2005).
16. P. Thane, 'Labour and Local Politics: Radicalism, Democracy and Social Reform, 1880–1914', in F. Biagini and A. Reid (eds), *Currents of Radicalism* (Cambridge: Cambridge University Press, 1991), pp. 259–60.
17. S. Bryher, *An Account of the Labour and Socialist Movement in Bristol* (Bristol, 1929), Part 3, p. 7.
18. W. H. Ayles, 'ILP in the South West', *Labour Leader*, 17 October 1912. Minutes of ILP Bristol Branch, AGM, 5 April 1913, Bateman Collection, Bristol University. It was claimed that all the 'paper' members had been struck off the list and this had left 616 actual members.
19. East Bristol, comprising the wards of St Phillips, St George West and St George East broke away from the Bristol branch in December 1910. Minutes of ILP Bristol Branch, 12 December 1910. It is not clear how many members were involved in East Bristol but Walter Ayles reported that there were 900 ILP members in Bristol altogether in 1912. W. H. Ayles, 'ILP in the South West', *Labour Leader*, 17 October 1912.
20. *Labour Leader*, 17 April 1913.
21. For details of the Bristol women's movement, see J. Hannam, '"An Enlarged Sphere of Usefulness": the Bristol Women's Movement, c.1860–1914', in M. Dresser and P. Ollerenshaw (eds), *The Making of Modern Bristol* (Tiverton: Redcliffe Press, 1996); E. Malos, 'Bristol Women in Action', in I. Bild (ed.), *Bristol's Other History* (Bristol: Bristol Broadsides, 1983).
22. Emily Blathwayt, *Diaries*, Gloucester Record Office, 1908.
23. *Votes for Women*, 14 June 1909, 14 January 1910.
24. There was no women's column between 1910 and 1912, but when it reappeared in 1913, it was edited by WSPU members, including Janie Allan and Helen Crawfurd. *Forward*, 1913.
25. For example, see Liddington and Norris, *One Hand Tied Behind Us*.
26. See Hannam and Hunt, *Socialist Women*, pp. 89–94 for a discussion of these controversies.
27. For the SDF, see Hunt, *Equivocal Feminists*. For the WLL see C. Collette, *For Labour and For Women: the Women's Labour League, 1906–1918* (Manchester: Manchester University Press, 1989).
28. Women's Labour League, *Annual Report*, 1911, 1912.
29. In the 1920s, she was the chairman [sic] of the St George and West Ward Women's Section of the Labour Party; was appointed the first female magistrate in the city in 1920 and was elected as a Labour Party councillor in 1929.

30. Collette, *For Labour and For Women*, pp. 84–5.
31. *Western Daily Press*, 2 March 1912, 21 July 1913.
32. Annie Townley was the wife of a trade unionist who was also active in the socialist movement.
33. *Common Cause*, 27 March 1914.
34. Holton, *Feminism and Democracy*, p. 107.
35. *Common Cause*, 23 May 1913.
36. Ibid., 3 October 1913.
37. *Labour Leader*, 13 March 1913.
38. Ibid., 27 February 1913.
39. *Common Cause*, 23 May 1913.
40. 'Interview with Representatives from East Bristol re EFF Work', n.d. quoted in Holton, *Feminism and Democracy*, p. 141.
41. NUWSS minutes quoted in Holton, *Feminism and Democracy*, p. 107.
42. Ayles had been elected to the City Council in 1912.
43. *Common Cause*, 17 October 1913.
44. ILP Bristol Branch minutes, 19 April 1913, 14 June 1913.
45. *Labour Leader*, 17 July 1913.
46. *Common Cause*, 27 February 1914.
47. 'Interview with Representatives', in Holton, *Feminism and Democracy*, p. 141.
48. Collette, *For Labour and For Women*, p. 73.
49. *Labour Leader*, 16 January 1913.
50. S. Bryher, *An Account of the Labour and Socialist Movement in Bristol* (Bristol: Bristol Labour Weekly, 1929), Part 3, p. 3.
51. ILP Bristol Branch minutes, 23 March 1912, 1 May 1912.
52. *Labour Leader*, 14 November 1912.
53. Women's Labour League, *Annual Report*, 1911, 1912.
54. See, for example, D. Tanner, 'Labour and its Membership', in D. Tanner, N. Tiratsoo and P. Thane (eds), *Labour's First Century* (Cambridge: Cambridge University Press, 2000), p. 250.
55. *Labour Leader*, 17 April 1913.
56. Bristol Socialist Society minutes, 6 May 1910.
57. ILP Bristol branch minutes, 10 March 1913.
58. Ibid., 20 November 1912 for the War on Poverty Conference.
59. Bristol Socialist Society minutes, 9 September 1910, 1 November 1910.
60. *Common Cause*, 23 January 1914.
61. *Labour Leader*, 17 April 1913.
62. Ibid., 12 February 1914.
63. Ibid., 7 May 1914.
64. Women's Labour League, *Annual Report*, 1912.
65. *Labour Leader*, 14 May 1914.
66. ILP Bristol Branch minutes, 17 May 1913.
67. *Labour Leader*, 17 April 1913, 23 October 1913.
68. Ibid., 20 March 1913, 3 October 1912.
69. Ibid., 29 January 1914.
70. Walter Ayles, 'What Labour is Achieving in Bristol', *Labour Leader*, 23 July 1914.
71. ILP Bristol Branch minutes, 16 April 1913. See also letter asking for 'ladies' to be appointed on visiting committees to mothers of schoolchildren about

medical inspection – the Women's Class was asked to take this in hand, 16 December 1912.

72. *Labour Leader*, 16 July 1914. In similar vein, Mrs Still of the WMIC wanted to 'get up a social to which males would be admitted'. ILP Bristol branch minutes, 1 May 1912.
73. Gordon, *Women and the Labour Movement in Scotland*, chapter 7.
74. *Common Cause*, 3 October 1913.
75. Cowman, *'Mrs Brown is a Man and a Brother'*, p. 135.
76. *Labour Leader*, 7 August 1913.
77. Ibid.
78. *Common Cause*, 25 September 1914.
79. Women's Labour League, *Annual Report*, 1914.
80. Ibid., 1917.
81. WLL, *Annual Conference Report*, 1916.
82. ILP Bristol branch minutes AGM, 22 April 1917. There was a vote of thanks to Mrs Townley for carrying out Ayles's work. Her husband was imprisoned in 1918 and his health never recovered.
83. Ibid., 5 September 1917.
84. Ibid., 1920.
85. Letter from Lucy Cox to Jim Middleton, 16 March 1932, Middleton Collection, Ruskin, Oxford.
86. Lucy Cox left Bristol to become secretary of the No More War Movement, an organisation in which Walter Ayles was also involved. As Lucy Middleton, she was elected as a Labour MP for Plymouth in 1945.
87. Minutes of the St George West Ward Women's Section, Bristol Record Office.
88. *Western Daily Press*, 16 December 1918.
89. Ibid., 10 February 1919.
90. D. Parker, 'A Proper Joiner. Marge Evans – memories of the Bristol Labour Movement', in *Placards and Pin Money* (Bristol: Bristol Broadsides, 1986).
91. K. Hunt, 'Making Politics in Local Communities: Labour Women in Interwar Manchester', in Worley (ed.), *Labour's Grass Roots*.
92. *Leeds Weekly Citizen*, 12 and 26 December 1913, 9 January 1914.
93. C. Collins, 'Women and Labour Politics in Britain, 1893–1932', unpublished PhD thesis, LSE, 1991, chapter 3.
94. Neville, 'The Women's Suffrage Movement'.

8

The Primrose League and Women's Suffrage, 1883–1918

Philippe Vervaecke

Often seen as the prime example of Conservatism's appeal to female audiences,[1] the Primrose League has been credited for easing the transition to female suffrage and mass democracy after 1918 for the Conservative machine.[2] Although not committed to any degree of parliamentary enfranchisement for women in its Victorian and Edwardian days, the League is cited as an organisation whose heavy, though not exclusive, reliance upon female political helpers arguably contributed to the process leading to female suffrage, as the ubiquity of Primrose Dames from the mid-1880s onwards legitimised women's active participation in politics.[3] The Primrose League, a Conservative body created in 1883 by Lord Randolph Churchill and his 'Fourth Party' associates, indeed counted a sizeable proportion of women in its ranks, who found themselves involved in an organisation that nonetheless chose to remain non-committal over women's suffrage, even at the height of the Edwardian suffrage controversy.

This chapter seeks to shift the focus away from the League's supposed long-term impact upon the 'Cause' and to look at the Edwardian climax of the suffrage controversy and its effect upon the movement. The narrative that emerges highlights the conflicts and tensions generated by the suffrage issue within the movement, and suggests that the Edwardian crisis of suffragism largely contributed to the League's post-1918 drift into effeteness. The League, a thriving organisation before the Great War, rallying thousands of women under its banner in its Edwardian days, then appeared as the chief Conservative organisation, but it steadily declined in the interwar years and never regained its pre-1914 strength once Conservative women were enfranchised. Why is it that the very organisation that enabled Conservative women to experience political apprenticeship badly suffered once they gained the right to vote? After 1918, the League's hegemonic position within the Conservative machinery was indeed at an end, and Conservative men and women started to join groups that were more fully integrated to the party structure proper. This chapter seeks to determine how far this process was related to suffragism and its impact upon an organisation that was so dependent upon female involvement.

The initial stage is to set the backdrop for the Edwardian crisis by looking at the ambiguous discourse on suffragism, womanhood and citizenship within the League in the years preceding the Edwardian era. Then, the discussion moves on to the height of the suffrage campaign and presents the reactions and effects produced by the suffragists' crusade on the League, both at central and local level. As the campaign for woman's enfranchisement gathered strength in the early twentieth century, the League's neutrality over suffrage became an increasingly awkward proposition. The movement's male and female elites became increasingly divided over the suffragist militancy. At local level, the impact was considerable, as the League's reliance on female support made it an ideal target for the shafts of suffragist propaganda, which did affect some female Tory canvassers who started refusing to work for anti-suffragist candidates. As a response to that crisis, League authorities chose to dissociate themselves from the League's public status as a mostly female organisation and to assert the movement's male dimension. Finally, the last part of the chapter consists in showing that suffragism coincided with increased gender-related tensions within the movement, a process which contributed to the rise of sex-segregated Conservative agencies and the corresponding decline of the League. The League, which remained adamantly open to both genders, then differed very much from the single-sex Conservative groups that emerged from the Edwardian years onwards and became dominant within the party after 1918. It is suggested that the interwar marginalisation of such a gender-integrative body as the League stems from Edwardian suffragism and the increased gender polarisation it fuelled within the movement. Previous accounts of interwar popular conservatism have explained the League's decline as the natural outcome of the Representation of the People Act of 1918, which required political parties to increase the integration of female voters into their structure. From that perspective, the League, as an organisation that publicly reasserted its independence from the Conservative Party proper in 1919, declined because the Conservative Central Office actively promoted Women's Unionist Organisations (WUOs), which unlike the League happened to be under its direct control.[4] The League's interwar decline may also be ascribed to infighting within the party during the Edwardian crisis of conservatism more generally, when tariff reformers and their opponents fought over control of the party machinery. In that conflict, the League toed as neutral a line as over women's enfranchisement, although it actively competed against tariff reform groups at local level, remained loyal to Balfour even after his departure from the leadership and was identified with sections of the party hostile to Chamberlainites. From that perspective, the tariff-reforming complexion of the party leadership after 1911 may rightly be seen as a damaging evolution for the League.

However, what we suggest here is that it is gender polarisation and not mere institutional adaptation to mass democracy, or ideological division over tariff reform, which caused the League's interwar estrangement from mainstream popular conservatism.[5] What is to be stressed is that from the 1880s gender relations were often of a conflictual nature within the League, and even more so during the Edwardian years. If indeed the League served as a political school for many Conservative women, the lesson they were taught constituted a caveat against the male complacency and female subservience which characterised the League's gender-integrative approach, which was gradually repudiated by female activists within the party.

'The alphabet of public duty': Primrose Dames and Victorian female citizenship

To understand the later impact of suffragism upon the League, it is necessary to delineate the movement's early attitude towards the question and to address the wider issue of female citizenship within the League. How was League neutrality over female suffrage articulated with women's prominence in the movement? On what grounds did Conservative women justify their involvement?

Both female suffrage and female citizenship proved divisive issues for the League. As regards suffragism, what first needs to be considered is how 'neutrality' was asserted, and how divisions over it appeared within the League. As for female citizenship, League ambiguities have to be highlighted, as the movement both promoted and circumscribed women's involvement in politics. Conservative women's activism within the League coincided with discourses and practices insisting on the womanliness of Tory militancy. Meanwhile, despite women's prominence within the League, which allowed political adversaries to stress its female identity, the League's structure and activities rested upon an approach to gender that remained safely patriarchal. While men kept control of the League, in particular through the exclusively male Grand Council, women shouldered most of the responsibilities at local level. Overall, the way the League functioned constituted an implicit endorsement of the separate spheres to which men and women were supposed to belong.

During its first two decades, the Primrose League was hardly affected by women's suffrage, a subject that was judged beyond the scope of the League's objects, as Grand Council, the League's ruling body, and its female arm, the Ladies' Grand Council, insisted that God, Queen and Empire were all the League was to stand for. Habitations, as local bodies of the League were called, were advised to rule women's suffrage out as potential subject of discussion after it was reported to the Ladies' Grand Council that a debate on the question had been scheduled in Cheyne.[6] In 1888, a pamphlet was issued by the Ladies' Grand Council to make the League's position clear. In *Why Should Women Care for Politics?* women's enfranchisement was brushed aside, while female support for the League was justified along various lines, including temperance, imperial fraternity with 'sister' countries, public morality, charity and religion.[7] Such arguments reconciled female participation in the League to Victorian women's traditional public duties, thus minimising the more controversial implications of Tory women's intrusion into party politics.

Unsurprisingly, the Ladies' Grand Council declined to take part in the suffrage movement, and in the women's movement, of the day. Invited in 1892 by the International Council of Women, a Chicago-based women's organisation, to send delegates to a World's Congress of Representatives, the Ladies' Grand Council turned down the offer, arguing that as part of a wider and mixed body, it had no power to appoint representatives.[8] In a similar vein, in 1888, Lady Sandhurst and Jane Cobden, two leading Liberal ladies, called in vain for the assistance of the Ladies' Grand Council to collect funds for their election as local councillors.[9] Consistently enough, the League did not co-operate with associations belonging to the women's movement, not even with like-minded groups like the Girls' Friendly Society, or the Victoria League, with which the League shared many wealthy patrons.[10] The only women's group with which the Ladies' Grand Council was recorded to co-operate was South Derry's Loyal Women of Ireland.[11] Clearly, for the League's female elites, the priority was unionism, not solidarity with the women's movement.

Leading League ladies also intended to remain aloof from the suffragist movement of the day. In 1886 Frances Power Cobbe, herself a Conservative, solicited help for the suffragist cause from her acquaintances in the Ladies' Grand Council, but her entreaties also failed to elicit a positive response. In her letter to Lady Amherst, Cobbe pointed out the anomalous position of Tory ladies in their enthusiasm for the

League, especially given the alleged ignorance of the newly enlarged electorate:

> The 2,000,000 new electors who will shortly register their votes, and thereby determine in great measure for years to come the destinies of our country, are, as you are well aware, men for the most part ignorant of politics, of economy; of law, of history, and even of the geography of the vast empire over which they will exert influence . . . As a Dame of the Primrose League, it will be your duty to counsel these persons, to win them from the misleading influence of demagogues, and to instruct them so far as may be possible in the alphabet of public duty. We call on you to reflect whether it be well that, while such are enfranchised, women, possessed of the same, or much higher, property qualifications, should be debarred from exercising the same rights? Are women who, like yourself, are deemed fit to instruct voters in their duties, not fit themselves to vote intelligently and honestly?[12]

Cobbe shrewdly reminded Lady Amherst of the suffragist leanings of leading Conservatives, who, according to her, should be lobbied by Primrose Dames to further the cause of female enfranchisement. League authorities nonetheless kept on shirking the issue, which could prove damaging to the movement, as became clear in 1889, when some well-known female figures of the League, including the Duchess of Marlborough and Lady Jennie Churchill, the mother and wife of the League's founder, signed a petition opposed to women's suffrage. This initiative created a stir among the League's female elites, and it prompted one anonymous Dame President to express her disapproval in the columns of the *Women's Suffrage Journal*. Her condemnation highlights the assumptions of some of the League's ladies, for whom commitment to the Tory cause via the League was expected to forward enfranchisement:

> When I became a Dame of the Primrose League, it was with the hope, a hope shared by many others, that if we worked successfully for the League, our reward would be the vote. In the division where I reside there is no doubt the dames of the Primrose League 'lifted in' the candidate, as he himself expressed it. Notwithstanding the really hard work of the Dames, they are still to be kept as 'hewers of wood and drawers of water', as one of our presidents [the Dowager Duchess of Marlborough] has protested against our being allowed our political freedom.[13]

This controversy proved how potentially divisive an issue women's enfranchisement was, as female promoters of the Primrose League had diverging opinions on the subject. The issue of women's rights to vote at parliamentary elections was thus avoided, but the view of citizenship circulated within the League had much in common with that lofty appreciation of the vote as an imperial – thus manly – trust which featured prominently among the Antis' arsenal of arguments against women's vote.[14]

Women's involvement in the League was all the same accompanied by the assertion of some degree of female citizenship. The extent of female participation in the League and the wide range of political work performed by Primrose Dames proved a powerful instrument for female enfranchisement. Primrose Dames, as once stated in the *Primrose League Gazette*, gained by their exertion 'useful converts' to the cause of women's suffrage, an issue that was not altogether concealed from Primrose League audiences, as Lord Salisbury and Sir Michael Hicks-Beach among others declared themselves favourable to some degree of female enfranchisement during Primrose League meetings, with hosts of Conservative ladies in attendance, while Arthur Balfour expressed support for women's participation in political debate.[15]

The League also served as a vehicle of political apprenticeship for Tory women. The League offered canvassing classes to its female members, and female speakers were regularly featured during habitation meetings, although some of these orators claimed that for womanliness's sake, their dabbling with public speaking was preferably to be performed within the context of informal gatherings:

> Public speaking is manifestly out of our province, so far at least, as the addressing of very large meetings is concerned. Neither by constitution, nor by taste and feeling are we adapted for the part of sharing in the gladiatorial combats of the platform.[16]

Primrose Dames and their Wardens, local district officers in charge of circulating Primrose League literature and collecting tributes, as subscriptions were called, indeed tended to relish At-Homes, those small-scale meetings during which they met with Associates, as rank-and-file members were named, and busied themselves embroidering League banners.

However, the League cannot be discarded as popular conservatism with just an ornamental feminine tinge about it. True enough, some Dame Presidents limited their commitment to a few cameo appearances to award Special Clasps to deserving canvassers.[17] But a sizeable proportion of local officials, acting as Ruling Councilloresses, Honorary Secretaries[18] or Wardens,[19] were women. Such female commitment and visibility contributed to gradually extend the boundaries of female participation to politics. For instance, when the advent of the Primrose Dame spurred debate on women's part in politics, well-known Primrose Dames wrote articles to legitimise their participation in this new Tory machine.[20] Through the League, some Conservative lady orators gained rhetorical proficiency on the platform, and the movement could boast such dedicated political entrepreneurs as Miss Milner, sister of a local Conservative candidate from York, who founded no less than twelve habitations in her area and who made regular platform appearances all over Yorkshire. Actually, Primrose Dames were often more active and committed than their male counterparts, who proved more receptive to the lure of Conservative clubs, male-only amenities offering the three Bs, beer, billiards and bridge.[21] This often gave rise to tensions between Conservative men and women, as both candidates and agents hailed women as more committed than their male colleagues. Within the League, women were often the most dedicated members. Evidence taken from the Garstang Habitation of the League shows that over a period of sixteen years of existence, female members were likely to be the most faithful activists, as 73 per cent of those paying their yearly tributes for more than ten consecutive years were women.[22]

Active female citizenship was also recognised and encouraged by League authorities, which canvassed female members entitled to vote for School Boards or local Councils.[23] Female voters were reminded of the relevance of such local contests over which loomed the threat of an increasingly secularised educational system, a process actively antagonised by the League. Primrose Dames and Associates were not only recognised in their civic rights and their role as guardians to the young. They were expected to be active militants, during and between elections, acting as political instructors to the newly enfranchised.[24] Primrose Dames also worked as canvassers, as women were considered particularly suited for such activities, for which womanly patience, courtesy and empathy with the electorate constituted crucial assets. ('The visiting lady, being well-known amongst the poor, will be listened to with more interest, and her words will carry more weight, than even the candidate himself', contended one leading Primrose Dame.)[25] Female involvement in electoral work actually increased over the years, as the League became more and more present in electioneering, which means that by the end of the century, female canvassers of the Primrose League had become stock characters of electoral contests.[26]

The League, although not part of the women's movement as such, was thus publicly identified with its female element.[27] The female identity with which the movement was rapidly associated explains why attacks on the League by political opponents often turned out to be of a gendered nature. For example, the League's medieval trappings were derided because of the appeal they exerted upon the female imagination as illustrated by this lampoon published in the liberal *Liverpool Review*: 'Stop, ye "buckram Knights" and silly "Dames",/Your masquerading with medieval names'. In such a perspective, the League's success could be ascribed to womanly subservience to fashion, but it could equally be debunked as a token of womanly deference towards religion and social hierarchy. The same paper later published taunts against Primrose Knights, which appear to be similarly based on gendered assumptions. During the 1885 elections, the *Liverpool Review* gleefully reported that a little band of Primrose League canvassers happened to be pelted with bricks and eggs by Radical miners in the Skelmersdale area. The incident, according to the paper, 'had a disturbing influence' on the Knights, who were said to find the Skelmersdale men 'rather energetic'.[28] What the episode suggests is a contrast between the male boisterousness of those working-class hecklers and the League's 'feminised' male members, who stand out as inexperienced and ignominiously rattled by an ordinary eruption of partisan violence. However, Radical jeers could also turn to sneers, and the League's female dimension could be portrayed in darker hues, especially when Primrose League ladies were accused of boycotting Radical shopkeepers. Liberal ladies were equally scathing about their Tory rivals, whose evasion of women's issues contrasted with Liberal women's groups, which debated suffrage and other women's issues.[29]

If the League did not directly address women's franchise, distribution of power within the League provides a clear indication of how female citizenship and its appropriate sphere were conceived within the movement. Up until 1918, Grand Council remained male-only, while the Ladies' Grand Council, although a generous contributor to the League's annual budget, remained under its supervision. Even if the League integrated women into Tory circles, these were treated as junior partners, and even sometimes as an unreliable workforce, as indicated by those disparaging remarks written by George Lane-Fox, the League's Vice-Chancellor from 1889 to 1912, to his cousin Jack Sandars, Balfour's private secretary, about the unpreparedness of Tory activists: 'The ignorance about the "Estates of the Realm" is nearly as great as about the Christian religion, even among educated people (especially women).'

Throughout its first twenty years of existence, the League was altogether spared from the type of divisions over women's suffrage that were experienced by Liberal ladies, who were split between rival suffragist and non-suffragist bodies.[30] In the Edwardian years, in a context of heightened polarisation over women's suffrage, the League's evasion of the issue became an increasingly untenable position.

The Primrose League and the 'subsidiary question' in the Edwardian years

While in the Victorian era the issue of female suffrage did not seriously disrupt the League, the same cannot be said about the Edwardian years. From the early century onwards, the League was faced with a difficult situation. Indeed, as the Conservative Party was divided by constant infighting between its protectionist and its free-trade wing, the League was also faced with the renewed salience of female suffragism. As suffragist groups gained strength and radicalised their methods, the days when the League was preserved from the controversy of female suffrage appeared to be over.

First of all, the League – and in particular its female membership – were explicitly targeted by suffragist activism. For example, on a poster published in 1908 by the National Union of Women's Suffrage Societies, the Primrose League is one of the groups threatened with boycott.[31] Prior to this, League members were identified as potential helpers to the suffragist cause, which explains why in 1906, the NUWSS asked Grand Council permission to get hold of the Rolls of Habitations, League documents with the names of local officers, in order to send circular letters calling on League female executives for help. Naturally, Grand Council turned down the offer, as it feared that suffragists might poach female workers away from the Conservative cause.[32] Calls for co-operation with suffragist groups also came from within the League, for instance when Frederick Rose, Kensington Habitation's former Ruling Councillor, suggested to Grand Council that the League should combine forces with the Women's Social and Political Union to obtain Women's Suffrage. Grand Council had to remind this suffragist enthusiast of the League's strict neutrality in regard to questions considered outside its province.[33]

What was the attitude of grassroots members of the League? There were signs both of sympathy with and condemnation of suffragettes, evidence that suffragism indeed divided Primrose League members. Suffragist rhetoric seems to have struck a chord among Primrose ladies, as incidents related to the suffrage controversy were more frequently reported to Grand Council by dismayed Ruling Councillors and Provincial Secretaries. For instance, in March 1909, the Deputy Ruling Councillor of the Streatham Habitation informed Grand Council that two members of the habitation had been arrested whilst trying to force an entrance into the Houses of Parliament. Grand Council subsequently urged the habitation to demand the Primrose suffragists' immediate resignation.[34] In October 1910, a member of the Fleet Habitation faced a similar fate after stating in a letter to Grand Council that she considered it her duty to support a socialist against a unionist candidate if the socialist supported women's suffrage.[35] In December 1910, North Cumberland's Divisional Council reported that some wardens had proved 'so keen about Women's Suffrage that they sat at home during the Election in Carlisle'.[36]

Simultaneously, Antis' feeling surfaced within the League as suffragists radicalised their methods. 'Since the last action taken by the suffragettes, I have come to think that no treatment is too bad for them', Mrs Grace Hutchinson wrote to Grand Council, to which she suggested devising a leaflet on 'Women's Suffrage' in order to 'ridicule the Radical chivalry'.[37] More than ever, leading Primrose League ladies were divided over the issue. Active membership of the Ladies' Grand Council included such well-known Antis as Lady Jersey, Viscountess Midleton and Lady Talbot, but also some of the most prominent Conservative suffragists, like Betty Balfour or Lady Knightley of Fawsley.

Inevitably, for Conservative suffragists, conflicting priorities meant that resignation was often the only option. In 1910, Betty Balfour resigned her Dame Presidency of Surrey's Chertsey Habitation because of the local MP's vote against the Franchise Bill. Betty Balfour chose to remain loyal to the League, as she retained her title of President of Ladies' Grand Council and kept on attending its yearly meetings until the war. But she publicly justified her action in Chertsey in a letter to *The Times*, in which she stated that it would have been an 'absurdity' for her to go on supporting Donald Macmaster, the MP involved in this controversy, who openly questioned the legitimacy of women's suffrage.[38] Macmaster replied to this statement by reminding Balfour that obviously her loyalty to the CUWFA had outweighed her commitment to the League. 'May it not be that there are duties even greater, more serious, and more pressing than voting for woman's suffrage?', Macmaster wrote, adding to support his case that he believed that a majority of women did not actually desire the vote.[39]

League authorities were aware of the damage that the suffrage controversy could entail, and they attempted to limit it in various ways. Keen to preserve unity within its ranks, Grand Council issued a joint statement with the Conservative and Unionist Franchise Association, which was published in *The Times* in 1909. In it, Grand Council insisted that 'women's suffrage was a question of opinion and not of principle', and was as such 'outside the scope of the League as a body'. Primrose ladies were allowed to sign petitions either in favour or against female enfranchisement, to take part in suffragist or anti-suffragist meetings. However, Tory suffragists were also reminded that they had to be prepared not to work against official Unionist candidates, whatever the candidates' personal position on the issue of suffrage.[40] Silent over suffragist pressure from without, the League was not to tolerate pressure from within. League authorities attempted to control the damage suffragism could bring about, first by taking a firm line against suffragist assertiveness. Faced with fresh reports of suffragist feeling within the League, Grand Council issued the following warning to habitation officers: 'Unless Wardens are prepared to place the Constitution and the Empire before a subsidiary question like Women's Suffrage, they should be called upon to resign.'[41]

But the League also reasserted its identity as a group open to male participation, in order to dispel the idea that the Primrose League was a women-dominated body. Grand Council started drawing attention to the fact that men were taking part in its workings, and that women could not be considered as the only committed activists within the movement. 'Those who are inclined to regard the Primrose League as a Ladies' Association will be interested in the Peckham return: in the work of that election, twenty-eight habitations took part, and there were 406 workers, of whom 267 were men and 139 women', Grand Council pointed out after a by-election in 1908.[42] Furthermore, as it had been observed for some years that the League found it difficult to attract young men into its ranks, an *Appeal to Young Men of England* was distributed. The leaflet was intended for young Tory 'cricketers, footballers and golfers' who were keen 'to play the game and come out like a man to help us in our campaign for God, King and Country', to see 'fair play for all classes, as contrasted with one-sided legislation by a Radical-Socialist Party' and 'to knock up a good score for the Empire'. It also encouraged the 'Young Men of England' who did not wish 'to wait until the enemy [had] opened our stable door and stolen our steeds' to feel concerned for the defence of the 'Mother Land, to which you owe so much affection and allegiance as to the human mother that reared you'.[43] At a time when the League's female component became less reliable, League authorities hoped to lessen the League's dependency upon its female workforce by enrolling more men, who were presented with a rather muscular version of popular conservatism.

To restore the movement's 'manliness', Grand Council also encouraged the creation of male-only bodies within the League. Grand Council for example supported the Knights' Imperial Chapter, which had been created in 1894. This gentlemen's club within the League organised dinners, with Conservative MPs, Grand Council members and public figures, like

Rudyard Kipling, on the guest list.[44] Grand Council actively promoted this new male-only agency for a number of reasons. First, the Knights' Imperial's generosity to the League counterbalanced the Ladies' Grand Council's usual largesse with the movement. Indeed, from 1904 onwards, the Knights' Imperial made a yearly donation of £500, which equalled the Ladies' Grand Council's own share of Primrose League finances. The Knights' Imperial could also be called to act as arbitrators in case of disputes between habitations.[45] In 1913, when the League's organisation came under review, Grand Council continued its support for the League's exclusively male body and it called its Provincial Secretaries to extend the local influence of Imperial Chapters.[46] Walter Long, who acted as the League's Chancellor at the time, made sure that a Primrose League representative was to accompany him during a tour to Canada, Australia and New Zealand to create Chapters on colonial soil.[47] Similarly, Grand Council also agreed to the creation of men-only habitations, such as the one gathering old boys from public schools, or that designed for graduates of the then exclusively male University of Cambridge.[48] This masculinisation pursued by Grand Council also affected the League's junior branches, and Grand Council registered with satisfaction the rise of Primrose League Boy Scouts, which appeared among its youth section for girls and boys, the Primrose Buds.[49]

How far did the suffrage controversy affect the League in terms of membership? To judge from figures recorded by the League's headquarters, the movement was in fact going through some form of Indian summer. While in the last years of Balfour's Conservative government, yearly enrolment stood at around 20 000 new members, this figure reached 60 000 in 1906, then 100 000 in 1910, and never fell below 40 000 before 1914.[50] It is hard to estimate if women proved more or less enthusiastic than men, as no data kept by Grand Council distinguished male and female Associates. But by 1910, the number of Dames (80 038) had almost caught up with that of Knights (87 235). The League's renewed popularity was linked to its Victorian motto still relevant to the Edwardian era. In an age of House of Lords reform, international tensions, rising domestic socialism and Liberal Education Acts, 'God, King and Country' offered a suitable rallying cry for Conservatives. With its principles visibly assailed, the League's blend of imperial, constitutionalist and religious conservatism was undeniably an asset, as the significant rise in membership figures shows. However, the rejuvenation experienced by the League barely concealed the seriousness of one Edwardian change in the conservative machinery, namely the rise of women's groups. From the Edwardian years onwards, the thorniest issue for the League was indeed how to deal with the rise of women-based political organisations, a phenomenon that gathered strength exactly when suffragette militancy was at its peak, and when tensions increased within the movement.

The League and the postwar demise of cross-gender party structures

The Edwardian years coincided with increased gender-related tensions within the League, and with the emergence of women-only Conservative groups, which attracted more and more women. The combination of both processes gradually weakened the League, and paved the way for its post-1918 marginalisation within Conservative groups.

First, during the years before the Great War, what disrupted the League was a greater degree of assertiveness on the part of Primrose Dames, who repeatedly denounced the absence of female representation in the governing body of the movement. As early as 1905, Honorary Secretaries asked Grand Council to have a greater say and share in the League's governing instances. Later, when the League was overhauled during the 1910–11 reform of the party, Grand Council briefly considered the possibility of admitting women among its elected representatives, but the proposal was pigeon-holed until it was finally adopted in 1918, a few months after women over the age of 30 were enfranchised by the Representation of the People Act. As late as 1918, the Ladies' Grand Council had to arm-twist Grand Council into taking that long-awaited decision, ironically enough at a time when it was Lord Curzon, a notorious Anti, who held the title of Grand Master of the League. The new rules devised in 1918 nonetheless limited women's seats on Grand Council to one-third of the number of yearly elected delegates.[51]

Grand Council's belated move showed how much gender and power within the League's governing bodies were prickly subjects. At habitation level, the League also had a long history of gender-related tensions, and gender relations were often tense. This could sometimes give rise to gender-segregated structures, such as Dames' habitations. There were few of these women-only bodies within the League, largely because Grand Council did not approve of such initiatives, smacking as they did of female independence. Still, as early as the 1890s, there were 33 such habitations, a somewhat meagre tally when compared to the 1200 habitations that were then in existence. The typical Dames' habitation was located in a medium-sized town or in a city, in London, the south and Lancashire and Yorkshire, where Conservative ladies of independent means were in sufficient number to organise a League habitation by and for themselves.[52] Dames' habitations also tended to be localised where local Conservative Associations were strong and in existence prior to the advent of the League. In such cases, Conservative men chose to keep women at bay by channelling their enthusiasm for the Tory cause towards separate bodies.

However, separateness was actively discouraged by Grand Council, which was keen to preserve unity and harmony between the sexes and consequently mistrusted women-only groups. In 1886, for example, the *Primrose Record* mooted the creation of a Primrose Club for gentlemen located in the League's London headquarters. In the following issue of the League's official newspaper, a 'Country Dame' wrote to suggest the creation of a Primrose Club for ladies, where female members of the League 'could get some luncheon or tea, have their parcels sent to, and meet their friends. I think it ought to be for ladies only, or else it would do away with the principal object, which is to have a place where a lady can go alone.'[53] Neither initiative materialised, given Grand Council's insistence that it was 'not desirable to divorce the sexes'. When rivalries between men and women belonging to the same habitation produced splits, which happened for example in Brighton in 1886, Grand Council suggested the following solution: 'let one habitation be that for the ladies managing with the assistance of some gentlemen, the other that for the gentlemen managing with the assistance of some ladies'.[54] While such incidents remained rare in the League's Victorian heyday, during the years corresponding to the height of the suffrage campaign, gender-based tensions greatly increased. Provincial secretaries reported growing resentment between Primrose ladies and gentlemen to Grand Council. In Cuckfield, League gentlemen talked of disbanding the habitation and of forming a men's Conservative association instead, 'as an opinion prevailed that women were of no political use', the League's provincial secretary told Grand Council.[55] In a context of exacerbated tension between Conservative men and women, Ruling Councillors were reminded that standard practice within the League required that joint gatherings should be preferred over female or male-only meetings.[56]

What caused concern in League high circles was the rise of rival, women-only Conservative groups. From 1905 onwards, provincial secretaries started reporting to the League's headquarters that in a number of localities, Primrose ladies scuttled their habitation for women-only associations. In Gillingham, Primrose ladies seceded from the habitation and formed a Women's Unionist Association after the male officers refused to grant them greater representation in the habitation's or the local part's Executive Council.[57]

George Lane-Fox, the League's Vice-Chancellor, was sufficiently preoccupied about this to call for Balfour's help. Lane-Fox, who remained a loyal supporter of Balfour and a critic of tariff reformers, first ascribed increased League disunity to Chamberlain's allies and their manoeuvres to gain control of the party:

> In a good many places, the Tariff Reform people are trying to get Primrose League women away from Habitations and into what they call Unionist Associations but which are really Tariff Reform affairs and it is now clear that all Fiscal people put their Fiscalities before the cause of either God or Country, and until they are put to death there will never be Union in our great party.[58]

But Lane-Fox later realised that the same policy was pursued by the National Union of Conservative Associations, which meant that the party itself was taking part in this strategy of bringing Conservative women into its fold. Lane-Fox pointed out to Sandars how counter-productive this could be for the party:

> The new so-called organisation of the National Union seems to mean in several places simply the formation of 'Women's Conservative Associations' to work against the Primrose League, which is not likely to benefit the party and is causing friction in places and any man who sets women fighting against women in the same army will do more harm than all the Radical associations ever did.[59]

Of course, Lane-Fox was to some extent right to perceive the rise of women's Conservative groups as a side-effect of the party's infighting between tariff-reforming Chamberlainites and Balfourites. The new bodies that then appeared had indeed a clear-cut position on the question of tariff reform, very much unlike the League's 'round-about, ill-defined' stance.[60]

For many Conservative women, if tariff reform could constitute the initial incentive to join those other groups, their move away from the League was also inspired by gender-related considerations. Indeed, Women's Unionist Associations and Women's Unionist Tariff Reform Associations (WUTRAs), which worked independently from men, could count upon a network of full-time female agents, as they were funded by women themselves, with the support of the Tariff Reform League or the Conservative Central Office. Conservative women were thus offered the chance to exert more influence over the local parties, and quite crucially over candidate selection, than the Primrose League could, given its institutional separateness from the party machine proper. Unlike the League, these new Conservative groups thus provided Conservative women with a heady mixture of influence over the party machine, financial and organisational autonomy from their male colleagues and freedom to discuss a wider array of subjects than the League allowed.

Faced with such ominous prospects of extinction, League authorities tried to stem the process in various ways. First, provincial secretaries were asked to do all they could to thwart the creation of local WUO branches. It soon appeared that the strategy failed, as this produced hostility towards the League among constituency agents, who often instigated the creation of WUOs.[61] The League then requested the party to broker a compromise solution between itself and those rival bodies.[62] By the end of the Great War, it was obvious that Grand Council was fighting a losing battle, and instead of opposing the rise of WUOs, which boasted thousands of members in the interwar years, the League started emphasising what by then constituted the League's specificity among Conservative agencies, namely its refusal of gender and age segregation. 'The Primrose League is the only Conservative organisation in which Father, Mother and Children can be members. It is an organisation for the family', insisted Grand Council in the 1930s.[63]

Even if many other factors explain the League's downfall, such as the growing irrelevance of its Victorian principles, with the postwar coinciding with increasing secularisation of political debate and indifference towards the Empire, the rise of gender-based structures was a serious blow to the League. League authorities tried to stem the rise of independent female organisations within the Conservative galaxy, but to no avail. For Conservative women, the League was an outdated organisational model, which offered them fewer prospects of political advancement than WUOs did. That the rise of gender-based party structures gathered momentum exactly when suffragist activism peaked shows that suffragism and its agenda of female empowerment not only disrupted the League, but also created a climate of gender polarisation that proved fatal to a movement defined by its insistence on welcoming both men and women.

Conclusion

If until the early twentieth century the Primrose League successfully curbed the divisiveness of the franchise issue within its ranks, the agitation engineered by Edwardian suffragists affected the movement. From 1905 onwards, many Conservative women chose to join WUOs because these groups proved more appealing to them, as they allowed access to the party machine, to party schools, and to party funds. The separation between men and women and the greater resources that these new associations offered to Conservative women explain why Conservative activists preferred to leave the League.

However, the battle for female empowerment did not end with the interwar success of WUOs, which reached one million members by 1934. Organisational separateness from Conservative men did not mean that Conservative women could finally exert the amount of influence that their sheer number justified. Throughout the interwar years, Conservative men and women continued to vie for influence over the party. Female agents were viewed with both jealousy and anxiety by male agents who tried to limit their scope of action, while many men resented the presence of women in the local parties' executive councils and selection committees.

As for the League, its evolution in the interwar years increased the gap that separated it from the increasingly female complexion of popular conservatism. Indeed, the party tried to formulate a programme designed to appeal to women voters, with a great deal of reforming zeal carried out in the direction of childcare, widows' pensions and health reforms. Conservative propaganda was also fashioned so as to consider women, with less emphasis placed upon imperial issues. Under the leadership of Baldwin and Neville Chamberlain, Conservative priorities shifted towards a feminised version of Conservatism, as some historians of interwar Conservatism have argued.[64]

But the League was little affected by this evolution. Indeed, it continued to neglect women's issues, and cantered its public discourse on anti-socialism, anti-alienism, imperial unity and the duties of citizenship.[65] Faithful to its prewar ethos of imperial grandeur and patriotic feelings, the League propounded its own male and traditional brand of conservatism, which was increasingly at odds with the party's official positions. This process of estrangement between the League and mainstream popular conservatism was reinforced by the League's rightward lurch, with Henry Page-Croft and Winston Churchill acting as the League's figureheads in the late 1920s. So in spite of a greater infusion of women on the League's Grand Council from 1918, the League came to embody a high-and-dry Conservatism that did little to accommodate women and facilitate their involvement in the movement.

Notes

1. Studies on Conservative women have usually treated women's inclusion in the Primrose League as a success story, and as evidence of Conservatism's

appeal to women. On the League's appeal to female audiences, see Beatrix Campbell, *The Iron Ladies: Why Do Women Vote Tory?* (London: Virago, 1987); G. E. Maguire, *Conservative Women: a History of Women and the Conservative Party, 1874–1997* (London: Macmillan/Saint Anthony's Series, 1998).

2. See for instance this statement by Martin Pugh: 'In view of their extensive traditional role as allied forces of the party in bodies such as the Primrose League and the Tariff Reform League it is not surprising that Conservative women adapted to the post-war system with little friction.' M. Pugh, *Women and the Women's Movement in Britain, 1918–59* (London: Macmillan, 1992), pp. 124–5.
3. For Martin Pugh, Primrose Dames 'reconciled Conservatives to women in politics long before 1918'. M. Pugh, *The Tories and the People, 1880–1935* (Oxford: Blackwell, 1985), p. 43.
4. Martin Pugh thus sees the League's decline as related to the necessity for the party not to leave such a mighty political machine outside the official party structure. For him, in the interwar years, the party 'simply adopted the practice, as well as the personnel of the Primrose League'. Pugh, *The Tories and the People*, p. 178. However, this begs the question of why it is that after 1918 Conservative men and women worked in separate bodies, and no longer in organisations open to both genders, as was the case within the League.
5. Recent studies on Conservative women have similarly highlighted the controversial dimension of gender within the party, while emphasising the difficulties encountered by female Conservative activists as far as their integration in the party was concerned. See for example D. Jarvis, 'The Conservative Party and the Politics of Gender, 1900–1939', in M. Francis and I. Zweiniger-Bargielowska (eds), *The Conservatives and British Society 1880–1990* (Cardiff: University of Wales Press, 1996), pp. 172–93; John Brennan, 'The Conservative Party in the Constituencies, 1918–1939', PhD, Oxford, 1994.
6. Primrose League Papers, Bodleian Library, Ladies' Grand Council (hereafter LGC), 27 April 1888.
7. *Why Should Women Care for Politics?* (London: Primrose League, 1888), Pamphlet Collection, British Library of Political and Economic Science (BLPES).
8. LGC, 9 December 1892.
9. LGC, 7 December 1888.
10. For the overlapping membership between the League and other imperial bodies, see 'Appendix 2: Female Imperialist Networks', in Julia Bush, *Edwardian Ladies and Imperial Power* (London: Leicester University Press, 2000), pp. 213–15. The League's imperialism was of a more sentimental complexion than the constructive imperialism advocated by the Victoria League, a women-only group that gathered both Unionist and Liberal Unionist ladies and which tackled such subjects as social reform, which the Primrose League neglected. On the Victoria League, see Eliza Reidi, 'Women, Gender, and the Promotion of Empire: the Victoria League, 1901–1914', *Historical Journal*, 45, 3 (2002), pp. 569–99.
11. LGC, 14 April 1893. A canvassing tour of northern England was arranged with those loyalist ladies from Ulster. Sisterly compassion with Ulster women reappeared within the League during the Home Rule crisis of 1913 and 1914. In 1913, the League set up a scheme to undertake the charge of the Ulster

women and children in the event of hostilities, with £12 000 collected for the purpose in April 1914, by which date the League started distributing 2 million forms of a Women's Covenant for Ulster. Irish women clearly formed an exception for the League, which usually abstained from co-operating with women's groups and from taking up women's issues. After the war, League authorities remained keen to be separate from the women's movement, and Grand Council refused to let League representatives take part in a women's demonstration of the League of Nations Union, or to let the Primrose League's name be appended to a message to America, arguing that the League 'belonged to both sexes'. Primrose League Papers, Bodleian Library, Grand Council (hereafter GC), 6 November 1913, 3 April 1914, 2 November 1921.

12. Letter from Frances Power Cobbe, 20 February 1886, Lady Amherst Papers, Coll. Misc 569, BLPES.
13. *Women's Suffrage Journal*, 2 September 1889, quoted in Patricia Hollis (ed.), *Women in Public 1850–1900: Documents of the Victorian Women's Movement* (London: George Allen & Unwin, 1979), p. 328.
14. The following remarks, made by Colonel Eyre, the local Conservative MP, at a meeting of the Wiverton Habitation, are a standard League pronouncement on the importance of the vote: 'They, as electors, were trustees of the most gigantic empire which the world has ever seen, and its prosperity was affected by the vote of every individual elector. It was a trust which should not be trifled with'. *Primrose League Gazette*, 28 November 1891, p. 9. For the Antis' insistence upon the imperial dimension of the vote, see Brian Harrison, *Separate Spheres: the Opposition to Women's Suffrage in Britain* (London: Croom Helm, 1978), p. 34.
15. For Salisbury's favourable pronouncement on women's suffrage, see *Primrose League Gazette*, 15 December 1888, p. 5. For Balfour, see *The Times*, 15 November 1895, p. 6. Typically, Balfour refused to take a clear stance over women's suffrage, arguing that it was too divisive an issue, and that as such it had to remain a matter of personal appreciation rather than official party policy. In the same speech, he questioned the legitimacy of women's appearance on electoral platforms, and preferred to see them perform patient work *between* elections. Still, Balfour recognised that 'women had a right to make their influence felt through the electoral machinery of the country'.
16. Mrs Courtenay Lord, wife of the Ruling Councillor of the Burnaby Habitation in Birmingham, *Primrose League Gazette*, 19 November 1887, p. 3.
17. One typical example of such absenteeism may be taken from the Garstang Habitation of Lancashire, whose Dame President, the Countess of Bective, failed to take part in habitation meetings. Preston, Lancashire Record Office, Garstang Primrose League Habitation (DDFz), Habitation Minute Book, 1894–1910.
18. Urban areas had the lowest proportion of female officers acting as Dame Presidents or Honorary Secretaries, as female deputy Ruling Councillors were called. For example, in London, Liverpool, Manchester and Blackpool, out of a total of 298 local officers, only 31 were women, while in such rural regions as Westmorland, Cumberland, Lincolnshire, Rutland, Monmouthshire, Wiltshire and Cornwall, the number of female and male officers was practically identical, *Roll of Habitations* (London: MacCorquodale, 1890).

19. Many women worked as League wardens who acted as cog-wheels within the organisation: their task was to keep Associates informed of the activities of the League and to collect subscriptions from them. Still, in rural habitations spanning larger territory, men were often preferred for the job. 'Although several Dames, at the special request of the council, were invited to canvass, it was considered best that all the Wardens should be men', as was reported to the Ladies' Grand Council by officers of the Bayham Habitation, which comprised 19 parishes in a 30-square-mile agricultural district of Sussex and Kent. LGC, 6 January 1886.
20. See for instance Susan Malmesbury, 'The Primrose League', *National Review*, May 1886, pp. 413–18.
21. See Jarvis, 'The Conservative Party and the Politics of Gender, 1900–1939', p. 178. On the gendered nature of Conservative sociability, see also Jon Lawrence 'Class and Gender in the Making of Urban Toryism, 1880–1914', *English Historical Review*, 108 (1993), pp. 629–52.
22. Preston, Lancashire Record Office, Garstang Primrose League Habitation (DDFz), Register of Members, 1894–1910.
23. LGC, 23 November 1888; GC, 4 October 1906, 18 October 1906.
24. Education was considered as a fitting pursuit for the League's female workers. 'Now the awakening political influence and capacity of women have found a just and fitting outlet in aiding the work of political education, which it is one of the main objects of the Primrose League to carry on all over the country', the pamphlet claimed, thus stressing women's educational mission within the League. Attributing this particular task to Primrose Dames enabled the League to euphemise the partisan dimension of its Dames' exertions, and to ascribe to women duties that seemed appropriate to their traditional role. *Why Should Women Care for Politics?* (London: Primrose League, 1888).
25. 'Lady Maidstone on Primrose Work', *Primrose Record*, 15 October 1885, p. 138.
26. I am grateful to Kathryn Rix for having pointed out this fact to me. On the relationship between the League and Conservative agents, see Kathryn Rix, 'The Party Agent and English Electoral Culture, 1880–1906', PhD, Cambridge, 2001.
27. This fact was noted by *Punch*, which published a cartoon representing two respectable ladies discussing in the street the latest election results: 'I am very glad Sir Percy Plantagenet was returned, Miss!', says the elder one, a remark that prompts the younger to inquire: 'Why, Are you a Primrose Dame?' 'No, Miss, – by my 'usband is!', replies the elder lady, *Punch*, 27 August 1892, p. 90. A cartoon entitled 'Candidate Catching' similarly represents the League under its female guise, as the drawing in question shows a Primrose Dame busy catching a candidate with a butterfly net, *Punch*, 14 May 1892, p. 239.
28. *Liverpool Review*, 5 December 1885, p. 6.
29. For a detailed comparison between Primrose Dames and their Liberal opponents, see Linda Walker 'Party Political Women: a Comparative Study of Liberal Women and the Primrose League, 1890–1914', in Jane Rendall (ed.), *Equal or Different: Women's Politics 1800–1914* (Oxford: Basil Blackwell, 1987), pp. 165–91.
30. For Liberal women's divisions over suffrage, see Claire Hirschfield, 'Fractured Faith: Liberal Party Women and the Suffrage Issue in Britain, 1892–1914', *Gender and History*, 2, 2 (1990), pp. 173–97.

31. For a published reproduction of the poster, see Lisa Tickner, *The Spectacle of Women: Imagery of the Suffrage Campaign 1907–1914* (London: Chatto & Windus, 1987), p. 17.
32. The League's Rolls of Habitations were equally coveted by tariff reformers, who in 1906 asked Grand Council for access to such a crucial source of intelligence, but to no avail, as Grand Council was careful to protect the League from such intrusion by rival organisations. GC, 8 March 1906.
33. GC, 7 November 1907.
34. GC, 4 March 1909.
35. GC, 6 October 1910.
36. GC, 22 December 1910.
37. GC, 6 February 1908. What Mrs Hutchinson had in mind was probably attempts by some Radical clubs to express sympathy for the suffragist cause.
38. 'Lady Betty Balfour and the Primrose League', *The Times*, 30 July 1910, p. 8.
39. *The Times*, 6 August 1910, p. 10.
40. 'Woman Suffrage. The Primrose League. Correspondence of the Conservative and Unionist Women's Franchise Association and the Primrose League', *The Times*, 27 October 1909, p. 9.
41. GC, 22 December 1910.
42. GC, 2 April 1908.
43. *For God, King and Country. A Primrose League Appeal to the Young Men of England* (London: Primrose League/James Truscott, n.d.), Pamphlet Collection, BLPES.
44. To judge from reports on attendance addressed to Grand Council, the Knights of the Imperial Chapter seems to have been a very Anti affair, as some of the party's most prominent Antis like Lord Curzon, Lord Cromer, Austen Chamberlain and Andrew Bonar Law were members. The Imperial Chapter had 1391 Knights on its roll in November 1904, with an aggregate membership of 1806 Knights since its foundation in 1894. GC, 28 November 1904.
45. An example of such gentlemanly arbitration on the part of Knights' Imperial occurred in North Devon in November 1905, when two habitations were on the verge of both falling into abeyance owing to rivalry between their women members. GC, 30 November 1905.
46. Confidential Draft Report to Grand Council, GC, 13 March 1913.
47. GC, 14 April 1913.
48. GC, 8 October 1908.
49. GC, 24 June 1909.
50. For tables showing yearly enrolment in the Edwardian years, see Philippe Vervaecke, *Dieu, la Couronne et l'Empire: La Primrose League, 1883–2000. Culture et pratiques politiques d'un mouvement conservateur*, Thèse, Lille 3, 2003, p. 230.
51. In fact, from 1918 onwards, women usually accounted for *more* than a third of representatives attending Grand Council meetings. For example, at the meeting held on 3 June 1937, there were 38 women present out of a total attendance of 71. GC, 3 June 1937.
52. See Pugh, *The Tories and the People*, Appendices V–XVIII, Table of Habitations, pp. 216–51.
53. *Primrose Record*, 17 April 1886, p. 390.
54. GC, 2 June 1887.
55. GC, 15 November 1906.

56. Letter to Sir Gerald Codrington, Ruling Councillor of the Codrington Habitation, from Henry Lancaster, Provincial Secretary for Oxfordshire, Berkshire, Gloucestershire, Wiltshire and Wales, 12 November 1910, Gloucester RO, D1610/X31,
57. Similar events were reported in Ipswich, Halifax, St Albans and Accrington, to mention but a few of the localities where such splits occurred. After a period of respite during the Great War, the process gathered pace from 1918 onwards, with Grand Council receiving frequent reports of similar conversion of League habitations into Women's Unionist Associations. GC, 4 March 1909, 3 March 1910, 5 June 1918, 4 July 1918, 19 February 1919.
58. Letter from George Lane-Fox to Jack Sandars, 4 January 1905, Sandars Papers, c. 751, fols 73–74, Bodleian Library.
59. Letter from George Sackville Lane-Fox to Jack Sandars, 10 January 1907, Sandars Papers, c. 753, fols 39–40, Bodleian Library.
60. These are the words used in an interview with members of Grand Council by Miss Garnett, Honorary Secretary of the Wharfdale Habitation of Yorkshire, to define the League's stance on tariff reform. League hesitations over the issue, according to Garnett, caused the departure of Conservative ladies towards other bodies. GC, 15 February 1912.
61. Agents were said to foil League attempts to revive dormant habitations, both before and after the war. GC, 16 January 1908, 7 June 1921.
62. Several meetings took place before and after the war, gathering representatives from the League, members of the Conservative Central Office and leading ladies from WUOs and WUTRAs, which combined their forces in 1913, thus mounting a serious challenge to the League. Female-only Conservative groups pledged not to interfere with existing habitations, and to co-operate with the League rather than compete against it. While at national level those rival governing bodies looked for appeasement, at local level, women nonetheless kept leaving habitations. GC, 14 August 1908, 7 February 1918, 7 June 1921.
63. GC, 5 July 1934.
64. On the feminisation of Conservative rhetoric and propaganda, see D. Jarvis, 'Mrs Maggs and Betty: the Conservative Appeal to Women Voters in the 1920s', *Twentieth Century British History*, 5, 2 (1994), pp. 129–52; Jarvis, 'The Conservative Party and the Politics of Gender, 1900–1939', pp. 172–93.
65. On the evolution of the League in the interwar years, see Matthew Hendley, 'Constructing the Citizen: the Primrose League and the Definition of Citizenship in the Age of Mass Democracy in Britain, 1918–1928', *Journal of the Canadian Historical Association*, 7 (1996), pp. 105–25; Matthew Hendley, 'Anti-Alienism and the Primrose League: the Externalization of the Post-War Crisis in Great Britain 1918–1932', *Albion*, 33, 2 (2001), pp. 243–69.

Part III
Beyond the Structure: Mastering and Discarding Organisational Structures

9
Unionised Women Teachers and Women's Suffrage

Susan Trouvé-Finding

'This year, 1911, is emphatically the women's year in the history of our professional Associations', exclaimed Mr Croft, suffrage motion mover at the Aberystwyth National Union of Teachers (NUT) conference.[1] For women elementary teachers the heyday inside the profession, in local and national instances, and outside, in the women's movement, was the decade from 1910.[2] 'The fact that this year, for the first time in history, every Union of Teachers, including those having a male membership, has a woman as its president, is a sign of the times and a proof that men recognise the merits and qualifications of women', enlarged Christabel Pankhurst.[3] While Isabel Cleghorn (b. 1852, Sheffield Council School Headmistress)[4] became the NUT's first woman president, Miss Eveline Phillips had become President of the mixed National Federation of Assistant Teachers (NFAT). A 'frenzy of delight' and 'feminine enthusiasm' greeted Miss Cleghorn's election as NUT Vice President for 1910 at the Plymouth Conference. 'Ladies could now feel that their functions in the Union were not merely those of paying subscriptions', she stated.[5] Women were coming to the fore in many local associations. Isabel Cleghorn had been elected Sheffield Association President in 1908, as was Kate Hogan in the East Lambeth Association.[6] Liverpool delegate to the NUT Conference since 1897, Miss Essie Conway (b. 1865) was elected President of the Liverpool and District Teachers' Association and member of the NUT Executive for 1910 and President of the powerful 10 000 member-strong Lancashire County Association (second only to the Metropolitan district) in 1911.[7] Miss A. K. Williams was elected as the first woman London teachers' representative on the NUT Executive Committee and to the chair of the influential London Teachers' Association (LTA) on the National Federation of Women Teachers (NFWT) ticket in 1911.[8] She was also treasurer of the London County Council Women Teachers' Union (LCCWTU), twenty members of which were elected to the General Committee of the LTA that year.[9] Miss Morgan became the first lady President of the North Devon Teachers' Association.[10] Mrs Mary E. Ridge became President of the 1300 Hackney Teachers' Association and Miss M. Waterman, on her election as President of the Kettering Association, remarked 'On looking round in Northamptonshire I find our near neighbours, Wellingboro', [Miss E Walker] and a distant association Daventry, have likewise chosen women for presidents for 1912. It is a sign of the times that woman is taking a place hitherto reserved almost exclusively for men in many of the movements around us.'[11] The first generation beneficiaries of generalised girls' education, these women had become pupil teachers, gained their teaching certificates and now, the respect and recognition of their peers brought them responsibilities as union executives. In their twenties by the 1890s, the eldest were in their forties and fifties by 1910.

Coming to the fore in their professional instances, women teachers appear to have been in the forefront among prominent suffrage campaigners[12] amongst whom Mary Gawthorpe, Teresa Billington-Greig and Emily Davison, former elementary teachers prominent in the WSPU must be named, whilst for some members of the public at least, women teachers' Militancy was a threat and a disgrace. 'Unless they are both blind and deaf, managers of Board schools must know that not a few of the teachers in the latter are not only members of the WSPU and similar societies, but have actually taken part in or openly advocated "Militant" outrages.'[13] But not all were suffragettes. In a pen-portrait, Miss Waterman, also President of Kettering NFWT since 1908, was declared 'a firm believer in the ultimate triumph of the Feminist movement . . . An ardent supporter of woman's suffrage, [she] as strongly deprecate[d] Militant tactics'.[14] Others took part in the demonstrations and campaigning. The LCCWTU (founded in 1898 as the London School Board Mistresses' Union) recorded in 1911 that 'council members have taken an active part in the past twelve months, and were prominent in the great demonstration which took place on the eve of the Coronation'.[15] The symbolic value of women teachers,[16] exemplifying the educated, responsible and publicly visible woman deprived of the vote, may have led the suffrage movement to over-emphasise their presence. Nevertheless, their quiet and dignified professional role inside the profession and among the people they worked and lived with, whose children they taught, must have worked in favour of the full recognition of the independent working woman, even without suffrage activism.

There appears to be a clear synchronisation between developments in the suffrage movement and the formation of specific women teachers' organisations. The two movements seem to have nourished and reinforced each other. There were, broadly speaking, three distinct periods in the developments in the teaching profession. Firstly, an awakening taking place concomitantly with the massive in-flow of women teachers in the last decade of the nineteenth century. The second period corresponds to the rising pre-eminence of women's issues, equal pay in particular, leading to tentative organisation with official transformation in 1900 of the NUT Ladies' Committee (1896) into a standing committee[17] and the launching of the unofficial Equal Pay League in 1904. The hardening of positions and more Militant period saw the latter's transformation into the broader National Federation of Women Teachers by 1907 to push for women's issues in general to be promoted within the NUT. By the end of the decade, the suffrage question was coming to the fore in professional meetings, culminating in the creation of a professionally specific single-issue group, the Women Teachers' Franchise Union (1912). The parallel time-lines indicate that the increasing strength and visibility of women in their profession mirrored that of the suffrage movement. However, research concentrating on the small militant NFWT may have over-emphasised the impact of suffrage on women teachers' professional development. It may well be that the suffrage movement itself was influenced to an extent by the nature of the women teachers' concerns and viewpoints.

Opening with a 1928 description by Miss Phipps[18] of the crucial 1911 NUT conference debate, an instance of the 'dominant narrative' on suffrage militancy,[19] Oram's work emphasises 'the extent to which questions of sex equality divided and disrupted the otherwise apparently respectable and moderate teaching profession'. The suffrage question is seen as being divisive, turning teachers against teachers, men against women. For Oram, 'the coming together of their professional concerns with the women's suffrage movement . . . caused a huge growth of feminist consciousness among women teachers'. The suffrage movement is considered as 'a focus for the development of teachers' awareness of their position as women workers'.[20] For Kean it was the *'lives of suffragette teachers'* (subtitle of her book) *outside* their profession that led them to 'bring their politics *inside* the NUT' (italics mine). Quoting Emily Phipps's words on deciding to quit the NUT executive in 1917, Kean comments, 'they provide answers to the question "why did the *suffragettes* leave the NUT?" but they do not explain why they remained *in the NUT* for so long – until 1919 when the NUWT was founded. To understand this we need to look at events *outside* the NUT' (italics mine). For Kean, militancy outside professional circles in favour of women's suffrage led women teachers to become politically active within the teachers' union, 'as a result of their politicization as feminists *outside* the NUT'.[21]

But it would be a mistake to believe that all women teachers were suffragettes or that only extraneous events were behind the forefronting of women's issues inside the union. As Agnes Broome, long-serving Chairman (sic) of the NUT Ladies' Committee (composed of the lady Executive members and ex-officio male union officers) put it:

> We must not forget that the women may roughly be divided into four groups: first, those who want the vote but are only prepared to take constitutional methods to get it; second, those who want the vote and feel it is their duty to do anything and everything to get it; third, those who are opposed to it altogether; and fourth, those who do not care twopence about it either way.

She explained the Ladies' Committee's delicate position:

> We women on the Executive have to represent as best we can these four groups, therefore we cannot possibly take up, as members of the Executive, a position on either extreme. We have our own opinions about the question which I think are generally well known.[22]

Inside the National Union of Teachers, women Executive members were torn between support for the suffrage cause stemming from their own position as women elected by members of the local mixed teachers associations and loyalty to the Union whose role in the defence of teachers and promotion of education they strongly believed in.

How much was suffrage a specific issue for women teachers? Was it merely part of a package of reforms including equal pay, the marriage ban and career prospects? The composition of the elementary school teaching profession and its professional bodies must be examined to understand the chronology of the emergence of women's issues and the suffrage question in particular in the profession. Such were the attractions of teaching and the demand for teachers that by 1899 three-quarters of the 82 000 elementary teachers were women. However in the absence of a systematic, planned national expansion education and training provision it was inevitable that they were unqualified or low-qualified young women.[23] These factors influenced the hierarchy within the profession with lower career expectations for assistant teachers, and led to a cleavage between qualified and non-qualified teachers, men and women, head teachers and assistants.[24] The decreasing percentage of male elementary teachers had twice as many training college graduates among them, but in 1911 there were only 13 per cent of all teachers who had been college-trained.[25]

Paradoxically, despite unequal pay scales and no premium for higher qualifications,[26] qualified women teachers considered themselves an elite, 'the aristocracy of women workers' as Miss Wood explained to the NFAT at Norwich in 1911.[27] Elementary teaching had become a select profession for upper-working-class and lower-middle-class women. Many pursued their studies by correspondence courses gaining the prestigious LLA from St Andrews.[28] London teachers were the country's *crème de la crème*. Only a small minority (1.7 per cent) of London's 17 500 teachers were non-certificated in 1914 and a sixth had no college training. There, the men, more highly qualified as a group on the national level, were in fact outnumbered almost two to one by equally qualified women.[29] This was not without incidence on the dynamism of London women teachers and their leadership of many campaigns. Other large towns such as Birmingham, Manchester, Liverpool, Leeds or Swansea witnessed the same phenomenon to a lesser degree. Mapping the districts in which women teachers were predominantly qualified reveals a pattern that appears to repeat itself in the geography of suffrage activity within the profession and that of suffrage activity in general.[30]

The differing social origins and outlooks, qualifications and responsibilities undoubtedly added to friction between men and women teachers.[31] The influx of large numbers of lower-middle-class women to elementary teaching was adding to the frustrated ambitions of their male and largely working-class colleagues whilst women's grievances also increased. Since women teachers were massively young and unmarried (by virtue of their youth and due to the growing reluctance to employ married women as teachers by some Education Authorities) but were also victims of pay discrimination and blocked career prospects, this may have led them to espouse the more radical points of view of the suffragettes.[32] Many of the nationally prominent women teachers were spinsters. However, those active in union and suffrage activity were not novices but members of the cohort of women recruited in the 1890s and by 1905–10 had fifteen to twenty years' experience. Cleghorn and Conway were in their forties by 1905.

Men were not only more qualified but also more unionised. In 1895, 83 per cent of all male certificated elementary teachers were members of the NUT, but only 35 per cent of their female counterparts were.[33] This was considered detrimental to the NUT's claim to represent the profession. The NUT Ladies' Committee, reporting in 1900, its first year as an official standing committee, on its principal *raison d'être* and first objective 'to endeavour to enrol all women teachers in the NUT', noted 'their numbers have increased from 10 000 in 1894 to possibly 21 000 in 1900, but there are still very many without the pale – probably 20 000'.[34] The NUT only admitted certificated teachers. This excluded a large number of women. But the recognition of women teachers' specific issues and separate corporate identity had begun. By 1904 57.7 per cent of certificated women teachers (97.5 per cent of their male colleagues)[35] were members of the Union, indicating a rapid change in the Union's make-up. The Executive, wishing to strengthen the union by its membership drive, may have got more than it bargained for.

Tropp credits the NUT's internal democratic workings with the ability to recognise and accept 'sectional antagonisms', allowing them expression within its ranks.[36] The NUT, with its federal structure, did allow different interests and strands to have a voice within its ranks. Assistant teachers, women teachers, married women teachers, head teachers, all had their own specific associations affiliated to the Union. However despite the Union's voting system of one member one vote, giving women an equal voice in Union affairs, the Union leadership did not recognise women's concerns and conferences were male-dominated. Conference reactions to the suffrage question and equal pay made this equal franchise seem illusory despite an increasing presence of women on the Executive. From two women of the 36 elected members in the 1890s (Cleghorn and Broome), their proportion rose slightly as the Executive grew: four out of 40 in 1901, five out of 43 in 1903, and seven out of 45 in 1906 (Agnes Broome – Ipswich, Isabel Cleghorn – Sheffield, Selina Dix – Coventry, Emma Goodwin – Southampton, Sarah Jobson – Chelsea, Annie Selvage – Louth, Hannah Williams – Cardiff). With the exception of 1907 (four), from 1904 to 1914 the number remained steady at six or seven.[37] However, the conservative Union was anxious to maintain its hard-won recognition by the educational establishment. NUT-sponsored MP, James Yoxall[38] received a knighthood and Dr Macnamara – whose antagonism towards women Executive members was widely known – became a member of Asquith's 1910 government. The NUT oozed respectability and social conservatism, while the activities of its local associations were often limited to 'soirées' and 'conversazione'. Nevertheless, women were beginning to concern themselves with professional issues. The well-attended Manchester 'Ladies Bureau' meeting on 13 October 1900 dealt with tenure, equal salaries for girls and infants' head teachers (equal to the salaries of elementary school head teachers, not equal between men and women), the charities (benevolent funds) and 'the need of a larger number of women representatives upon the Executive'.[39]

In view of the socio-demographic pressures within the profession, the ensuing awareness of women teachers' contribution and their unjustified exclusion from matters concerning their professional status was even more acute. More concerned with decorous tea parties than bread and butter issues, the NUT Ladies' Committee's membership drives involved Local Associations Ladies Bureaux 'At Homes' during which local worthies spoke to teachers and light refreshments followed. The principle of allowing one item dealing with ladies' questions to be placed on local associations' agenda was envisaged at the first conference of women teachers organised by the NUT on 21 March 1896, when women's representation on the Executive and a meeting of ladies at conference were mooted (to no avail for the latter).[40]

Equal pay and combined departments were the issues through which the visibility of women teachers in their professional instances became transparently inadequate. Established in reaction to the NUT Ladies' Committee's inability to push forward demands, the Equal Pay League (EPL) first met in Manchester (on 27 April 1904, with 34 members by October[41]) and Liverpool. It was set up by assistant elementary teacher Teresa Billington, Joseph Tate (Birmingham) and Miss L. E. Lane (London). Between 1898 and 1903, Lane had challenged women's unequal entitlement to NUT provident fund benefits.[42] It was intended to take the campaign beyond teaching to other categories of women workers, such as the Postal Clerks and Telegraphers in Manchester; a meeting with Mrs Pankhurst, then a member of the Manchester Education Committee, was planned presumably to raise the issue of unequal pay for women teachers.[43] By the spring of 1905, Billington, its secretary and principal organiser, moved a resolution for a petition 'in favour of the passing of the Women's Enfranchisement Bill during the present session'.[44] The short-lived Manchester branch seems to have evolved along the lines of her personal development and collapsed on her leaving teaching to become a full-time ILP organiser. In 1906, the National Federation of Women Teachers took up the issue of equal pay that had foundered with the Manchester branch of the EPL. It lobbied within the NUT for women's professional issues to be mainstreamed, to influence the NUT executive on the issue of equal pay by canvassing candidates as the EPL had done from its inception.[45] In May 1907, a London branch was established.[46]

The NUT Ladies' Committee appears to have waned between March 1901 and March 1906, when it was resuscitated. By then both the suffrage movement outside and professional militancy inside the profession were making it impossible to ignore women's issues. The only business on the agenda at the Ladies' Committee first reconvened business meeting on 5 May 1906 was a letter from the Women's Co-operative Guild and combined departments. They 'did not see their way to sign' the United Manifesto in favour of Votes for Women and uncontroversially but weakly recommended 'the [NUT] Executive to support a Parliamentary vote for women on present Municipal Lines' and requested the NUT General Secretary to deputise the Board of Education to maintain women as separate heads of girls' and infants' departments in response to the growing tendency to appoint one, male, head teacher. The NFWT achieved a measured success with the NUT's condemnation of such combined departments (Resolutions 18, 1907 Oxford NUT Conference and 29, 1908 Hastings Conference) and different salaries paid to qualified teachers who had been college-trained or not, but failed to obtain a salary resolution placing men and women on an equal footing (1906 Scarborough and 1908 Hastings Conferences). The impact of the NFWT on the NUT was rapidly felt. Within two years, the latter had begun to fear the loss of women members they had had such difficulty attracting in the first place.

The contradictions inherent in the policy of the Union, campaigning to encourage greater membership among women teachers, but doing nothing to advance women's specific demands, were apparent. Women began to complain at the idea that they contributed to the Union funds but were not receiving any benefit from their membership. Indeed, they were specifically excluded from the benevolent fund's top category. 'We women are not wanted by the men either at Russell Square [NUT headquarters] or in the local associations (except, of course, to prepare tea!) but our subscriptions appear to be required . . . Surely, those who help to pay the piper should help to call the tune! . . . Fellow women members, let us determine to have more representatives at Russell Square, and a woman president as a start' complained an 'old stager' in the NUT weekly.[47] Another maintained that 'the time has come for us to make it known that as we help to keep the Union going so also do we want fair representation, not just a set of men who look after the interests of the masters only, and who let women's affairs go to the wall'. Parallels with the suffrage campaign were drawn:

> Surely I need say no more in view of the recent disappointment of those in favour of women's suffrage! Yet, hopes had run high, as 400 MPs had promised support – of some kind! I am afraid the support to women teachers promised by some candidates for the Executive – before election – is of the same 'academic' kind. Women teachers should combine in their own defence – there is no other way. Let London mistresses join the London County Council Mistresses' Union and provincial ones the National Federation of Women Teachers, and strengthen our hands. I fear we must 'work out our own salvation', and first let us have more women on the Executive.[48]

'Can't we take a leaf out of the suffragettes' book and see if noise and continued agitation will wake it up in our interests?' suggested another.[49]

By the summer 1907 a worried Ladies' Committee was preparing a 'Women's conference':

> The Committee discussed the matter at great length. They were of the opinion that there is great dissatisfaction among the mistresses throughout the country, as they feel that the Union has not done all that it might have to protect the interests of the Women Teachers, and it is feared that unless some step is soon taken to show the women members that they are being considered and that their interests are our concern, we shall have our ranks largely diminished. The Committee also felt that the holding of a Conference would to a large extent prevent the women teachers taking *irresponsible action.*[50] (Italics mine)

Grace Peake, Chairman of the Gloucester Association, declared that 'a number of our Committee are going to join the National Federation of Women Teachers, for we feel that probably it may be of service to us in the future.'[51] Most alarming to the NUT Ladies' Committee may have been the loss of the quality and commitment of valuable experienced women. Professional issues brought women to organise outside the official channels, but still within the NUT, attempting to remedy the internal democratic deficit against which they considered they were labouring.

The attempt to contain and control the debate at the December 1907 Women's Conference in the context of increasing suffragist activism led grassroots militants to complain. The proceedings were closed to all but the 55 invited women members. The London Branch of the NFWT, prompted by Miss Lane, protested that they were not representative, had not been elected (therefore had no mandate), and that the 45 men from the Executive present had voted (inferring the Conference's name was a misnomer).[52] The NFWT London branch nevertheless supported Isabel Cleghorn's candidacy for NUT vice president in 1908. On her election the following year, she thanked the Women's Federation, the London Mistresses' Union and the Ladies Bureaux jointly for their help and encouragement.[53] Cleghorn continued to want to revive meetings of 'ladies only' whilst trying to get in touch with and 'guide' the Women's Federation:

> They are endeavouring – in many places successfully – to form branch Associations. If these . . . could be treated as we treat ladies' bureaux – looked upon as sub-committees of local Associations – induced to enrol

> only members of the NUT, I can quite see some future good in the Women's Federation, whereas now it is a menace.[54]

While encouraging the 'furthering of good relationship between the two bodies' the elder ladies continued to believe that 'Ladies Bureaux might be changed into branches of the Women's Federation'[55] when patently their respective functions were different. Conceding that further women's conferences were obviously needed, the first 'business' meeting open to all lady teachers concerning uncontroversial topics was agreed for the Easter NUT Conference at Morecombe in 1909.

The EPL functioned as a loose, informal pressure group, perhaps because it did not have time to become structured. Its successor, the NFWT, did. The name itself indicates its ambition. The NUT was preoccupied above all by questions of professional status in relation to other 'professions'. The more adamant NFWT and the moderate LCCWTU can be considered as complementary women's lobbies within the national union. The London group, with a large number of married women members, was both geographically limited and more moderate. When the NFWT held its first independent congress at the Plymouth NUT Conference in 1910,[56] the danger the growing militancy of younger women represented to the NUT was recognised. Under pressure from members, the NUT was obliged to consider the status of women within the profession. The official women's business meeting at Conference had discussed the situation of married women teachers,[57] departing from more neutral questions previously addressed (infants' schooling, domestic subjects in schools) considered appropriate for discussion by women. The Ladies' Committee sent out unofficial contacts to persuade the 'Women's Federation' (as they called the NFWT) to join the Executive at the Conference Women's Meeting in the coming year. The latter declined. Anonymous letters in the WSPU *Votes for Women* that autumn suggested women NUT members refused to pay the two shillings from their union dues used to pay the salaries of NUT-sponsored MPs 'though not a single woman among the 35 000 who belong to the Union has a vote, and the Union has never made the slightest effort to obtain the vote for women who contribute three-fifths of its funds'.[58] Sir James Yoxall, defending his parliamentary record on woman suffrage had received 'communications from teachers . . . whom I know very well, long and earnest members of the Union, complaining about the inactivity of the Executive and the Union in this matter'. He pointed out that 'the Executive thought it would be going outside the proper limits of the Union's work to take part in the Trafalgar Square Meetings etc.',[59] referring obliquely to women teachers' participation in marches and demonstrations.

Over the winter of 1910–11 the debate had moved from equality of rights and representation within the Union to the broader suffrage question.

Hotly debated at NUT conferences four years running from 1911, suffrage came to be seen as central to the advancement of women's issues within the Union. Describing an undated incident in which a Leicester militant demanded her subscription back when her branch refused to discuss franchise, Kean comments: 'For some NFWT members their first militant suffrage action was not directed against the state but against the NUT.'[60] As the debate on the Conciliation Bill moved forward so did the position of the NUT Ladies' and Executive Committees. At their behest, and bypassing usual procedure, a suffrage motion was introduced at the 1911 Aberystwyth Conference to express 'its sympathy with those members of the NUT who desire to possess and exercise the parliamentary franchise, but because they are women, and for that reason alone, are by law debarred from it'. The Conference floor's refusal to suspend Standing Orders to consider the question owed as much to the way in which it had been introduced as to the subject, but the 'rowdy, disgraceful scene' (so Yoxall said) when the proposer, former NUT president Mr Croft, was refused a fair hearing, ensured the enduring notoriety of the Conference and hardened women's resolution to campaign for suffrage within the NUT.

Following the defeat of the motion to suspend standing orders, a women's meeting was convened by the Ladies' Committee to 'discuss the . . . best method of bringing the matter forward at the next Conference in *a constitutional manner*'[61] (Italics mine) at which the chair, Agnes Broome, and NUT President Isabel Cleghorn congratulated the women for their 'wonderful self-restraint'. Cleghorn analysed women delegates' reactions.

> I have met a number of women who had been up to now . . . the apathetic ones; I have also met some who are anti: others who are anti I do not think object to the vote but object to some of the methods . . . The way that affair was treated has altered their opinions, and we have many more suffragists in Aberystwyth today than if it had not taken place. I am myself a more advanced suffragist to-day than when I came.

Her advice to women showed how suffrage and women's union membership were linked in her mind:

> Go back to your Local Associations . . . and tell them you have found out, a great many of you, that you have been doing wrong in working for the suffrage movement and forgetting your Union, therefore losing influence in your Union . . . Work to get in the non-members: then

> work in your Local Associations and get resolutions passed, not only on the suffrage but on any question that you think right as coming from the women teachers.[62]

Addressed by Croft and Yoxall, the women were told by the latter to be patient but steadfast. 'It is still a far cry from the harem to the forum – a far cry from the position of being more or less a slave to becoming an equal, and during that transition process it takes a long time for those who have hitherto been slaves to acquire the gumption of the governing class.'[63] The best way to further the suffrage cause in the Union was the argument that by putting even greater numbers of voters behind the voice of the MPs the Union funded, women's suffrage would increase the weight of the Union in Parliament. 'Let it be brought forward by the most suitable person present, not the most extreme, not the most bitter, not the most resentful, not one who will say things in the course of a speech which will irritate men. Use the wisdom of the serpent combined with the innocence of the dove.'[64] They were encouraged to double the number of women delegates from 500 (out of over 2000) to 1000. 'Every woman will go home from this Conference a missionary. It will be a splendid object lesson to the women that they must unite and if they want to see their views represented they must send women to represent them', exclaimed Miss Byett, who had seconded the conference suffrage motion, proposing a motion be sent to the prime minister in lieu of the one hoped for from the whole NUT, stating 'this meeting of women representatives of the National Union of Teachers assembled at Aberystwyth desires to express its emphatic approval of the Bill to remove the sex disqualification for the exercise of the franchise, shortly to be introduced'.[65]

It appeared that Cleghorn, Byett and Yoxall's advice for unity, patience, diplomacy and hard work was being heeded. The London Women Teachers (LCCWTU) followed Cleghorn's argument, 'believing that ability to use the vote would tend to improve their position and influence, have identified themselves with the peaceful and constitutional methods adopted by suffragists during the past two years'. They had therefore spoken at meetings and attended the demonstrations in Trafalgar Square.[66] Its 'president, officers, council, and a contingent of members, headed by the Union's banner (the gift of Mrs Morgan Dockrell), joined in the great women's procession which marched on Saturday, June 17 [1911] from the Embankment to the Albert Hall.'[67] The NFWT London branch backed candidates for NUT election advising members 'to ensure a good attendance and a fair discussion' in local associations when the Executive's Motion on Women's Suffrage was brought.[68] Mrs Dockrell, LCCWTU president, spoke to the NFWT on 'Women as Citizens' in February 1910. She argued, like Cleghorn, that suffrage involved:

> not alone the economic and social status of women teachers, but the whole future status and efficiency of elementary education, namely, *the pressing need of unity among teachers* in adopting means for the removal of women's political disabilities . . . Women teachers, therefore, have a double responsibility. As women, and as teachers . . . and no fear of scorn or ridicule should deter them from individually and collectively using *all lawful means* for obtaining their political enfranchisement.[69] (Italics mine)

Continued emphasis on unity and the importance of constitutional methods hint at the threat of secession and the discredit violent tactics in the suffrage movement were causing. Threats of women leaving the NUT and forming a union of their own over its non-advocacy of equal wages for equal work continued.[70] 'The Union with half its members women does not even admit a grievance here. Not only does it not officially admit it, but also the men do not believe there is a grievance', wrote Agnes Dawson.[71] Equality of professional rights threatened to split women from the NUT; suffrage helped to keep most of them within the folds. Whilst inequalities in terms of workload, responsibilities, pay and promotion were more or less ignored by the NUT executive and women found it hard to push for improvements, the suffrage issue did achieve some degree of response within the national instances as women came to the fore. Adhering to the universal principle of equal rights was easier when it did not affect one's personal status as a privileged (male) member. Votes for women would not change the status quo in the profession and did not upset the apple-cart, whereas equal pay would.

Within the NUT women's activity increased over the autumn and winter of 1911–12. There were a record ten women candidates for the thirty-six seats on the NUT Executive (Agnes Broome, Essie Conway, Jane Wood, Mary Ride, Selina Dix, F. McKenzie, A. K. Williams, Isabel Cleghorn, Hannah Williams, Emma Goodwin). Regardless of their platform, the women's ticket was put forward. 'We should have liked to have seen more women teachers out in the field this time. The large percentage of women [members] ought surely to justify an equal number with men of women teachers for selection.'[72] Seven were elected. Photographs of 118 women delegates to the Hull Conference prominent in their national and local associations were published.[73] The intense activity in the local branches of the NUT enabled the Parliamentary Franchise for Women resolution to be tabled thirteenth after more pressing professional issues. At the West Lambeth Teachers' Association Amy Williams argued that 'They were only now being asked to carry out in a wider sphere what they had already carried out within their own local Associations.'[74] Teachers exercising full democratic rights within their union and gaining increasing elective responsibilities expected the same rights as women in the national arena. Some argued, however, that women's representation in the Union and the suffrage question were not linked.

> It must be made evident that the struggle of Women Teachers to get their rights in the control and conduct of the NUT is quite a separate question from woman's suffrage. The one is a domestic question: the other is purely political. The bulk of Women Teachers have very wisely kept the great suffrage question out of Union affairs, but have struggled most valiantly for their undoubted rightful position in the Union . . . So far as results have shown the executive of the NUT was anxious to increase the membership and funds, and did not dream of Women Teachers doing other than paying up and holding their tongues.
>
> It has surprised them somewhat to find that Women Teachers are now demanding their fair share of the work and administration of the NUT. This movement, coming as it does at the time of the woman's suffrage agitation, has led the smaller intelligences to think that the suffragettes are attempting to capture the Union . . . Let us therefore make it plain that the Women Teachers' agitation in the NUT is not a political or suffragette [sic] question but is the just demand of the female section of the union for proportional representation and power.[75]

Whatever the viewpoint, separate or linked, both were part of the same phenomenon – the inexorable rise of the educated woman.

With such intense activity in the run-up to the Hull Conference in 1912, it is not surprising that 'excitement ran high at Conference on Wednesday. Delegates assembled with a sense of something interesting being about to happen. The air was electric – for the franchise debate was to come.'[76] A NUWSS meeting called on the NUT to support woman suffrage 'in the interests of their own members and those of the state generally'.[77] As an indication of the weight the Executive was now prepared to put behind the motion, its retiring president, Isabel Cleghorn, proposed and the incoming one, Mr Dakers, seconded.

> I am a householder, said Miss Cleghorn, I pay rates, but I have no vote. The man who cleans my windows (oh, oh!), the man who digs my

> garden, the caretaker who lights my fire – each has a vote, but I am classed with paupers and lunatics and infants. I have not a vote, though taxation means representation. It is not fair (hear, hear). You are not asked to sympathise with any party and any particular Bill, or any particular method (dissent and cheers). You are asked to sympathise with those women in our union who possess the necessary qualifications that the men have for voting, but who because they are women have not the vote. We teach in the schools: we have to teach the children citizenship, loyalty, patriotism, and all that is necessary to make them good citizens, but we have not the vote to enable us to take part in making the laws (Cheers).[78]

The parliamentary franchise for women teachers enfranchised inside their professional body was a logical struggle she told the floor. 'A large section of their members asked for their sympathy in their endeavour to get outside the union what they already had inside the union – equal voting power.'[79]

Reactions were similar to those the previous year. The sympathy motion provoked uproar seemingly caused by fears of the Union being held hostage to suffrage. The reassurances proffered to the NUT at the fringe NFWT conference by Miss Thomas, its president, confirm this. 'They did not as suffragists wish to capture the National Union of Teachers. The vote was a sign of equality, and they wished their men folk to recognize their equality and joint rulership.' The moderate stance adopted by the NFWT and resolution moved by Miss Lane and Mrs H. Plumb echoed the Executive motion.[80] Nevertheless with 72 394 teachers represented, of whom 40 955 were women (58 per cent), a number of them pronounced suffragists, and despite the intense activity to move suffrage and elect women to the committees and as delegates, the conference voted not to vote on the motion by 36 225 votes to 22 284. 'Thus has a year's hard work ended in a three to two defeat; thus opens so far as the *Woman Teachers' World* is concerned another year's effort to secure justice for the women teachers and all law-abiding women of the country', regretted the moderate journal commenting 'that the Militant tactics have contributed largely to this defeat is probably too true'.[81] It was not Militant activity within the Union that caused these regrets, although in the conservative and establishment-linked NUT this was frowned upon, but that of women in the suffrage movement at large. It is significant that the conference passed a resolution proposing that disqualifications debarring (all) teachers from becoming members of their own Borough and County Councils be removed,[82] proof that local political activity (on educational grounds) was not frowned upon.

Debates within the women's groups in the teaching profession repeatedly emphasised legal and constitutional tactics and followed arguments on citizenship and the state close to WFL tenets and practice, but also to a certain extent, arguments on the vote as a panacea for social evils, a position advocated by the NUWSS. Suffrage arguments within the NFWT repeatedly evoked the social responsibilities of teachers.

> Why should they teach girls how to think for themselves and explain citizenship, and yet not hold out the hope of some day aiding by their vote the ideals they would like to attain? . . . Women teachers [have] a double responsibility. Their influence, their efforts for the good of the community [are] hindered and nullified by reason of the disqualification, but no fear of scorn or ridicule should deter them from all lawful means of obtaining their political freedom.[83]

It was thus their professional duty and also their social duty to be concerned about women's issues. Without the vote, they could not fulfil either. The suggestion that the Women's Freedom League had 'the greatest influence' within the NFWT, which in turn modelled its internal democracy and organisation on the former, has been made. The NFWT's Emily Phipps was a long-standing WFL member and two other NFWT members were WFL branch secretaries.[84] But Agnes Dawson, another of its leading members, was a NUWSS member. The extremely procedural NUT, the NFWT's emphasis on the value of internal democracy and the struggle to impose direct self-government by women rather than committee rule by men in the LTA in 1912 (men, perhaps under pressure from such an exclusive female assembly, opposed any debate on equal pay),[85] all corresponded to the WFL's internal workings. While the NUWSS had a federal structure familiar to women members of the NUT, the NUWSS's links with the working class and the Labour Party meant that women teachers, more generally from lower-middle-class backgrounds and keen to emphasise the respectability of their profession, would have preferred the WFL, whose stated aims in addition to women's suffrage – 'to use the power thus obtained to establish equality of rights and opportunities between the sexes and to promote the social and industrial well-being of the community'[86] – closely resemble women teachers' concerns and preoccupations about their role as expressed in discussions for example on questions of infant teaching or domestic science classes at the time. Women teachers' actual membership of the various suffrage groups needs further examination.[87] It may be that just as suffrage influenced women teachers, women teachers influenced suffrage practice and principles.

It was in this context following the Hull Conference and in response to the unexpected defeat of the motion proposed by the Executive, that women teachers, 'after much hesitation and some reluctance',[88] set up the Women Teachers' Franchise Union (WTFU) 'to get fair play for women teachers in the educational world; to organize women teacher suffragists and sympathizers so as to make their point of view felt in their own organisations'.[89] E. Lane urged the small (110-strong) but active NFWT London branch to send a firm resolution for the next conference and to prepare a meeting for 18 June on parliamentary franchise with speakers from inside (Mrs Morgan Dockrel, Miss Lightman) and outside teaching (Mrs Philip Snowden)[90] at which suffragist teachers called upon the Executive to 'reaffirm and send to the Local and County Associations its resolution on the Parliamentary Franchise for women teachers'.[91] Their hesitation was over adding to the already numerous suffrage societies. 'They thought, as one of the objectives of the National Union of Teachers is "To secure effective Parliamentary representation for its members", the NUT would work on their behalf.'[92] The NUT executive had come round to supporting the votes for women campaign since 1910–11, on the advice of their moderate Ladies' Committee, which seems to have been surprised and outflanked by the intensity and span of women teachers' support for the issue. But the local teachers' organisations and national conference had not gone their way, as the objectives on the WTFU rule card spell out: '(a) To secure full rights of citizenship for all Women Teachers. (b) To further the education of the public on Women's Suffrage from the Women Teachers' point of view. (c) To secure adequate representation of Women Teachers *on all Committees and at all Conferences of the various Teachers' organisations*'[93] (italics mine). Suffrage was the first aim but it was a catalyst that had demonstrated that a voice in professional affairs was also needed. 'Women Teachers, attend your local associations, and take your part in gaining freedom for yourselves, and dignity for your profession.'[94] A say in Union affairs was a way of bringing forward women's say in national affairs and vice versa.

> You need the Vote for your own sakes, not merely because politicians cannot attend to the wants of the voteless, but because nothing is so likely as political enfranchisement to break down the tradition that women's work is inferior and therefore should be ill paid. If you want to be judged on your merits, you must work for the vote.[95]

The WFTU was inclusive and non-restrictive, cross-party and interdenominational, encouraging women teachers of every status to participate in every kind and at every level of teachers' associations and apparently doing away with the qualification proviso for membership operated by the NUT and the NFWT. Its rules allowed that 'all Women Teachers be eligible for full membership'. With a view to promoting women's participation in the decision-making processes of their union their organisations agreed to work together rather than to encourage rivalry. Prominent NFWT members Agnes Dawson, Ethel Froud (WSPU) and omnipresent Miss Lane belonged to the WTFU Committee but its permanent officers (Hannah Townsend, Miss Llewhellin or Miss Follett) and other long-serving committee members (Nancy Lightman and Mrs Tidswell) were less well-known in the women teachers' organisations giving priority to suffrage activity outside.[96] At its first meeting Agnes Dawson (NUWSS) was chair and Hannah Townsend (WSPU) secretary. Other prominent members included Adelaide Jones (WFL) and A. K. Williams (LTA president). Overlapping membership and officials, common speaker and electoral agreements were the rule. 'The intention was not to detach members from existing "Women's Unions" but rather so to "*educate*" their members "*rouse*" them to take greater interest in all matters affecting their professional welfare'[97] (original punctuation). The aim was to increase the representation of women in their professional bodies: co-operation and collaboration were the by-words: 'with a view of strengthening the chances of women for Com[mitte]e in different districts we endeavoured to support the same candidates as the LCCWTU and WTFU provided they are members of the NFWT.'[98] Kean argues that 'the campaign for NUT support for the parliamentary franchise . . . had its origins *outside* the educational state apparatus in the political relations between women and the state. In taking their argument *into* the NUT the feminists made explicit links between their role as women teachers and their political role in society.' The WTFU was set up 'with the intention of forcing the NUT to campaign for . . . the franchise. It was the political experience of such women *outside* the union that led to their consciousness of different methods of organization to those favoured by the NUT. It also led them to increased militancy and to an increasing estrangement from the NUT'[99] (italics mine). In view of the chronology and stated aims, the WFTU and increasing militancy appears to have stemmed as much, if not more, from the situation inside the union.

At the NUT's 1913 Weston-super-Mare Conference suffrage continued to dominate proceedings. Lord Haldane, member of the Asquith government, was invited to speak, evidence of cordial relations between the Union and the cabinet, but also perhaps of a lack of understanding of the force of opinion on the suffrage issue or the women's temerity. The subject, boys' education, could not have been more provoking to women to whom and for whom girls' education meant so much. A pencilled note on the *Eastern Daily Mail* press cutting on the incident, held in the NUWT archives, reads 'Before meeting began Dakers [retiring President] announced that Haldane would see deputation re suffrage at 5 o'clock. Bentliff [incoming President] told Haldane if this announcement had not been made for every one thrown out there would have been 20.'[100] Half a dozen hecklers protesting at the government's treatment of 'suffering women' (a reference to forcible feeding) interrupted the Lord Chancellor's address and left the hall voluntarily, were asked or forced to leave.[101] The deputation consisted of Mrs Burgwin, Mrs Sandford and Miss Truelove, who spoke against the granting of the franchise to women, followed by an impressive array in favour, eight retiring or former lady members of the NUT Executive: Cleghorn, Broome, Conway, Dix, Goodwin, A. K. Williams, H. Williams, Wood; two NFWT Committee members: A. Dawson and Thomas; and Miss Gittens. 'They emphasised especially the educational side of the question. They claimed that the lack of the vote placed them in a false position, and deprived them of the force and power they ought to have.'[102] In addition 'NUT Suffragists' held a large meeting at the Town Hall chaired by Miss A. L. Brown and addressed by Mrs Dice, Miss Margaret McMillan and Mr Harben and adopted the Executive resolution that the full NUT conference refused: 'That this conference expresses its sympathy with those members of the National Union of Teachers who desire to possess and exercise the Parliamentary franchise, but because they are women and for that reason alone, are by law debarred from it.'[103]

Despite the NFWT's continued defence of equal pay (Agnes Dawson proposed the general conference motion on the issue),[104] the NFWT was accused of being 'a Suffrage society masquerading as a teachers' organisation'. Ethel Froud reacted strongly to this reduction of their aims: 'We recognise that *Woman Suffrage is the solution of the many injustices under which we labour* [italics mine] and we therefore make Woman Suffrage one of the planks of our platform. Strange that the remaining six objects go unchallenged and only the seventh is such a heinous offence!'[105] Promoting women's issues within the NUT, the NFWT's declared 1914 objectives were: 'combined action. To secure better pensions and earlier optional retirement for women teachers. To secure equal pay and equal increments for men and women teachers of the same professional status. To secure the maintenance of each girls' and infants' dept. under its own head mistress. To bring all women teachers into the National Union of Teachers and secure more women on the National Union of Teachers executive. To secure representation of women on all educational authorities. To secure for women teachers the Parliamentary franchise.'[106] So entwined were the issues of suffrage and professional status, it could equally have been said of the WTFU, defending equal pay, that it was a teachers' organisation masquerading as a suffrage society.[107]

At the Lowestoft NUT Annual Conference in April 1914 'a great deal [was] to be heard about woman suffrage', noted *The Times*'s Special Correspondent in the only article in its columns directly linking women teachers and suffrage, 'and some resentment is felt among members of the union that the Conference is now regularly exploited by suffragists and anti-suffragists alike.'[108] The April 1914 issue of *The Suffragette* announced 'Great Campaign at Lowestoft'. The issue dominated the event, at least outside the conference hall. Five suffrage organisations were present. Both Mrs Pankhurst and Mrs Fawcett were due to address meetings in the town. On the Saturday evening, Militants tried 'to take possession of a meeting of the local secretaries of the union' addressed by Yoxall 'but they were ejected after some disturbances'. On Sunday, at the official church service attended by the Mayor and Corporation, the Bishop of Norwich was harangued in the pulpit on the torturing of women in prison, while other women rushed up the aisle and knelt in prayer.[109] It is not clear whether these women were teachers but the occasion, a teachers' conference, may have led the public to assume so.

Inside the conference, discussions were dominated by women's rights questions of equal pay and suffrage.[110] Despite the NUT's executive and 38 branches (out of 500 or so county and local associations[111]) supporting resolutions 'expressing sympathy with those members of the union who by reason of their sex alone are debarred from the franchise'[112] discussion was acrimonious. 'Great disorder then ensued as to procedure on the next business . . . Delegates all over the hall shouted their opinions and questions at the president.'[113] East Ham teacher Miss A. G. Hewitt warned of women teachers' frustration:

> Don't let it go forth to the civilised world that the enfranchisement of two-thirds of the members of this great union was not worth discussion. The women were ready to come out of the union as a sign, but they did not want to come out. They wanted to preserve the solidity of the union, but they could not go back to their associations and tell their women who were ready to revolt that that motion had been carried.[114]

An amendment proposed by the Waterloo branch deplored the fact that time was being 'wasted' discussing the issue in a union which existed for professional purposes; the motion adopted by the conference declared that suffrage was outside the scope of the union, by a majority of 16 449[115] out of 88 376 members, of whom 52 079 were women (59 per cent).[116] The parallel NFWT conference 'adopted a resolution protesting against forcible feeding and drugging and calling upon the Government to take steps to remove the cause of the women's agitation'.[117] It naturally again demanded equal pay for equal work. Equal pay, not suffrage, was to lead to the final break between the NFWT and the NUT. On 19 September 1914 the Ladies' Committee recorded the WTFU suffrage motion ('That in order to promote Object V of the NUT viz., "To secure the effective representation of educational interests in parliament" this Conference is of the opinion that women members should be granted the Parliamentary Franchise on the same terms as men') and once more recommended the Executive adopt a 'sympathy' motion, with the exact wording of those that had been on the NUT conference agenda since 1911. With the outbreak of war, equal pay supplanted suffrage. From 1917 Miss Phipps, disgusted by the NUT's continuing support of unequal pay scales in the male-dominated discussions that were to lead to the 1920 Burnham scales, decided to abandon her position on the NUT executive and the NFWT condemned 'the action of the National Union of Teachers in attempting to make compulsory a scale of salaries which was not based on those principles'.[118]

The suffrage campaign had not divided women teachers. It grew out of growing concerns over increasingly visible inequalities in professional rights as the numbers of women teachers grew and union membership expanded. The suffrage issue demonstrated to the female majority how the male minority in the profession were clinging to an outmoded concept of the Union's role and strength. 'Suffrage came to symbolise the struggle of women teachers in getting their views heard and fairly represented.'[119] Women teachers imposed not only a new agenda but also new political practices in their professional lives, managing to question the routine conduct, the committee-management of Union affairs. If the proportion of women members on the NUT executive rose to between 8 and 10 members from 1915 until 1920, it is argued that this was largely due to 'the caucusing and political climate created by the feminists'.[120] Benefiting from the enforced absence of mobilised male colleagues, women stepped in to positions of responsibility; but this was also the result of the inexorable rise of a generation of professional women. For the majority their professional personae had led them into the fray. Working from within their main union, in repeating patterns of multiple membership and responsibilities, they increased their visibility and maintained pressure from various angles on the NUT executive. Despite setbacks in conference (which were not necessarily anti-suffrage *per se* but a question of the proper role of union activity) these moderate leaders gained support for responsible woman suffrage. Equal rights did not have such success. The two issues had become inextricably linked throughout the rise of suffrage as a concern for women teachers. The ambiguity and intertwining of professional and political issues did a disservice both to the suffrage cause and to that of equal professional rights. Working together, women teachers supporting either or both appeared as one to the opposition irrespective of the differences of opinion between the strands. Criticism of Militant tactics was not limited to the activities of Militants. The pleas of the moderate women dissociating themselves from such illegal activity indicate the irritation they felt. It was thought the militancy helped neither the cause of suffrage nor that of professional status and respectability. It was quiet committee work, responsible leadership in the unions and firm, qualified, diplomatic statements as enfranchised union members which they saw as the best argument for their parliamentary enfranchisement. The opportunity of belonging to several professional organisations led to a beneficial plurality in which overlapping membership between women's groups seems only to have become an impossible duality when the NUT's position on equal pay and married women teachers did not evolve, leading eventually to the transformation of the NFWT into the National Union of Women Teachers in 1920.

Notes

1. *Ladies' Committee Reports*, 20 May 1911 (NUT records).
2. Two other of the only four women elected president of the NUT to date, Essie Conway and Jane Wood (BA, Head Mistress Secondary School for Girls, All Saints, Manchester), were elected in 1918 and 1920. Leah Manning was the first married chairwoman in 1930 (Labour MP 1931 and 1945).
3. *Woman Teachers' World* (official organ of the London County Council Women Teachers' Union), 12 October 1911.
4. 1895–1919 NUT Executive Committee member and on consultative Committee, Board of Education, from 1907. *Oxford Dictionary of National Biography* (Oxford: Oxford University Press, 2004).
5. *The Schoolmaster*, 2 April 1910, p. 583.
6. *Woman Teacher* (linked with the NFWT), 19 March 1912, p. 55.
7. *The Schoolmaster*, 1 January 1910, p. 27; *Woman Teacher*, 12 September 1911, p. 47; *ODNB*. She was to be adopted as the first NUT sponsored woman parliamentary candidate in 1918. Forty-Ninth Annual Report of the Executive 1919, p. 236.
8. NFWT (London Branch) General Meetings (NFWT Archive, 783), 30 September 1911.
9. *Woman Teachers' World*, 14 September 1911, vol. I, no. 1, p. 8.
10. *Woman Teacher*, 13 February 1912, p. 400.

11. *Woman Teacher*, 16 January 1912, p. 333; 13 February 1912, p. 416; 27 February 1912.
12. O. Banks, *Becoming a Feminist: the Social Origins of First Wave Feminism* (Brighton: Wheatsheaf, 1986), pp. 11–12, bases this affirmation on a figure of 20 out of her sample of 98. However, her sample is composed of 'the best known of the feminists' (p. 10) on the national level. Work on the local scale might reveal a similar incidence of women teachers given their professional eloquence, social conscience and administrative skills. As Banks recognises 'many women in relatively humble positions' (p. 10) were not included in her overview.
13. *New Age*, 13 August 1914, pp. 358–9.
14. *Woman Teacher*, 30 April 1912, p. 149.
15. *Woman Teachers' World*, 14 September 1911, vol. I, no. 1, p. 8.
16. A. Oram, 'Women Teachers and the Suffrage Campaign: Arguments for Professional Equality', in June Purvis and Sandra Stanley Holton (eds), *Votes for Women* (London: Routledge, 2000), pp. 210–11.
17. Standing Order No. 28, NUT Executive Committee meeting, 5 May 1900 in *Ladies' Committee Reports*, 19 May 1900.
18. NUT Executive Committee member 1915 and 1917. Militant NFWT Council member.
19. June Hannam, Book Review of Laura E. Nym Mayhall, *The Militant Suffrage Movement: Citizenship and Resistance in Britain 1860–1930* (Oxford: Oxford University Press, 2003), Institute of Historical Research, www.history.ac.uk/reviews/paper/hannam.html.
20. A. Oram, *Women Teachers and Feminist Politics 1900–1939* (Manchester: Manchester University Press, 1996) pp. 1, 103. See also Oram, 'Women Teachers and the Suffrage Campaign'.
21. H. Kean, *Deeds not Words: the Lives of Suffragette Teachers* (London: Pluto 1990), pp. 26, 63; H. Kean, *Challenging the State? The Socialist and Feminist Educational Experience 1900–1930* (Basingstoke: Falmer Press, 1990), p. 123.
22. NUT *Ladies' Committee Reports*, 29 May 1911.
23. S. Trouvé-Finding, 'Teaching as a Woman's Job: the Impact of the Admission of Women to Elementary Teaching in England and France in the late 19th and early 20th Centuries', *History of Education Journal*, 34, 5 (2005), pp. 483–96; Oram, *Women Teachers*, Table 2, 'Number of Teachers of Various Grades in Public Elementary Schools 1900–1938, England and Wale'; H. Corr, 'Sexual Politics in the National Union of Teachers 1870–1920', in P. Summerfield (ed.), *Women, Education and the Professions*, History of Education Society Occasional Publication, 8 (1987), pp. 53–65; H. Kean, 'Women Teachers, Experience and Theory', *Oxford Review of Education*, 23, 3 (1997), pp. 407–10.
24. A. Tropp, *The School Teachers: the Growth of the Teaching Profession in England and Wales from 1800 to the Present Day* (London: Heinemann, 1957), pp. 156–7.
25. *Times Educational Supplement*, 2 May 1911, 'The Training of Teachers. New Difficulties. Their Solution'.
26. *Times Educational Supplement*, 2 April 1912, 'The Threatened Dearth of Teachers'.
27. *Woman Teacher*, 3 October 1911, p. 93.
28. Periodicals for women teachers are replete with advertisements for these courses. Official photographs portray them in gown and mortarboard, badges of status.

29. *Times Education Supplement*, 1 December 1914, 'Education and Local Patriotism: XII London'.
30. J. Hannam, ' "I had not been to London": Women's Suffrage – a View from the Regions', in J. Purvis and S. Stanley Holton (eds), *Votes for Women* (London: Routledge, 2000), pp. 226–45, examines the political geography of the suffrage movement *per se* concentrating on suffrage activities within suffragism and underlines the complex strands entering into women's political identity but does not examine their professional status and activities (p. 242).
31. A. Oram, 'Inequalities in the Teaching Profession: the Effects on Teachers and Pupils, 1910–1939', in Felicity Hunt (ed.), *Lessons for Life: the Schooling of Girls and Women 1850–1950* (Oxford: Blackwell, 1987), pp. 101–23.
32. Kean, *Deeds not Words*, p. 17.
33. Tropp, *The School Teachers*, p. 157, n.46.
34. Draft Circular Letter to Secretaries of Local Associations and District Unions, *Ladies' Committee Reports*, 7 July 1900.
35. Oram, *Women Teachers*, Table 1, 'Membership of the National Union of Teachers 1900–1929', p. 226.
36. Tropp, *The School Teachers*, p. 159.
37. NUT, *Report Books* (London: NUT, for the given years).
38. General Secretary of the NUT 1892–1924.
39. *Ladies' Committee Reports*, 20 October 1900.
40. *Ladies' Committee Reports*, 20 June 1907.
41. NUWT Archive, Manchester and District Equal Pay League Minute Book 1904–1905.
42. Kean, *Deeds not Words*, p. 16.
43. NUWT Archive, Manchester and District Equal Pay League Minute Book 1904–1905, handwritten notes signed 'TBG [Teresa Billington-Greig] 1957'.
44. Manchester and District Equal Pay League Minute Book, 10 February and 10 March 1905.
45. Ibid., 27 April 1904.
46. NFWT (London Branch) General Meetings (NFWT Archive 783), 7 May 1907.
47. *The Schoolmaster*, 25 May 1907, p. 1020.
48. *The Schoolmistress*, 14 March 1907, p. 373.
49. Ibid., 28 March 1907, p. 406.
50. *Ladies' Committee Reports*, 22 June 1907.
51. *Ladies' Committee Reports*, 15 November 1907.
52. *Ladies' Committee Reports*, 18 January 1908 and 20 March 1908; NFWT (London Branch) General Meetings, 8 February 1908.
53. NFWT (London Branch) General Meetings, 26 September 1908; *The Schoolmaster*, 2 April 1910, p. 618.
54. *Ladies' Committee Reports*, 20 June 1908.
55. *Ladies' Committee Reports*, 18 July 1908.
56. *The Schoolmaster*, 2 April 1910, p. 581.
57. *Ladies' Committee Reports*, 19 November 1910.
58. *Votes for Women*, 28 October 1910 and 13 January 1911, recorded in the *Ladies' Committee Reports*, 19 November 1910 and 21 January 1911.
59. *Oxford Times*, 11 February 1911; *Ladies' Committee Reports*, 18 February 1911 and 20 May 1911.
60. Kean, *Challenging the State?*, p. 136.

61. *Ladies' Committee Reports*, 20 May 1911.
62. Ibid.
63. Ibid.
64. Ibid.
65. Ibid.
66. *Woman Teachers' World*, 15 November 1911, p. 309.
67. *Woman Teachers' World*, 1 November 1911 p. 243.
68. NFWT (London Branch) General Meetings, 30 September 1911.
69. *Woman Teachers' World*, 14 September 1911, vol. I, no. 1, p. 8; 29 November 1911, p. 353.
70. *Ladies' Committee Reports*, 21 October 1911.
71. *Woman Teacher*, 26 September 1911, p. 70.
72. *Woman Teacher*, 5 March 1912, pp. 26–7.
73. *Woman Teacher*, 9 April 1912, pp. 104–6; 23 April 1912, p. 141.
74. *Woman Teacher*, 10 October 1911, p. 113.
75. *Woman Teacher*, 21 November 1911, p. 197.
76. *Woman Teacher*, 16 April 1912, p. 115.
77. *Woman Teacher*, 9 April 1912, p. 109.
78. *The Standard*, 11 April 1912.
79. Ibid.; *The Schoolmaster*, 13 April 1912, p. 719.
80. *The Times*, 8 April 1912, p. 8.
81. *Woman Teachers' World*, 12 April 1912, p. 944.
82. NUT, Executive Committee Minutes, Resolutions of Conference, Hull 1912.
83. *The Woman Teacher's World*, 17 April 1912, p. 992; *The Times*, 8 April 1912, p. 8; *Woman Teacher*, 9 April 1912, p. 106.
84. Kean, *Deeds not Words*, pp. 19–20; A.J.R. (ed.), *The Suffrage Annual and Women's Who's Who* (London: Stanley Paul, 1913), p. 115.
85. WFTU, *The Referendum*, 'Address delivered by Mrs Kate Dice, at the WFTU, on February 21st, [1913]'; Oram, 'Arguments for Professional Equality', pp. 120–3.
86. *The Vote*, 8 September 1909, p. 1.
87. See Oram, 'Women Teachers and the Suffrage Campaign', pp. 209–10; Hilda Kean and Alison Oram, ' "Men must be educated and women must do it": the National Federation (later Union) of Women Teachers and Contemporary Feminism 1910–1939', *Gender and Education*, 2, 2 (1990), pp. 149–51.
88. *Woman Teachers' World*, 4 September 1912.
89. A.J.R. (ed.), *The Suffrage Annual* (1913) p. 134.
90. NFWT (London Branch) General Meetings (783).
91. Letter from Miss H. M. Townsend, *Ladies' Committee Reports*, 22 June 1912.
92. A.J.R. (ed.), *The Suffrage Annual*, 1913, pp. 133–4.
93. NUWT archive (518), Special documents: WTFU Rules (n.d.)
94. WFTU, *Why the Women's' Suffrage Resolution is Legitimate NUT Business*, n.d. [1913].
95. R. F. Cholmeley, *Teachers! Why Women's Suffrage Matters to You*, NUWSS, reprinted by WTFU, n.d. [1913].
96. WFTU, *Why the Women's Suffrage Resolution*, n.d. [1913]; WFTU, *1915 Annual Report*; WTFU, *Fifth Annual Report 1917*.
97. NFWT (London Branch) General Meetings (783), 28 September 1912.
98. Ibid., 20 September 1913; 26 September 1914.
99. Kean, *Challenging the State?*, pp. 138, 136.

100. 'Lord Haldane's address to NUT – principles of the proposed scheme foreshadowed – Interruption by suffragettes', *Bristol Times and Mirror,* 26 March 1913, p. 7, NFWT archive (551).
101. Ibid.
102. Ibid.
103. Ibid.; Agnes Dawson's report to the NFWT (London Branch), 26 April 1913.
104. *Bristol Times and Mirror,* 26 March 1913, p. 7.
105. *The Schoolmistress,* 5 June 1913, p. 184.
106. Ibid.
107. WTFU, *Equal Pay for Equal Work* (n.d.) [1913].
108. 'Woman Suffrage and the Teachers', *The Times,* 13 April 1914, p. 13.
109. Ibid.
110. 'The National Union', *Times Educational Supplement,* 5 May 1914.
111. NUT, 'List of Associations', *Year Book 1914.*
112. *The Times,* 13 April 1914, p. 13.
113. *Eastern Daily Press,* 17 April 1914, p. 10.
114. Ibid.
115. *Times Educational Supplement,* 5 May 1914, 'The NUT at Lowestoft, April 13–16'.
116. *The Times,* 13 April 1914, p. 13.
117. Ibid.
118. *The Times,* 11 April 1917, p. 3.
119. Oram, 'Women Teachers and the Suffrage Campaign', p. 220.
120. Kean, *Deeds not Words,* p. 71.

10
Avant-garde Women and Women's Suffrage

Lucy Delap

> 'At this present time there is no feminist movement in the country, but only a suffrage movement – and chaos.'[1]

In this chapter, the early twentieth-century formulations of 'feminism' are explored, as an identity developed in active defiance of 'suffragism'. While some suffragists later came to identify as feminists, for a brief period feminism provided an intellectual and political space for a very different kind of Edwardian politics, heavily influenced by the modernist Anglo-American avant-garde.[2] I consider the replacement of the 'double affiliations' of suffragism (suffrage-socialist, suffrage-liberal) with the single term 'feminism' amongst some Edwardian women in Britain, and what this meant for suffrage politics. Many of the 'advanced' or 'vanguard' women who came to describe themselves as feminists were motivated by their former experiences as suffragists. They retained a complex relationship with suffrage organisations, unable to ignore or move on from suffrage, yet unwilling to let it dominate or eclipse their political ideals and intellectual forums.

Edwardian suffrage affiliations were notoriously conflictual and prone to splintering. Teresa Billington-Greig (1877–1964) was perhaps the foremost critic of suffrage politics within what became the feminist avant-garde. She had been an Independent Labour Party (ILP) organiser and campaigner on equal pay issues in Manchester. Like her friends Dora Marsden and Mary Gawthorpe, she became a committed Women's Social and Political Union (WSPU) and later (following a damaging split in 1907) a Women's Freedom League (WFL) activist, serving prison sentences in Holloway. However, she quickly became disillusioned with the autocracy within suffrage groups, and the refusal of some within the movement to discuss controversial issues of gender relations. Billington-Greig resigned her post, and published in 1911 a devastating critique of the Militant suffragists, *Emancipation in a Hurry*.[3] While she had advocated in 1907 that feminists should establish an 'Independent Woman's Party', Billington-Greig became increasingly disillusioned by the suffragist belief in what she termed 'emancipation by machinery'.[4] Bruised by her outcast status following *Emancipation in a Hurry*, she came to believe that 'advanced' feminism was a more promising basis for an emancipatory movement than suffragism. She recognised that, as yet, no one was quite sure what 'feminism' meant: 'Women and men who regard themselves as advanced feminists are all at sixes and sevens as to principles, theories, objects and methods . . . the way is strewn with half-enunciated new ideas and half-obsolete old ones.' Writing in the socialist-modernist paper *The New Age*, she therefore proposed a 'free feminist platform', equivalent to the 'open review' style of *The New Age*, to try to elucidate what feminism was about.[5]

Other *New Age* feminists agreed. Beatrice Hastings (1879–1943), the paper's literary editor, had gained a reputation from 1907 as a formidable feminist, supporter of Militancy and proponent of women's autonomy in reproduction. Hastings found Teresa Billington-Greig's denunciation of suffrage politics compelling:

> If Mrs. Billington-Greig, or any capable organiser, would give women the opportunity of joining a real feminist league, with no calls to glory . . . no deadly commercial dealings, no ostrich tactics, I believe we might prevent the threatened temporary collapse of the woman's movement. People scarcely bother to argue against it now.[6]

While feminism has become a term which can be projected back onto the activities of suffrage activists at the start of the twentieth century, it was a term which many of them fought shy of, or only adopted when it had become a more mainstream, politically neutral term. In its initial uses, 'feminism' came to occupy a similar space to the idea of the 'new woman' of the 1890s, signifying a radical, subversive grouping closely associated with the avant-garde and radical movements that flourished before World War One. It connoted rupture, including for some, a break with various strands of the suffrage movement. With this agenda in mind, in late 1911, the first British journal to term itself 'feminist' was launched. *The Freewoman* was a three-penny weekly review, edited by Dora Marsden and Mary Gawthorpe, both former WSPU activists. Marsden (1882–1960), formerly a teacher in Manchester, had been drawn to the extremely active suffrage scene. After some involvement as a WSPU speaker and activist, she resigned her teaching position in 1909 in order to march to the House of Commons. A photo of her battling, hatless, with policemen was printed on the front page of the British *Daily Mirror* under the headline 'Arrest of Miss Dora Marsden, the "Standard-Bearer" '.[7] Briefly a national celebrity, she went on to become a paid WSPU organiser in London and Lancashire. Marsden enjoyed the political theatre of Militant suffragism, being arrested for actions such as throwing balls labelled 'bomb' through the windows of political meetings, and hiding in rooftops to interrupt speakers. WSPU leaders were not, however, impressed with her inability to consult them over such actions. Their attempts to curtail Marsden's independence led to a bitter dispute over her ability to take autonomous decisions. She later wrote that even during their suffrage activism, she and colleagues such as Mary Gawthorpe (1881–1973) were sceptical of it: 'At the very kernel of the [Manchester suffrage] community was a tiny group which in its intimate moments and as an unholy joke called itself the S.O.S. They were Sick of Suffrage.'

Marsden claimed that all those who had 'personality, conspicuous ability, or undocile temper' were milled from the movement by the WSPU leadership, who worked in the style of an 'Eastern potentate'.[8] From around 1910, Mary Gawthorpe became an invalid following her suffrage activism and hunger strikes, and she was gradually side-lined in the movement, though she did not care to publicise her ambivalence about suffragism. Making more public protest, Marsden resigned from the WSPU, with great bitterness, in January 1911. Her career had been marked by frustration at the anti-democratic and bullying leadership style, and exemplifies the tensions which caused other members such as Billington-Greig, Edith How-Martyn and Charlotte Despard to secede in 1907 to form the Women's Freedom League. Marsden herself hoped to publish her feminist journal as a supplement to the WFL periodical, *The Vote*, but apparently came to feel that even this link to suffrage politics was too close for comfort. Even the supposedly democratic WFL had become too dominated by its leader, Charlotte Despard, for her liking. *The Freewoman* was therefore a political independent, and it became the focal point for a group of avant-garde women who were both shaped by their involvement in suffragism, and yet also in active rebellion against its principles. Rebecca West, who as a teenager had worked closely with Mary Gawthorpe in the WSPU, became the paper's literary editor. The journal attracted writers and readers as diverse as the novelist Dorothy Richardson, the unashamed proponent of free sexual unions and free motherhood Françoise Lafitte (later married to Havelock Ellis), the flamboyant socialist H. G. Wells, and trades union organiser Ada Nield Chew. The paper survived, under various names, from 1911 to 1919, and it became a leading publisher of modernist fiction and poetry. To be 'a freewoman' became an identity enthusiastically taken up by readers of the paper. Readers quickly incorporated it into their vocabulary and apparently identified with it. 'Freewoman' implied a personification of feminist ideals that was clearly attractive and memorable. In its early years, 'feminist' or 'freewoman' were identities and political spaces that developed across the grain, so to speak, of the suffrage movement. Its avant-garde connotations are difficult to pin down politically, since left–right designations are notoriously unstable and misleading amongst such circles. What is clear, however, is that for a brief period amongst Edwardian women, roughly 1911 to 1915, what it was to be a 'feminist' was intimately connected with being 'avant-garde' – and in a different way, closely bound up with suffragism. Indeed, the 'freewoman' identity has been described by historians as 'a composite of the "modern woman" and the "militant woman" '.[9]

Despite the clear gendering of identities such as 'freewoman' or 'new woman', one of the distinguishing features of being a 'feminist' was its gender neutrality. To be part of avant-garde or bohemian circles in the early twentieth century indicated an openness to the joint efforts of men and women to share their cultural and political spaces. In 'advanced' circles, the replacement of 'woman's movement' by 'feminist' marked a new openness to the activism of men. An initial advertisement for *The Freewoman* in *The New Age* had noted:

> Literary contributions will be sought from men equally with women, and it is hoped that the paper will find male readers as readily as women. It is considered that any theory of feminism which regards itself as the private province of women's interests is an absurdity, and that any reputable theory must hold that the interests of men are involved at least as equally as those of women.[10]

It was no accident that a feminist review should seek readers from amongst the eclectic radical, socialist, and modernist readership of *The New Age*. The journal attracted male and female readers who regarded themselves as 'radicals' and iconoclasts in one dimension or another, a readership described by John Carswell as 'uncommitted, progressive and for the most part young'.[11] The editors of *The Freewoman* suspected that many of these readers were alienated by the patronising tone the *New Age* editor, Alfred Orage, adopted towards feminism and women's suffrage. Orage, a friend of Mary Gawthorpe from their shared participation in the avant-garde Leeds Arts Club, commented to her that 'My view is that there are not enough writers who understand feminism to run a paper; still more that there are not enough readers to keep it going.'[12] Feminism, in his view, was likely to be 'superfluous'. Nonetheless, writers associated with *The New Age* (many of them men) did indeed flock to *The Freewoman*, and the two existed in a productive state of friendly rivalry. As an open review, *The Freewoman* hosted opinions from all viewpoints, including anti-suffrage. It became known above all as a site where sexual matters, from masturbation to inversion, could be discussed. This focus became one of the most characteristic and controversial features of 'advanced feminism'.

However, this sexual explicitness, and the satirical spats with avant-garde socialists made it hard to also please readers used to the more women-dominated suffrage papers, where sexual matters tended to be discussed only within social purity idioms, satire was almost unknown, and conflicting ideas were kept relatively low-key. One reader wrote to the editor:

> The indelicacy of many of the letters and articles makes these unpleasant reading for normal people. Mrs Hinde thinks it is a pity that the main idea of being a 'freewoman' should be the continual harping on sexual matters.[13]

Following accusations from Olive Schreiner and others that *The Freewoman* was male-dominated, and propagated 'the tone of the brutal self-indulgent selfish male',[14] Dora Marsden announced that around half of the contributors were male. Very few of the men who worked actively within the suffrage movement openly identified as feminists or supported the avant-garde *Freewoman*. It seems likely that such men already felt uncertain about their acceptance within suffrage societies, though individuals such as George Lansbury, Henry Nevinson and Frederick Pethick-Lawrence were high profile in their support. Their membership of separate 'men's leagues' may have left them feeling 'belittled' and divorced from the suffrage 'storm centre', but this rarely translated into the kind of open criticism that became a hallmark of feminism.[15] As men, they may have felt that critical comments were too easy to associate with the open antagonism of the male anti-suffragists (Antis). The men who felt most comfortable as 'advanced feminists' (or at least as the interlocutors of feminism) – men such as Floyd Dell, H. G. Wells, David Eder, Randolph Bourne, Harry Birnstingl and Charles Whitby – were often of Fabian or socialist background, were sometimes interested in exploring homosexuality, or were flamboyantly bohemian literary experimentalists. This chapter examines mainly female avant-garde feminists while bearing in mind that an active purpose of the feminist identity was to draw men into what had been 'the women's movement'.

Relations with suffragists

The Freewoman was initially advertised in suffrage papers as well as *The New Age*, and subscription lists reveal readers from all the main suffrage groups, as well as occasional suffrage branch subscriptions.[16] It clearly fascinated suffragists, even though, as one declared in a national paper, *The Freewoman* 'no more represent[s] the general opinion of suffragists than, say, the opinions of the Mormons represents the Christianity of the Church of England'.[17] It is clear that many had not understood the purpose of the paper, which was to uncouple feminism from suffrage. The WSPU supporter and Girton scientist Hertha Ayrton wrote to Mary Gawthorpe upon its launch, 'I wish you a very great success with your new review, which I shall of course take in and read – your name as editor is sufficient to ensure that, and the high aims with which you start are a further inducement. I only wish you had waited till after we had actually won the vote, because then a lot of money would have been released which would have made it quite easy for you to obtain the money you need to establish it.'[18]

But only a week later, Ayrton was shocked by the apparent anti-suffrage stance of the first issue:

> Miss Gawthorpe, Your vile attack on Miss Pankhurst in *The Freewoman* fills me with amazement and disquiet too deep for expression. That you, you, who talk so glibly of seeking first and foremost TRUTH AND LIGHT should follow a Mrs Billington-Greig in attacking a former colleague at the first opportunity – this is indeed a disillusionment. You, who have worked and suffered for the cause, are now betraying it, just when it is about to triumph, out of some petty personal spite . . . How dared you ask me to subscribe without giving me the faintest hint as to your changed attitude towards the whole suffrage question, and especially towards the Women's Social and Political Union?[19]

The personal rancour of attempts to distinguish feminism from suffrage are evident. Marsden herself was unable to keep her discussions philosophical, and often made personal attacks on suffrage leaders, particularly those of the WSPU. Aside from the personal bitterness, there were two main strands of criticism of suffragism that emerged amongst avant-garde feminists. First, there was a strong sense that the WSPU leadership were working for their own aggrandisement rather than for the vote. Organisationally, the movement was a failure because the leaders worked to gain resources and power, and crushed out what could have been the emancipatory power of participation in a movement for social change. As Marsden put it:

> Before the 'birth' of the 'leaders', before the trumpets, banners and catchwords, a phenomenal advance was quietly being made: It was 'actual' in individual women. Then arose 'leaders', who reduced it to a 'cause', a fixed idea, stationaryness and consequent stagnation . . . The blight of the 'leader' has brought the 'movement' to a standstill. The 'Women's Movement' is the 'Women's Halt'; with the failure to move forward, the energy that was in the impulse forward, makes them spin like spinning-tops about the pivot of the idea.[20]

Marsden analysed the emotional landscape of suffragism, portraying Militancy as meeting a need for excitement:

> a want in the lives of women which is all the more insistent because it is rarely put into words. Unless exceptional ability has opened up unusual avenues of interest, or unless they chance to be under the influence of some other satisfying emotion, women are haunted with the vague realisation that they do not count much otherwise then passively: they feel non-responsible and unnecessary save as accessories.

Women's emotions became 'like a tightly wound spring'. Through suffrage, 'from being nobody amongst very ordinary somebodies she feels she has become a person among those who count: name in papers, a celebrity: government solemnly discussing how by stretching its powers to the utmost it can deal with her: a problem.'[21] These sentiments of excitement, Marsden felt, were being cynically exploited by suffrage leaders, who were 'content to say as in the jingle, "we want, we want we want the vote", with as little as possible about "why" and "what form".' As most 'vanguard' feminists agreed, creative and inspired Militant acts, such as the hunger strike, still had the potential to transform women from passive parasites to active individuals, but this was being reined in by the organisational imperatives that dominated suffrage. Some saw this as a class problem; Ada Nield Chew, a trade union and NUWSS organiser, was clearly irritated by the dominance of suffrage by 'a small and privileged class', utterly out of touch with working women.[22] She was willing to concede that the vote might awaken women to other kinds of injustice, but that it was unlikely to do so if suffrage organisations were run along autocratic lines. Avant-garde women were not detached from the industrial and labour struggles that had become increasingly divorced from suffrage after the

WSPU had moved from Manchester to London in 1906. While the avant-garde was elitist, in search of 'superwomen',[23] superior powers were imagined to be creative, and unrelated to class. Marsden wrote:

> The inverted scale of value which holds good in social class conventions, whereby the parasite is ludicrously considered as of higher class than the producer, has made us fear to speak of class; or, if we speak of it, only to imply that the 'lower' classes are better than the 'upper'.[24]

Many of the leading avant-garde women were themselves from impoverished origins and struggled to locate themselves within the class system. They were comfortable with the language of elites, but felt as a precondition that 'rich' and 'poor' must be abolished, and all should earn their own living.

A second strand of criticism also emerged that had more substantive concerns with suffrage as a goal, and which can be read as a difference over political philosophy. Though most suffragists and feminists produced texts that operated at a level of political discourse that falls outside of formal political philosophy, they did nonetheless engage with contemporary political theory. Drawing, for example, on anarchist ideas, some feminists came to see the orientation towards the state as a failure of the women's movement. They disliked the construction of citizenship as duty and service that predominated within the suffrage movement, an idea of citizenship that had been influenced by the political idealism and moderate municipal socialism that prevailed amongst Edwardian reformers.[25] In particular, as a WSPU member Mary Knight made clear in an article in the *Westminster Review*, feminists disliked the heaviness with which state demands for more births, more housework and better quality child-rearing were laid upon women. Giving women political representation would help, Knight believed, but in more fundamental terms, what 'advanced' women needed was an individualist rejection of self-sacrifice.[26] The journalism of Teresa Billington-Greig and Dora Marsden centred on their rejection of the state as the main conduit for women's emancipation. Both preferred introspective and individualistic politics, more closely allied to modernism than to idealist ideas of service and duty.

Knight was able to maintain her anti-statism from within her suffrage organisation, and this suggests that there was less of a clear divide at the level of ordinary members between the 'advanced' women Knight described, and the more conventional suffragists. Suffrage journals continued to comment on the ideas circulating within the feminist avant-garde – those ideas freely discussed within *The Freewoman, The New Age,* the Freewoman Discussion Circle (a London-based study group), and in the cheap restaurants of Bloomsbury where feminists gathered to discuss and disagree. *Common Cause,* the NUWSS official journal, welcomed *The Freewoman*'s 'plain speaking and clear thinking', though the editor did not like the emphasis on sexual experimentation that was so characteristic of the avant-garde.[27] There was of course no absolute divide between suffrage-feminism and those who termed themselves 'feminist' in order to distinguish their politics from suffragism. Some who wrote to *The Freewoman* persisted in seeing suffrage and feminism as inseparable, or in conciliatory mode, tried to substitute their own account of the emotional landscape of suffragism. One WSPU activist, Mrs Eleanor Jacobs, continued to contribute to *The Freewoman* and *The New Age,* despite their criticisms of suffrage – indeed, there was a surprisingly committed readership of suffragists who still found feminism attractive, indicating perhaps an ability to move across ideological 'divides' at the personal and grassroots levels. Eleanor Jacobs responded to Marsden's attack on the sentimentality of suffragette leaders with her own defence of political passions:

> The fact is you are a reaction against emotionalism. Well, have you realised that the suffrage movement, and especially the Militant suffrage movement, is a reaction too – against the commonplace, sordid civilised life? That's what it was to me and I expect I'm not abnormal. We *wanted* emotionalism, and it was good for us, at any rate it made us happier – makes us happier. Idealism, comradeship, self sacrifice (*with* a 'self' to sacrifice – I liked that article) – they all helped. Suffrage with some of us is a religion (– *not* a narrow 'getting a vote' you know). When I was a girl I tried the ordinary kind of religion as an escape from the earthly commonplace, as is common, but it was never any use – too vague, too selfish, too introspective. Women's emancipation and Socialism gave hope in the world . . . Well, though I am a WSPU religious suffragist, I am a hater of gush and sentiment. I am known as phlegmatic and reserved. Though I know myself to be emotional in certain directions. No hero worshipper – yet have I felt a vague stirring of affectionate admiration in my heart when Christabel comes forward to speak! And I am a Celt. But there must be a thousand more just like me. Have you ever come across us? I don't think you quite know us? . . . Anyway, you *ought* to know something of us.[28]

Clearly, suffragists were interested in their own emotional responses, and quite open-eyed about the psychic and even erotic needs their commitment fulfilled. The introspection and desire to transform women's psyches of avant-garde feminism was not in itself unwelcome to suffrage-feminists, though the importance accorded to the realm of formal politics continued to divide them.

Avant-garde feminism

The divides over suffrage sustained the development of feminism, and slowly enabled a new intellectual space to be developed within the women's movement; one commentator described suffrage as 'the forcing house of feminism'.[29] Nonetheless, it is hard to distinguish 'avant-garde', 'éclairiste' or 'vanguard' feminists as a group. Many referred to themselves as 'advanced feminists' or 'advanced women', but included quite different political beliefs under this description. Some combined avant-garde beliefs with a continuing willingness to work within the confines of suffragism. Others wanted to emphasise their self-consciousness of being 'advanced' and 'ultra-modern', and saw disengagement from mass politics as part of this. The term 'avant-garde' has been predominantly associated with artistic and cultural innovations, but for Edwardians also carried political connotations from its mid-nineteenth-century meaning of revolutionary political radicalism.[30] 'Avant-garde' indicates a discourse or social imaginary within feminism, rather than a movement. It can be understood as a primarily textual space, rather than a tightly drawn circle. It thus serves as a heuristic device rather than a precise political affiliation; it loosely designates the interests of a number of thinkers who regarded themselves (in some contexts) as feminists. It certainly does not indicate that there was no disagreement within this grouping, which was marked by splenetic controversy. 'Avant-garde' does, however, usefully characterise some features of feminist discourse: the idealisation of originality, rejection of forebears and sense of rupture with the past, the denial of essences and eternal truths, anti-conventionality, artistic experimentalism and so on.

For the thinkers and activists included in this 'avant-garde' realm, the term 'feminist' needed no prefix to indicate these concerns. By itself, 'feminist' had come to indicate an engagement with 'modern' concerns of the psyche, individuality and sexuality.[31] What was the content of feminism that distinguished it from suffrage? Edna Kenton, an American *Freewoman* subscriber and experimental theatre writer, argued forcefully:

> Feminism is not a concrete thing, to be touched with hands or seen of eyes; *it is any woman's spiritual and intellectual attitude toward herself*

> *and toward life. It is her conscious attempt to realize Personality*; to make her own decisions instead of having them made for her; to sink the old humbled or rebelling slave in the new creature who is mistress of herself . . . Feminism in its essence – if it is anything – is a great personal, joyous adventure with one's untried self . . . To attempt consciously to realize Personality, to seek the personal and the larger meanings of life, is, as nearly as it may be defined, the spiritual urge back of the feminist movement.[32]

To seek trivial political rights was overshadowed by this interior journey. Dora Marsden described 'rights' as 'nothing more than a collection of fables made up to amuse children in nurseries'. In egoist terms, one simply had to *take*, rather than *ask for* freedom: 'A people with free instincts would have nothing to do with a despicable whining about rights; they would rise up to take and hold – what they *can* take and hold.'[33] Teresa Billington-Greig made the most sustained case against the women's movement's prioritisation of suffrage and inclusion within the state, in two articles published at the end of 1911 in *The Freewoman* and *The Contemporary Review*. She claimed that 'The channel of politics is all too narrow and shallow for [feminism] . . . Feminism would re-make society, would set up new standards, would destroy old customs, would establish a new morality. It frankly sets out to do great deeds of destruction and reconstruction. It asks a new world.'[34] Feminists were to expect, and revel in battling against, the fierce resistance to this kind of revolutionary change. The suffragist, by contrast, had 'sought the line of least resistance for her advance, and has reduced her creed to a minimum to take advantage of it'. This meant that 'The great mass of women suffragists are suffragists, and nothing more.' No feminist revolution would follow the gaining of the vote; indeed, Billington-Greig suspected that newly-enfranchised women, left 'raw and unskilled' by the failure of the suffrage movement to engage in political argument, were more likely to work against women's interests. Suffrage activism 'shuts out study, thought, independence, the quickening force of personal conviction; it opens the door to obsession and to ignorant intolerance. In place of mental activity, we have blank minds.'

This assessment of suffrage-feminism went hand-in-hand with a deeper political critique of the compulsions and powers of the state. The democratic political machine, Billington-Greig argued in *The Freewoman*, was coercive, party-dominated and corrupt, by its very nature. Democracy represented the tyranny of the majority, as well as being bureaucratic and unresponsive to 'the living thought of the living race'. She conceded: 'If government exists, women are of course entitled to share in it. Their right is not the question at issue here.' But she was convinced that feminists needed to imagine a system outside of the 'governing machine' in order to achieve 'full human liberty for women'.[35]

Although this might imply a humanist commitment to the equal liberty and development of all, avant-garde feminists sought to delineate those women (or 'superwomen') who might form the 'vanguard' of feminism through their possession of 'personality', and their ability to listen to and express their 'inner voice'. A mass movement, along suffrage lines, would only invite the mediocre into politics. Teresa Billington-Greig proposed in 1911 that the feminist movement of the future must be 'a movement to make possible supermen and superwomen'.[36] Her politics were infused with a typical modernist fear of the crowd; as she argued in the *Contemporary Review*, 'Under present conditions, control by the multitude must mean control by ignorance, mediocrity and commonplace. . . . The rate of advance under democracy is measured by the average intellect and activity; and with us the average is still low.'[37]

Beatrice Hastings explicitly sought to bring 'people who matter' into the feminist movement, because she believed that 'Numbers are negligible nowadays. Statesmen know perfectly well how to control numbers.'[38] For women to have children without reference to men's support, to dress without care for convention, to gain a job, to know themselves spiritually, to give free rein to their creative impulses – all these things were far more important than suffrage, and would probably only be achieved by, at best (as Dora Marsden estimated), one woman in four. Her first *Freewoman* editorial had commented: 'There must be, say ten [freewomen] in the British Isles.' These ten had a duty to develop their genius and individuality, even if at the expense of others, 'because *it is by way of the few that come those innovations which later will be the higher law for the many*.'[39] Feminism was not understood in these early stages as a democratic and egalitarian movement. Given the intellectual context, this was not surprising. While modernists are portrayed by historians such as John Carey as ground-breaking in their elitism,[40] an elitist approach and tendency to dismiss popular political participation was fairly common currency amongst Edwardians. Elitism spans Fabian, new liberal and avant-garde feminist political discourses. The Fabians had tended to regard the poor as positively disqualified from participation:

> it is difficult for their atrophied brains to grasp an idea. Even if they could, their devitalised natures and anaemic bodies would be incapable of working for it. This explains why *no socialist has or ever will come from the slums*.[41]

This attitude can also be found within the pro-democracy suffrage movement. The Fabian and suffragist Ethel Snowden commented that 'the majority never wants what is good for it; never will keep abreast of the times. The history of the ages has ever been the story of an intelligent minority dragging on the huge mass of an ignorant and unthinking majority.'[42] The characteristic beliefs of the feminist avant-garde were not entirely iconoclastic, nor even entirely opposed to suffrage, but drew on the available political languages of their time.

Transatlantic feminism

Feminism gained cultural capital through its association with the idea of 'the new' and 'the modern', and for many British feminists, this was captured by the connotations of being 'American'. When the British journalist, W. L. George attempted to convey what it was to be feminist in 1913, he described it as 'one vast, incoherent, lusty shout . . . so young in liberty, so American and so intoxicated with novelty.'[43] There were in fact very close links between advanced women in Britain and the United States, with many close working relationships being formed. Individuals such as Mary Gawthorpe, Harriet Stanton Blatch, Rebecca West, Crystal Eastman, Mina Loy and Randolph Bourne moved freely between the two countries, and others kept up long correspondences. Dora Marsden, though she did not visit the United States, was surprised by how widely read and known *The Freewoman* was across the Atlantic. She had always aimed to transcend the national perspective of suffrage and *The Freewoman* was positioned from its first issue as a cosmopolitan magazine.

Suffragists had, of course, worked through transnational relationships, prompted initially by the transatlantic anti-slavery movement, and also by strong links in the temperance and social purity movements.[44] Since the early years of the twentieth century, they had co-operated through the conferences of the International Woman Suffrage Alliance. But overtones of rivalry remained; NUWSS leader Millicent Fawcett was dismissive about the American suffrage movement, branding the United States constitution 'the most conservative on earth'.[45] She stressed the distinctiveness of 'English' national character, and its role in shaping British suffragism.[46] It seems that some suffragists regarded the two national contexts as competing for both contemporary influence and historical legitimacy, rather than genuinely occupying a shared space. Though there was a rhetoric of sisterhood within suffrage periodicals, a strong sense of rivalry also emerges, particularly in the somewhat laboured explanations of why

Britain was still at the forefront of the suffrage struggle, despite the suffrage victories in the American Western states.[47]

Irritated by British suffragists' claims to be the 'storm centre' of the world movement, *The Freewoman*'s initial publicity stated 'It is believed that feminism would be conceived in truer perspective if the English movement could keep in review the forms of activity in which the impulse finds expression in countries other than our own.'[48] Marsden came to see the Anglo-American element as essential for both her British and American readerships, declaring 'I am hoping to be able to make the paper into an Anglo-American Review in a literary sense as well as a commercial. We in England know practically nothing about the new spirit of America.'[49]

It seemed, though, that in the United States, feminism was more compatible with suffragism. The editor of the literature department within the National American Women's Suffrage Association (NAWSA), Frances Bjorkman, wrote of her 'delirious joy over *The Freewoman*. It has been really funny to see one after the other of us pick it up casually and immediately become rooted to the spot for hours.'[50] Marsden responded with surprise that suffragists should find it so compelling. Bjorkman wrote back with a revealing description of what it was to be a suffragist while also inhabiting the political avant-garde circles of New York:

> [we] are not suffragists 'pure and simple.' Miss [Jessie] Ashley is a socialist [militant suffragist crossed out] with strongly I.W.W. tendencies and insurgent towards the Socialist Party's attitude towards women. Mrs [Mary Ware] Dennett is a Single Taxer with strong Socialist sympathies. I belong to the Socialist Party, but find it impossible to become interested or to have any sympathy with Party tactics, having a sense more for the philosophical principles of Socialism in the broadest sense than in the mere establishment of the economic system of Socialism. Really, we are all much more feminists than suffragists, although we are all three anxious to see suffrage put through as speedily as possible.[51]

As within the British suffrage societies, there was a sense of 'sick of suffrage' within NAWSA. Bjorkman commented 'Suffrage here is absolutely booming, but feminism has hardly so much as lifted its head. Whenever I feel the former to be an insupportably dull and obvious business, I take a dip into *The Freewoman* and emerge refreshed.'[52] The American suffrage movement was conceived as a broad church, open to both those who supported the vote alone, and those who identified as feminists.

After a damaging split between 1870 and 1890, the NAWSA had come to tolerate rebellious and critical factions. In 1912, for example, it became official NAWSA policy that its officers could abandon non-partisanship and work with any political parties of their choosing.[53] Where British critics had felt compelled to resign from suffrage groups on differences of principle and tactics, the NAWSA made no such demands. Bjorkman and others in the Literature Department were able to express their *ennui* with suffrage, their lack of faith in their own suffrage journal, and to publicise *The Freewoman* in a personal and semi-official capacity.

Nonetheless, Bjorkman recognised that her suffrage colleagues might not welcome the attempt to situate NAWSA as 'feminist'. In 1912 she had arranged to reprint some articles from *The Freewoman* as a pamphlet titled 'Bondwomen', and wrote to Dora Marsden of her delight in being able to embrace the 'feminist' identity openly for the first time: 'The advertisement [sic] in the back of "Bondwomen" is something quite new. We've never advertised ourselves before as purveyors of "feminist" literature. I live in joyous anticipation of a protest from some of our members, who take their "suffrage neat" – I'm so thankful to Miss Marsden for teaching me that word – when they learn about the National's *Freewoman* affiliations.'[54]

Bjorkman felt her suffrage work to be 'idealess', and presented her department's literature as 'rainbow flyers' which give 'the main suffrage argument in words of one syllable and screaming type on bright colored paper'.[55] Though she wanted to bring working-class women into the women's movement, she was clearly dissatisfied with the 'lowbrow', tabloid style methods used to gain a mass following. While she saw suffrage as 'a most effective instrument for fomenting general feminine revolt and for focalizing the rising forces of feminine discontent', she was extremely ambivalent about her work with the NAWSA:

> If you could know the 'row' that we at headquarters have just been through . . . which centered in this very matter of 'idealessness' you would realize how rich was our appreciation of your last two utterances on the subject. As editor of the literature department, I confess to a blush of shame remembering all the 'woman in the home, votes and babies, votes for mothers' stuff which we are so disingenuously putting out; but I try to console myself with the thought that occasionally we print something that is REAL – instance, 'Bondwomen.'[56]

Bjorkman's irritation at the 'mass marketing' of suffrage, and the conservatism of suffragists who would not align to feminism continually surfaced in her letters to the *Freewoman* office. This Anglo-American conversation became a substantial and ongoing channel of communication and exchange, as *The Freewoman* came to be represented by American enthusiasts such as Edna Kenton and Floyd Dell, became more widely distributed in the United States, and encouraged a number of transatlantic intellectual exchanges to be set up, within its pages and through private correspondence. For a brief period, before the war ushered in a more confining intellectual environment and made transnational periodical publishing more difficult in material terms, avant-garde feminism was constructed as a space that was free of the rivalry and strongly national ethos of the suffrage movement. These exchanges created the possibility of a shared intellectual field for feminists, and certainly the 'egoist' and modernist ideas of avant-garde feminism were firmly in circulation in both countries by 1914. In 1916, bibliographies of feminism in the United States still listed *The Egoist* (the successor to *The Freewoman*), as well as other avant-garde periodicals such as *The Little Review* and *The Masses* as essential reading for feminists.[57]

The political argument of advanced feminism had a profound influence upon attempts to define feminism in the United States. A contributor to *The Forum* in July 1914 argued that 'Woman's prime function in the social organisation, like man's, is to be a self: this at any cost, even at the price of foregoing her other important function of motherhood . . . Woman's primary right [is] full majority and self accountability; full freedom to test her strength as woman and to bring her feminine individuality to supreme and perfect unfolding.'[58] An American feminist, Rose Young, acknowledged in *Good Housekeeping* that the nature of feminism was still an open question in 1914, but she regarded it as beyond question that feminism concerned individualistic self-development, spiritual freedom, and an end to self-sacrifice.[59] Suffrage, then, was almost nowhere to be found. In typically blunt terms, the American anthropologist Elsie Clews Parsons summed up the advanced feminist case: the vote would do 'a little [good], but only a very, very little. It doesn't do men so very much good, does it? It's more important for women to get rid of their petticoats than to get a vote. And it's still more important for them to get a good job.'[60]

Anti-suffragism

Given the uneasy relationship between suffragists and the feminist avant-garde, how appropriate is it to describe the latter as anti-suffragist? Certainly, committed suffragists regarded many feminists as the best advertisements anti-suffragists could hope for. It was felt by many 'Antis' that suffragists were made more vulnerable to accusations of immorality and degeneration by their links to a wider feminist movement. The high profile anti-feminist Ethel Harrison (wife of Frederic Harrison) thus referred to the suffragists as 'the Feminist party', and the anti-feminist writer Ethel Colquhoun also elided the two.[61] In fact, the distinction between 'Anti' and feminist was not especially clear. Rose Young pointed out that

> Being an anti-suffragist by no means opposes one to far-reaching feministic conviction as to the individual development of women . . . Dora Marsden, the most professedly individualistic woman in England today, the most relentless in her jeers and jibes at the spiritual subjection of women, is harshly, sneeringly anti-suffrage. So is individualistic Emma Goldman in this country . . . Being a suffragist by no means implies being a feminist.[62]

There was clearly hostility towards suffragism within the 'feminist avant-garde', but along very different lines from the 'Antis'. Politically, anti-suffragists and suffragists shared many beliefs, centring on a sense of women's civic contribution based on ideas of service and duty. The progressive 'Forward Policy' Antis, led by Mrs Humphrey (Mary) Ward, clashed with the more misogynist stance adopted by the leader of the Anti-Suffrage League, Lord Curzon.[63] Mary Ward emphasised women's abilities to translate their skills in housekeeping to a civic level – the level of *local* government only, she emphasised. But in many senses, her understanding of the basis of women's citizenship was not dissimilar from that of her opponents, the suffragists. Mary Ward occupied the same ground as those many suffragists who ascribed to women a benign moral influence. Ward argued that women should gain 'their full share in the State of social effort and social mechanism. We look for their increasing activity in that higher State which rests on thought, conscience and moral influence', while rejecting their actual participation through voting. For Ward, 'women must claim a right – but only the right to serve'.[64] Women's service through municipal or national 'housekeeping' was the common ideal that linked the suffragists to the Antis, and was the nub of what motivated feminists of the avant-garde variety to reject suffragism. Neither the progressive or reactionary wings of the anti-suffrage movement held any attraction for the feminist avant-garde, and no political alliances were formed between these two dimensions of opposition to suffrage.

The trajectory of avant-garde feminists in relation to suffrage differed. In the 1913 publicity for the successor to *The Freewoman*, it was clearly conveyed that

> *The New Freewoman* is NOT a Suffrage Paper.
>
> It Is the only journal which treats of the philosophical base of the insurrectionary movement.
>
> It Is a philosophic Crucible in which all authoritarian morality is dissolved.
>
> It Is an intellectual acid, eating up the empty concepts which consume the energies of the workers to no purpose; Rights, Justice, Liberty, Equality, Fraternity and the rest.
>
> It Is a journal which will make rebels into men to be reckoned with.[65]

The modernist preference for rebellion, their lack of faith in rights, their preference for a politics of elitism, had become dominant, and rejecting suffrage had become a prime way to signify this. Dora Marsden declared in 1914 that 'suffrage is wholly a matter of indifference.'[66] The transformation of *The Freewoman* from 'a weekly feminist review' in 1911, to its new title of 1914, *The Egoist, an Individualist Review* has frequently been read as a triumph over feminism of misogynist modernists such as American Ezra Pound, who became the paper's highly assertive literary editor. Dora Marsden, however, provided another explanation, centred on suffrage:

> Far from being erratic the development of the FREEWOMAN-EGOIST has been in one unbroken line . . . Claims are the reproaches of the powerless: whines for protection. All the suffragists' 'claims' are of this order, and it was to disentangle the journal from association with these and with the long list of whines, Free Speech, Free Love, Free Assembly and what-not, that 'Freewoman' became EGOIST.[67]

Dora Marsden came to believe that voting was a mistaken goal for women. It tied them more closely into a corrupt system, and in asking that such powers be granted to them, it made suffragists into the clients of powerful men. But without the impetus of a suffrage commitment, Marsden, like Teresa Billington-Greig, eventually withdrew into private life and political inaction. Feminism, especially in its egoist formation, could not sustain a mass movement, and came to have a much more generalised, conventional meaning during World War One and afterwards. It began to emerge as an innocuous synonym of 'women's movement'; a 1915 British textbook for Roman Catholic students, for example, discussed women's powers of social reform and service under the title *Christian Feminism*.[68] The restrictive atmosphere of wartime Europe and America brought to an end the unique conditions of a relatively free press, and intensely felt political commitment allied to intellectual and artistic creativity. In the new atmosphere, it seems that introspection came to hold less promise for feminists. Nonetheless, the ideas of avant-garde feminists did not entirely fade away in the changed atmosphere of Britain at war; they are clearly present, for example, in Wilma Meikle's 1916 book titled *Towards a Sane Feminism*.[69] Her plea for 'sane feminism' was a vanguard call for women to abandon domesticity and motherhood as their ideals. In keeping with her avant-garde predecessors, Meikle saw the vote was a relatively trivial issue, a red herring for feminists.

Some within 'advanced' circles, however, retained their commitment to suffrage. Beatrice Hastings, for all her dislike of women's parasitism and the sentimental morality of suffragism, still identified as a suffragist. But she supported Militants for quite unusual reasons – not so much for their claims about justice and representation, but rather for the opportunity Militancy gave to women to free themselves of obedience to the law, to find it within themselves to throw off tyranny. She made her case in terms of will and personality, rather than justice and social change. This was by no means a unique position, though it was a minority one. Writing under many different pseudonyms in *The New Age*, Hastings presented herself, and was read, as a sometime critic of Militant suffragism, sometimes as an exponent, sometimes as an anti-feminist suffragist, and on several occasions as a man. Her suffragist and feminist identities were playfully explored in a manner disconcertingly different from the serious and politically committed suffragist periodicals.[70]

The idea of women's emancipation supported by all Hastings's 'voices' was based on a consistent claim that women needed to take freedom for themselves, that it could not be granted by men or the state. Her campaign against the Criminal Law Amendment Act of 1912 had led her to be highly sceptical of the influence of women in public life. This Act, which gave police increased powers of arrest against men suspected of procuring girls for the 'White Slave Trade', had been campaigned for by many suffragists, and was welcomed by them as a sign of their political influence. Hastings regarded white slavery as a dangerous fiction, and railed against the purity and equal moral standards so dear to most within the suffrage movement. This made her deeply unpopular in some suffrage-feminist circles. Her 1910 book, *Woman's Worst Enemy: Woman* was typically 'avant-garde' in its denigration of women's weakness of will and lack of personality. It was read as damaging to the cause of suffrage; *Votes for Women* refused to review it, and Hastings complained bitterly that it had been 'officially' boycotted. Hastings's relationship with suffrage was complex, and after 1912 became increasingly strained. While suffrage-feminism had been a possible 'double identity' when feminism was first coined, it was extremely hard to sustain as a political position.

Others in the avant-garde simply found suffrage confining and boring. Teresa Billington-Greig wrote of the 'deadly apathetic dullness' of the suffrage movement. Rebecca West, who had been active as a 'flapper dogsbody' with the WSPU between 1907 and 1909,[71] wrote to Dora Marsden about *The Freewoman* in 1913: 'Can't we stop attacking the WSPU? The poor dears are weak at metaphysics but they are doing their best to revolt, and the discussion concerning the parish pump could be no duller than the discussion of the Pankhurst soul. It will plunge us into the same interminable quibbling correspondence as at the beginning of the last Freewoman . . . I think it would be much better to drop it.'[72] Nonetheless, West did not think that voting was a mistake for women. Looking back from a vantage point of the late 1920s, she wrote that while *Freewoman* feminism had been born from discontent with suffragism, this was misplaced 'as an accusation against the Pankhursts and suffragettes in general, because they were simply doing their job, and it was certainly a whole time job'. West therefore remained convinced that the suffrage movement was limited but worthwhile, while noting that in 1911, 'there was equally certainly a need for someone to stand aside and ponder on the profounder aspects of feminism.'[73] Mary Gawthorpe was also unimpressed by the direction that suffrage politics had taken, but she was unwilling to resign from the WSPU, and came to resent the philosophical anarchism of Dora Marsden. She continued to take sporadic part in suffrage demonstrations, and to work for the Pankhursts even after her emigration to the United States.[74] Nonetheless, her autobiography, published in 1962, stressed not her high-profile suffrage work, but rather the socialist and eclectic origins of her activism, through the Labour Church, ILP, Clarion clubs, Leeds Arts Club and Theosophical Society. Suffrage commitments were portrayed as emerging out of this context for a limited time; a mixture of socialist and labour politics, plus a utopian cultural politics described as 'the germ of a new future' remained the bedrock of Gawthorpe's political activism.[75]

Conclusion

How much did their relationship to suffragism divide, unite and define avant-garde feminists? The high-profile critique of suffrage served to publicise the invention of 'feminism', gaining letters and editorials in national newspapers – in this sense, the debate about the boundaries of 'feminism' and suffragism was welcomed by avant-garde women. Since building a social movement was not their goal, they were indifferent to the divisive power of suffrage schisms and controversies. Teresa Billington-Greig had made it clear that she sought an extended debate amongst the 'discontented and disgusted feminists' who had given up on the suffrage struggle and sought a deeper form of rebellion. She hoped that 'Organised lectures, discussions and debates on a free platform should prepare the way for a vigorous rational development in feminism.'[76] Activism was put off to the far future, and this can be understood as leaving this strand of feminism marginalised in a practical sense, though not in intellectual terms. Nonetheless, the feminist introspective focus, their emphasis on psychic, economic and cultural emancipation, was extremely influential, both within early modernism, and as prefiguring later feminist concerns in the twentieth century. The early articulation of a space outside of suffrage enabled activists and intellectuals to think about deeper issues, not just of public policy, but of personal, sexual and psychic liberation.

The Freewoman was intended to be an open review, and however strange this was to readers used to the partisan, campaigning suffrage periodicals, it was a space that thrived on controversy and disagreement. The contentions over suffrage were therefore bread and butter to avant-garde feminism, and enabled the crystallisation of alternative political philosophies – egoist, individualist and elitist. Though other traditions fed into avant-garde feminism, the experiences and ideas of suffragism were a necessary precursor to the creation of avant-garde feminism, and a continuing stimulus to debate throughout the first two decades of the twentieth century. The term 'feminism', however, became too strongly associated with the politics of the women's movement to adequately convey the avant-garde critique. 'Feminist' was adopted after World War One by both the 'old' equalitarians and the 'new' maternalist camps; neither grouping reflected avant-garde concerns of rupture and iconoclasm. The avant-garde vision of feminism as central to the creative impulse had faded and writers such as Virginia Woolf declared: 'Let us write that word in large black letters on a sheet of foolscap; then solemnly apply a match to the paper.'[77]

Notes

1. T. Billington-Greig, 'Feminism and Politics', *Contemporary Review*, November 1911, reprinted in *The Non-Violent Militant: Selected Writings of Teresa Billington-Greig*, ed. Carol McPhee and Ann FitzGerald (London: Routledge & Kegan Paul, 1987), p. 226. This chapter summarises the arguments developed at greater length in L. Delap, *The Feminist Avant-Garde: Transatlantic Encounters of the Early Twentieth Century* (Cambridge: Cambridge University Press, 2007).
2. E. Francis, *The Secret Treachery of Words: Feminism and Modernism in America* (Minneapolis: University of Minnesota Press, 2002).
3. T. Billington-Greig, *The Militant Suffrage Movement: Emancipation in a Hurry* (London: F. Palmer, 1911).
4. T. Billington-Greig, 'For Sex-Equality', *New Age*, 30 May 1907, p. 73; 'Feminism and Politics', *Contemporary Review*, November 1911.
5. T. Billington-Greig, 'A Free Feminist Platform', *New Age*, 30 March 1911, p. 525.
6. D. Triformis [B. Hastings], 'To Your Posts, Feminists!' *New Age*, 16 February 1911, p. 368.
7. *Daily Mirror*, 31 March 1909, p. 1. For further biographical details on Marsden, see L. Garner, *A Brave and Beautiful Spirit: Dora Marsden 1882–1960* (Aldershot: Avebury, 1990); B. Clarke, *Dora Marsden and Early Modernism* (Ann Arbor: University of Michigan Press, 1996).
8. D. Marsden, *The Egoist*, 15 June 1914, pp. 223, 224.
9. Clarke, *Dora Marsden and Early Modernism*, pp. 47, 98.
10. *New Age*, 23 November 1911, p. 95.
11. J. Carswell, *Lives and Letters: A.R. Orage, Katherine Mansfield, Beatrice Hastings, John Middleton Murray, S.S. Koteliansky, 1906–1957* (New York: New Directions, 1978), p. 35.
12. Orage, copied to Marsden by Gawthorpe, Dora Marsden Collection Princeton University Library (henceforth DMC, or indicated by roman numerals (box number) followed by folder number), 8 September 1911: II, 1. On the Leeds Arts Club, see T. Steele, *Alfred Orage and the Leeds Arts Club, 1893–1923* (London: Scolar Press, 1990).
13. Hinde to Marsden, DMC July 12 1912: III, 2.
14. Schreiner to Havelock Ellis, 7 August 1912, in *The Letters of Olive Schreiner 1876–1920*, ed. Cronwright-Schreiner (London: Unwin, 1924), p. 312, Quoted in L. Bland, *Banishing the Beast: English Feminism and Sexual Morality 1885–1914* (London: Penguin, 1995), p. 265.
15. S. S. Holton, *Suffrage Days: Stories from the Women's Suffrage Movement* (London: Routledge, 1996), p. 184.
16. L. Delap, '*The Freewoman*, Periodical Communities, and the Feminist Reading Public', Princeton *University Library Chronicle*, 61, 2 (Winter 2000), p. 236.
17. Catherine Furley Smith, *The Morning Post*, 26 July 1912, p. 5
18. Ayrton to Gawthorpe, 19 November 1911, DMC: II, 25.
19. Ayrton to Gawthorpe, 26 November 1911, DMC: II, 25.
20. D. Marsden, 'Views and Comments', *New Freewoman*, 15 November 1913, p. 203.
21. D. Marsden, *The Egoist*, 15 June 1914, pp. 225–6.

22. A. Chew, *The Freewoman*, 18 April 1912, p. 435.
23. L. Delap, 'The Superwoman: Theories of Gender and Genius in Edwardian Britain', *The Historical Journal*, 47, 1 (2004), pp. 101–26.
24. D. Marsden, *The Freewoman*, 16 May 1912, p. 502.
25. For a fuller description of the intellectual roots of the 'politics of conscience' that dominated the women's movement, see S. Pedersen, *Eleanor Rathbone and the Politics of Conscience* (New Haven: Yale University Press, 2004).
26. M. Knight, *The Westminster Review*, 1909, July, p. 39.
27. *Common Cause*, 30 November 1911, p. 600.
28. Mrs E. Jacobs to D. Marsden 4 January 1912: III, 3.
29. A. H. to D. Marsden, UD: III, 1.
30. Renato Poggioli, *The Theory of the Avant-Garde* (Harvard: Belknap Press, 1968), pp. 5–12; P. Peppis, *Literature, Politics and the English Avant-Garde: Nation and Empire 1901–1918* (Cambridge: Cambridge University Press, 2000).
31. L. Bland, *Banishing the Beast: English Feminism and Sexual Morality 1885–1914* (London: Penguin, 1995); N. Cott, *The Grounding of Modern Feminism* (New Haven: Yale University Press, 1987), chapter 1; C. Stansell, *American Moderns: Bohemian New York and the Creation of a New Century* (New York: Henry Holt and Co., 2000).
32. E. Kenton, 'Feminism Will Give Men More Fun, Women Greater Scope, Children Better Parents, Life More Charm', *Delineator*, July 1914, p. 17. Original emphasis.
33. D. Marsden, *The Freewoman*, 12 September 1912, p. 321.
34. McPhee and Fitzgerald, *The Non-Violent Militant*, p. 227 and *passim*.
35. Billington-Greig, *The Freewoman*, 21 December 1911, 'Women and Government', reprinted in McPhee and Fitzgerald, *The Non-Violent Militant*, pp. 236–9.
36. Billington-Greig, *The Militant Suffrage Movement*, p. 213.
37. Billington-Greig, 'Feminism and Politics'.
38. D. Triformis [B. Hastings], 'To Your Posts, Feminists!', p. 368.
39. D. Marsden, *The Freewoman*, 25 April 1912, p. 444, emphasis added.
40. J. Carey, *The Intellectuals and the Masses: Pride and Prejudice Among the Literary Intelligentsia, 1880–1939* (London: Faber & Faber, 1992).
41. R. C. Bentinck, in *Women's Fabian Tracts*, ed. Sally Alexander (London: Routledge, 1988 (1910)), p. 144.
42. E. Snowden, in *Woman: A Few Shrieks!* ed. C. Smedley (Letchworth: Garden City Press, 1908), pp. 124–5.
43. W. L. George, *Women and To-Morrow* (London: Herbert Jenkins, 1913), pp. 177–8.
44. J. Rendall, *The Origins of Modern Feminism: Women in Britain, France and the United States 1780–1860* (Basingstoke: Macmillan, 1985); P. G. Harrison, *Connecting Links: The British and American Woman Suffrage Movements, 1900–1914* (Conn.: Greenwood Press, 2000).
45. Quoted in C. Bolt, *The Women's Movements in the United States and Britain from the 1790s to the 1920s* (New York: Harvester Wheatsheaf, 1993), p. 247.
46. See Fawcett's chapter on 'England' in Theodore Stanton (ed.), *The Woman Question in Europe* (New York: G. P. Putnam's Sons, 1884), discussed by Sandra Stanley Holton, 'British Freewomen: National Identity, Constitutionalism and Languages of Race in Early Suffragist Histories', in E. J. Yeo (ed.), *Radical Femininity; Women's Self-Representation in the Public Sphere* (Manchester: Manchester University Press, 1998), pp. 153–4.

47. Emmeline Pethick Lawrence, 'Across the Atlantic', *Votes for Women*, 11 October 1912, p. 25.
48. *New Age* advertisement for *The Freewoman*, 23 November 1911, p. 95.
49. D. Marsden to F. Bjorkman, 11 January 1913, Mary Ware Dennett Papers. Schlesinger Library, Radcliffe Institute (henceforth MWDP).
50. F. Bjorkman to the editors of *The Freewoman*, 24 February 1912, MWDP.
51. F. Bjorkman to D. Marsden, 20 May 1912, MWDP. Jessie Ashley was a lawyer, and partner of the IWW leader Bill Haywood. Mary Ware Dennett, formerly a noted arts and crafts leatherworker, worked in the 1910s to secure civil liberties, and women's rights to birth control in the National Birth Control League. See N. Cott, *The Grounding of Modern Feminism*, p. 90; C. Chen, *The Sex Side of Life: Mary Ware Dennett's Pioneering Battle for Birth Control* (New York: New Press, 1996).
52. F. Bjorkman to G. Jardine, 16 August 1912, MWDP.
53. Cott, *The Grounding of Modern Feminism*, p. 29.
54. F. Bjorkman to G. Jardine, 16 August 1912, MWDP.
55. F. Bjorkman to D. Marsden, 25 July 1912, 20 May 1912, MWDP.
56. F. Bjorkman to D. Marsden, 20 May 1912, MWDP.
57. P. J. Smith, *The Soul of Woman: an Interpretation of the Philosophy of Feminism* (San Francisco: Paul Elder and Co., 1916), pp. 65–6.
58. G. Burman Foster, 'The Philosophy of Feminism', *The Forum*, 10–22 July 1914, pp. 18, 22.
59. R. Young, 'What is Feminism?', *Good Housekeeping*, May 1914, pp. 679–84.
60. E. C. Parsons, *The Journal of a Feminist*, ed. Margaret C. Jones (Bristol: Thoemmes Press, 1994), p. 67.
61. E. Harrison, 'Then and Now', *Nineteenth Century and After*, December 1909, p. 1052; E. Colquhoun, 'Woman and Morality', *Nineteenth Century and After*, January 1914, pp. 128–40.
62. Rose Young, 'What is Feminism?', pp. 679–80.
63. J. Bush, 'British Women's Anti-Suffragism and the Forward Policy, 1908–1914', *Women's History Review*, 11, 3 (2002), pp. 431–54, p. 431.
64. Ward, quoted in B. Sutton-Ramspeck, in *Victorian Women Writers and the Woman Question*, ed. Nicola D Thompson (Cambridge: Cambridge University Press, 1999), p. 211. See also M. Faraut, 'Women Resisting the Vote: a Case of Anti-Feminism?', *Women's History Review*, 12, 4 (2003), pp. 605–21, p. 605.
65. *Daily Herald*, 6 December 1913, p. 6.
66. D. Marsden, *The Egoist*, 15 June 1914, p. 224.
67. Ibid., 15 June 1914, p. 225.
68. Margaret Fletcher's *Christian Feminism*, reviewed in the *Times Literary Supplement*, 2 December 1915, p. 443. Similarly, the *Oxford Essays in Feminism* edited in 1917 by the progressive publisher Victor Gollancz suggests little distinctive avant-garde content to 'feminism', and indeed, Gollancz strongly distanced 'feminism' from the 'extremism' of its 'vanguard' thinkers. *The Making of Women: Oxford Essays in Feminism*, ed.Victor Gollancz (London: George Allen & Unwin, 1917).
69. W. Meikle, *Towards a Sane Feminism* (London: Grant Richards, 1916).
70. E. Jacobs, *New Age*, 14 April 1910, p. 573.
71. R. West to J. Marcus, August 1977, reprinted in B. K. Scott (ed.), *Selected Letters of Rebecca West* (Newhaven: Yale University Press, 2000), p. 461.

72. R. West to D. Marsden, June 1913, DMC, I, 26.
73. R. West, 'The Freewoman', *Time and Tide*, 16 July 1926, reprinted in D. Spender (ed.), *Time and Tide Wait for No Man* (London: Pandora Press, 1984), pp. 63–8.
74. Holton, *Suffrage Days*.
75. M. Gawthorpe, *Up Hill to Holloway* (Penobscot, Maine: Traversity Press, 1962), p. 197.
76. Billington-Greig, 'A Free Feminist Platform', p. 525.
77. V. Woolf, *A Room of One's Own and Three Guineas* (London, Vintage, 1996), p. 221.

Index

References to secondary sources in the text are in bold type

www.ingramcontent.com/pod-product-compliance
Ingram Content Group UK Ltd.
Pitfield, Milton Keynes, MK11 3LW, UK
UKHW041910040925
462611UK00003B/185
* 9 7 8 1 3 4 9 5 4 4 9 1 2 *